IOANNIS G. TSATSARIS

THE
REVELATION
AFTER
IOANNIS

THE MAN OF THE EARTH AND THE HEAVENS

Nature and Man

Human biology

its natural and para-natural

functionality

EPISTOS PUBLICATIONS

EPISTOS Publications, 22 Zinonos St., 104 37Athens, Greece
Correspondence address: 21 Amerikis St., 106 72 Athens, Greece
Fax: (01)9940668, E-mail: info@epistos.gr, Internet site: www.epistos.gr

Published by Epistos Publications 2000

First published in Greek as *Η Αποκάλυψη μετά του Ιωάννου* (I Apokalipsi meta tou Ioannou) by G. Tsatsaris Publications, Athens, 1997. Second edition by G. Tsatsaris Publications, Athens, 1998. Parallel second edition in Greek for USA by Seaburn Books, New York, 1998. Third expanded edition by Epistos Publications, Athens, 2000.

The present translation is based on the third edition
plus a glossary prepared by the author

Translated from the Greek by Jane Assimakopoulos
Edited by Professor Themistocles Politof, Ph.D.

Supplementary editor: Daniela Ageli
Comments in the form of footnotes bearing the initials [A.V.] linking parts of this work
to existing medical knowledge are by Athanasios Voreakos, M.D.

Managing editor: Katy Papayiannis

ISBN 960-90834-1-2

Films by Bibliosinergatiki
Cover films by Dot Repro
Printed and bound in Greece by Epikinonia Ltd

"You shall know the truth

and the truth

shall set you free."

OUR LORD JESUS CHRIST

(John, VIII.32)

C O N T E N T S

PREFACE BY IOANNIS

As the author of this book I have no particular desire to influence those of you who read it, since you do so in your own personal interest and not in mine. As I am performing a missionary function on Earth, I have an obligation to create these writings, revealing the unrevealed with regard to the biological perception of Man on this planet. And it is everyone's personal interest as well as his right to control and decide what he must do for himself; this does not concern the author. Because I know that the Laws of the Creator of All things in the Universal worlds must not be disrupted. And as the Creator has granted free will to every individual so that each may function and create for himself, each of his actions is judged individually by the All-Universal Law of Justice.

And so, in beginning this book, as my *Position as an *Element of creation and revelation commands me, the Rules of the concepts concerning Man compel me to enter rather mysteriously into their individuality. And this mysterious Position commands me to employ this particular style of writing, which revolves around the central axis of *Higher Sensory Attunement. as is required by the concept of creation on all levels of animate Orders, and to express myself as a special knowledge-holder newly appeared in this location called the globe and, according to Universal nomenclature, **Noudra**[1] **Earth**.

For this reason, do not feel that this is something foreign to you, due to the difficulty you might encounter in studying the first or the second chapter, or certain phrases in what is to follow, or even the texts of communications that I have received from the great Positions of the Universes and included in this book, so that you too as individuals will seek out emotionally the pathways leading to the open Gates of the *Heavens. It will be good for you to put some effort into this, and to feel that you are offering yourselves something very worthwhile by studying this book. Because you are in it, revealed in your invisible state. And be assured that you will hear the call of your soul telling you to read and reread... And then you will meet the Me of human Perception on Earthly levels and the Why that creates incompatible relationships. These two terms, the **Me** and the **Why**, with their enormous resilient emotional momentum, cause Man to become involved in lower-level egocentric entanglements, to enter into unreasonable confrontations, and also to feel constantly wronged.

I will now transcribe a message that explains how I, Ioannis carry oyt my communications with the higher Positions, exactly as described by the great Order **Indonyoi Soo**, creator of the Pan-Universal mechanism connecting

---

[1]Noudra: from the Greek Nous=Mind and Dratto=grip.

universal frequencies, which facilitates direct communication between myself and all the Positions of intergalactic functions and frequencies, so that I may present to you some of their accounts incorporated into this book, in the preface, the epilogue and elsewhere.

ON THE UNIVERSAL NETWORK OF COMMUNICATIONS FROM INDONYOI SOO code 01-15-15

Introduction of **Indonyoi Soo** by the Position **IN** Δ (Delta) from planet Z of sun Lambadias of the Higher Universe:

A group of entities who approach the codes[2] of individualities through mathematical calculations and connect lines of trans-Universal networks

INVOCATION BY IOANNIS

From the Earth where I am at present carrying out my missionary work, as ordained by the sovereign Position of the Laws, in search of nourishment for my Soul, I turn my eyes upward. Then the infinite Positions make their presence felt so that I experience the immense pleasure of encountering my pan-Universal relations at various time intervals. In this way your call sent a message to my *Essential Visual field so that I directed it upward. And I saw you, Indonyoi Soo, and you gave me your code. I express to you my infinite joy and I ask you to

---

[2] Code is the name associated with an entity in the universe. It pertains to the frequencies of the space, time and level where the entity is currently found and enables the establishment of communication.

send me a message concerning the function of my Position here on the Earth of the Sun Karya[3], events that will occur on this Earth, and your own missionary function in the Universes. With infinite gratitude I convey to you my humble salutations.

Ioannis

INDONYOI SOO code 0I-I5-I5

*"**Elethros** and **Myas Abassias**. We are representatives of the triadic Order of the infinite S, the All-Universal Soul that unites the disjointed lines of free individualities into organized communities on creative paths. We bow to your accomplishments and we humbly approach your frequencies in order to transmit the full extent of our Word as a reply to your continuing solar call, in accordance with the message given to you by the Seven Sovereign Fathers, carrying out your function and supporting Life in your heptaform hands.*

Ioannis, the multi-fold connections you have achieved with all material levels of the Universe have transcended the barriers of the descending Rules. Our Orders have brought you into ascending contact with interplanetary and interstellar Orders during the past four solar years. And it has offered the all-encompassing unification of expression and utterance with

---

[3] From the Greek kara=head.

genetic Orders of other stars and heavens, which no appearance or likeness has ever brought or will ever bring together in terms of space and dimension, since they are entirely different, distant and unapproachable, in so far as the nature of their Logical[4] Positions is concerned. It has brought about the union of the invisible representatives with the star of your spirit in a network suitable for the restructuring of their bio-molecular formations, with Ioannis as a central axis, and a central distributor of this trans-Universal, trans-celestial network.

The "translation" is realized through cyclonic transporters[5], appertaining to the emissions of the universal systems, which receive and transform sonic waves of expression into vibrations of the biological language of the Universal Order to which the communication is addressed, creating the fields of biological re-formation that unite the centers of Universal individualities or mechanisms, beginning with You!

In our functional capacity we have adorned the Universe of this network with the care it was determined it should have, through the infinite wisdom of Ioannis, and have consolidated this structure into a transmission of the true essence of things. Birth! Births throughout the Universe! Under your Command! We remain the keys, eternally toiling.

Behold! Few people of this Earth will achieve any progress.

---

[4] Pertaining to Logos, where Logos is the vibrational expression of the Natural state and existence of an individuality.

[5] System of transport in the form of cyclones, i.e. atmospheric molecular circuits.

Many will undergo regressions to lower biological levels that will come about because of this universal transition, taking the form of conflict among nations enslaved by confused thinking. The extent of the collapse will be immense. Even more than in war, beings will succumb to selfish fanaticism and self-destruction. During the coming years, only support from their strong wills may partially and temporarily alleviate undue hardship. Although physical signs will not fail to rekindle hopes for life and happiness on Earth, Life will be in a state of entombment, and suspension!

Our cosmic Life Position excludes the possibility of our departure from you. You are in our mind's code. Thence the obtrusion. In your Name, beyond harm and without worry as we carry out our work, we become both receptors and donors in the network of our labor, fixed within eternal time. With your permission, we come into existence.

We thank you for your kind hospitality. May the hospices of Your Word be blessed with the glorious apostolic love of the Heavens, of the Fathers and their Servants. Amen."

Indonyoi Soo

PREFACE
BY ANTONIS BOUSBOUKIS
Linguist

Ioannis G. Tsatsaris has ascended to a highly cognizant state with regard to the rules of creative Nature. As of today he has traversed —and continues to traverse— an incomparable orbit of internal progress with unselfish aspirations. Armed primarily with his advanced emotional development and visionary perception, he has spent a lifetime observing human behavior. He has sought out and analyzed its motives, while studying the relevant literature. His active participation in the many facets of life has furnished him with a solid knowledge stemming from direct experience during his functional development. This visionary ability of his has allowed him to see the other side of the mountain and to develop a higher awareness. And so as not to confine his valuable knowledge to the narrow circle of those fortunate enough to see him or to consult him about their personal problems, it was decided to publish this book as an offer to a wider public.

Nature, in its "theoretical" dimension at its optimum operational level, is the cosmic womb with infinite potential. Lately this is also the view of Quantum Physics... Nature is much greater than the visible, since the lesser is born of the greater, according to the necessity of creative process. According to Heraclitus: "Nature loves to hide." This is what the great Ionian asserted, with the authority of his wisdom and personal experience. And what does Nature try to hide? Its "Laws!" And what are these Laws? Seeds in a potential state that, nevertheless, do not die when they germinate. They are conserved for the perpetual sowing, which is destructible, whereas they themselves are indestructible. The manifestations of the Laws are the phenomena themselves at their prescribed times. Their knowledge dictates an inductive process, since it starts at the level of manifest Creation and ascends to the space of the seminal BEING.

With his devotion to the primary goal in his life, the Revelation of Knowledge, Ioannis has managed inductively (through research, observation, study, prayer, vision) to enter the channels of social Nature and shed light on "anthropocentric" Laws and be enlightened by them. The author of this book is not simply a person apart, endowed with special energy. He is the gleaner and initiator of knowledge regarding man. He traces man's physiology, his *physiognomy, his teleological function and his mission throughout the entire course of his existence: from the cells to the glands, controllers of his bio-psychology, and the various centers of operation, up to the *Etheric outer regions of his existence. Marriage, childbearing, childhood, puberty, adulthood, the psychology of man and woman, problems that shape behavior, forces that hold man back and create disharmony in health and social adaptability, suggestions for rooting out dark complexes and restoring man to the right course, are the central themes around which these writings revolve.

The title of this work will understandably create a sense of comparative as well as "competitive" parallelism with another title, the well-known "Revelation" of John the Evangelist. But while the latter work reveals the forthcoming and "ever-present" events within the framework of human history, the work by Ioannis G. Tsatsaris brings to light elements that constitute and structure human nature and help it move forward or impede it and cause it to retrogress. And as he himself states, when human creativity retrogresses, it provokes Nature and causes it to enter catastrophic orbits. These are elements that reside at the deepest levels of human constitution and that interconnect in various ways, depending on the individual case, shaping the personality at surface level in its hidden as well as visible form. The revealing —always partial— of these forms and the mutual influence of one on the other justifies the title of the book, since the author offers it as new knowledge.

The creator of this book is, as he writes, in communication with "Divine Authorities and Fathers of the Worlds of Light." He accomplishes this through prayer, which allows him to tune in to the frequencies of incorporeal beings. From these Positions (always according to his own testimony) he draws knowledge which he includes in the present writings. It consists of experiences locked within the individual who has them, and is therefore not subject to inspection by a third party. This communication could also be interpreted as an echo, as a reverberation of super-conscious thoughts and tendencies resonating from within "rocks" hidden in the depths of the inner "divine invisible." Here in the inaccessible recesses of the Soul lies archetypal knowledge drawn, it appears, from the collective super-consciousness of humanity which Jung —in his time— called the "collective unconscious." And as we know, many knowledgeable ancient Greeks strove to attain the "divine inaccessible" of the Soul, among them the great Heraclitus, who attempted, through his dynamic initiative, to give us its definition: "No matter how deeply you traverse the Soul, you can never discern its limits, even if you follow all its paths; that's how deep its meaning is."

Today, in fact, it is accepted in the field of quantum mechanics that the experimenter influences the behavior of the object under experiment by the simple process of observation. Thus, the options adopted by any micro-particle are determined each time according to the observer present. Since the results of a given experiment at the borderline of the existence of matter are no longer objective, but bear the seal of the individuality of the experimenter, this subjectivity-in-objectivity is to be expected, especially in the realm of the study of the Inner Man and of research on the Soul.

But in the realm of the Inner Man observation is not enough; direct participation is essential. In this case it is *Psychic emotion that develops the link with the environment and allows the individual to be a participant in whatever he is observing or experiencing. "The notion of participation as opposed to observation has recently been adopted by modern physics, whereas it was well known to all researchers in the realm of mysticism. Mystical knowledge cannot be acquired through observation, but through total participation of the Being of the mystic [...] they have taken this to its limits, that is to a point where observer and observed, subject and object, become literally an indivisible entity." [6]

Through progress in physics, the convergence of the theory of relativity and quantum mechanics becomes apparent. This will form the foundation for a new awareness of the relationship between time and space. John Gribbin wonders: "Is it possible that this new theory will break away from the field of physics and cross over into metaphysics?" The biologist Lanell Watson, ever since he came up against phenomena that could not be explained from a scientific point of view, recognized the existence of "para-natural" forces that he tracked to the world of transcendental physics. According to what his friends in theoretical physics confided to him, "the objective world of time and space does not exist and science is thus obliged to work with probabilities and not with data, since the latter constitute an illusion. No theoretical physicist in quantum mechanics any longer speaks of improbable things. A kind of "static mysticism" has been developed and it is now difficult to distinguish between physics and metaphysics. This approach facilitates the work of the biologist, who is faced daily with mind-puzzling problems."[7]

---

[6] F. Capra, "Tao and Physics."
[7] L. Watson, "The Mysteries of Time."

Our understanding of human existence becomes greater and greater. Today the brain is no longer considered to be simply a static mass of flesh. Slowly but surely its perpetual activity in the physical world, which is empowered by its electromagnetic aura, is becoming apparent. The halo of saints is now recognized as a feature common among men. It varies only according to the intensity of its light. Visionaries who have seen it have tried to portray it, and though we consider it to be an imaginary projection honoring the saintly personage, in our days, technology has proven them right...

Holography, a new branch of physical science, places Man and every being as a virtual presence within the entire dimension of the Universe, whereas his physical Position is the condensed point of his existence. According to B. I. Verdasky, every animate being on earth "gathers from the entire heavenly space a large spectrum of radiation of every kind, of which visible radiation is only a minuscule part."[8]

Thus, from the above, it becomes apparent that Ioannis's engagement in psychological physiology is not a futile step. It is penetration into areas that exist but are unknown to the "positive" way of thinking, whose horizons are set on the visible, the sole tangible element. Besides, according to Jung, yogis and others looking inward, "during their states of ecstasy attain states well beyond (so-called) normal categories of thought."[9]

---

8 In B. N. Pushkin - A. P. Dubrov, "Parapsychology."
9 J. Jung, "Man and His Symbols."

Ioannis points out that the Soul needs to be nourished like the Body. When we do not nourish it we "do not function normally." And since we do not function normally, then "we can neither feel life nor essentially live it." A prerequisite for harmonious functioning on the individual and social levels is to know our Souls ("know thyself"). Knowledge of the nature and the needs of the Soul comes from the observation of both personal behavior and the behavior of others, as well as from experience drawn from the circumstances we encounter. This knowledge, according to Ioannis, is deemed necessary and beneficial to everyone, but mandatory for those who serve as responsible social agents, such as priests, teachers, psychologists, psychotherapists, doctors, judges, politicians and others.

The presence of Ioannis in the field of teachings concerning Inner Man has a practical orientation in the philosophical sense of the word, which denotes "ethical and social behavior." It does not, however, have a moralizing character, nor is it limited to the framework of practical teachings. It is firmly based on knowledge, not only of the soul's moral nature (ethos), but also of its expression during its functional contact with the body it drives and animates. And all this is given through precise description combined with well-chosen terminology.

Ioannis's educational level is not the product of formal schooling. According to his autobiographical notes in the text, the need to gain a livelihood deprived him of the benefit of a formal secondary and higher education. However, the resourceful way he reacted to events compensated for this deficiency. Apprenticeship in the field of human psychology furnished him with knowledge and a particular ease of expression in the formulation of ideas and of psycho-philosophical thought.

Ioannis makes unusual use of language in an entirely personal style of expression. The originality of the ideas he puts forth renders the presentation somewhat hard to follow at certain points, due to the novel ideas being revealed. The cutting-edge position in which his thoughts evolve —we are talking about a "supernatural physiology"— justifies such a linguistic medium. At certain points, in fact, one is surprised by the specificity of expression, as it demonstrates a spirit that has intimate knowledge of and is entirely conversant with the subject being presented.

This lack of much "formal" education was for Ioannis a positive element allowing him to concentrate on the study of his subject free of any scholarly interference. Thus, deviating from the beaten track, he opened his own avenues of research.

His awareness of the rare and very interesting knowledge he possesses leads the writer to present himself as an individual with a particular mission and function. If this is considered an exaggeration, as might be expected, we would do well to remember Archimedes who, clad only in his enthusiasm, saw the way and shouted the famous "Eureka!" And we would also do well to remember that other superlative utterance: "Give me a place to stand and I will move the Earth."

And again let us not forget the self-proclaimed divinity of Empedocles who, at the beginning of his opus "Catharsis" announces that he is God. Yes! " Be glad for I among you am an immortal God, not a mortal." I must confess to the reader that I preface this work not in my capacity as a scientist but as a long time listener to the teachings of Ioannis regarding Inner Man.

From these Soul-nourishing encounters I have gained many morsels of internal knowledge against a background of psychological interpretation. I believe that this knowledge is quite valuable for everyone, but especially for those who delve beneath the surface of things...

Antonis Bousboukis

PREFACE
BY ATHANASIOS VOREAKOS
Psychiatrist

I had the unexpected pleasure of meeting Ioannis G. Tsatsaris at a certain moment about eight years ago through one of my colleagues at the time, a radiologist, as I too was practicing that discipline before I finished medical school. And my acquaintance with him brought to my own attention certain subjects that created in me the need and the desire to seek understanding of the particular set of human characteristics called Man, both with regard to myself and in connection with the social function called marriage, which encompasses man, woman and the creation of children. This, as I realized shortly after meeting the author of this book, Ioannis G. Tsatsaris, led me to the portal of the vast mystery permeating man, woman and children. And then I said: "Knowledge is infinite for the ignorant and a welcome joy for the Knowledgeable who serve it." Soon a strong inner desire gave me the impetus to complete my studies as a medical doctor.

My academic studies in medicine helped me to acquire many kinds of knowledge pertaining to human existence and also to formulate many questions which, during my meetings with Ioannis over a period of time, he answered for me, explaining things in terms of simple bio-functional states of Man.

Subsequently, my systematic research as a doctor brought me into contact with many cases of pathological illness, and I often came up with the same answers that had been given to me by Ioannis. My specialization in psychiatry contributed to my efforts to join the quest for the meaning of human origin, nature and progress.

"I seek man," Diogenes said, knowing full well that no one can find him in his true *dimension. Because, however much medicine defends itself outwardly, I have the impression that it simply continues to concern itself with the maintenance and management of unhealthy and unnatural states, in which the individual is unable to perceive anything more than what he is offered for consumption.

All the truly astonishing accomplishments of medicine aim at the improvement of the quality of life — a life, however, that medicine itself defines as healthy or unhealthy, in collusion with other forces composing the social fiber of a controlled and dominated environment. For instance, penicillin, the electronic microscope, molecular biology, neuro-transmitters and so many other discoveries did not avert new epidemics due to invasions of "smart" viruses, nor did they solve the mystery of life-threatening cancer. On the other hand, isolated "cases" become exceptions to the established rules and undergo remission from incurable diseases or appear to behave in a way that deviates from scientifically oriented perception. The tremendous gap between specialization and holistic perspective, the laboratory and individuality, and medical awareness and ethics, sometimes makes the obvious hard to discern. The doctor must possess a great amount of information in order to solve a disease-equation, overriding his own position in treatment but also the participation of the patient.

For I am under the impression that true disease has not as yet been defined, seeing as it extends far beyond the criteria set by science. No matter how well doctors may heal patients, they feel that there is something missing with regard to the individual they are treating. Although I have had many answers from Ioannis regarding this deficiency, doctors are unable to define it, mainly because they are unable to convince themselves that they themselves are healthy. If you cure an infection, you have not eradicated the microbe in the environment, but only in the patient. If you operate on a perforated stomach, you have not cured the lesion, but you have managed to diminish the threat to life by creating a new deficiency in the wholeness of the individual: a mutilated stomach!

The question thus arises whether medicine is a science of health or a science of survival. And whether life is primarily survival. The image of the patient who, before entering the temple of Asclepius, slept for many nights in the courtyard of the temple expecting to see the Holy Snake in his dreams, is often evoked. He alone had the right to be healed by the divine Asclepius. For in those days a healer was not simply a warrior against death. He was also a mystic and an apostle. He held the keys to an invisible world, a world where everything functions through Faith, the Knowledge of God and the total support of the "supreme" being. And while doctors taking the ancient Hippocratic oath begin by saying "I swear by Apollo the physician, by Asclepius, by health, by Panacea and by all the gods and goddesses, making them my witness, that I will carry out my duty,...." they forget in short order all about tradition and the quintessential knowledge it contains, and stray toward new articles in medical journals in search of new and more perfect techniques.

There are many things around us that can lead us to "absolute" Wisdom and Knowledge. There are also many elements inside us that can lead us to absolute ignorance, and we all strive to learn to think through the unsolved mysteries of eons. The more man progresses, and the more new discoveries he makes, the more these mysteries increase. Knowledge becomes broader but not deeper; anxiety with regard to life and death, pain and the quest for happiness, justice and injustice, good and evil, have remained the same from when the Earth was flat to when we conquered the moon and split the atom. No "enlightened" scientist has been able to alleviate the accumulated confusion ruling over us.

The way of analytic scientific thought reveals its nakedness in the presence of men who have approached Knowledge axiomatically (based on principle and intuition) and have demonstrated the existence of phenomena that have, sooner or later, been accepted. Now, at the dawn of the third millennium, we are in need of such an axiomatic Position, that will unify existing knowledge on a new basis, a stable and humanitarian one, that will bring us a little closer to the Absolute and to the Creator. For it is Faith in the Creator and the humble recourse to the Knowledge He offers that govern human history.

These thoughts are recorded so as to create a starting point for us to at last think about ourselves, about the family, about society, about the space and the spaces referred to as "Universes," from a different vantage point. And this important opportunity is offered us in this book by Ioannis G. Tsatsaris.

It is therefore with pleasure, but also with humility, that I assume the task of introducing such a book, whose first reading will be bewildering, whose second will be unsettling, and whose third will touch off deep feelings, hidden away for centuries since the creation of our individuality.

And the honor became even greater when I was asked to intervene in the text with certain elements of "established" knowledge in medicine, by way of explanation of terms and as comments. Therefore, a certain amount of text written by myself, attempting to provide certain conventional knowledge we already accept, has been included in the text in the form of notes, followed by my initials in brackets. As you shall see, these pieces of text are small building blocks of a mosaic that is just becoming apparent, in the face of man's need to overcome the barren logic of disorientation that the established scientific community has been attempting to disseminate until now. For "to arrive at simplicity you must travel round the world."

In conclusion, a strong desire compels me to remind you of the words of our Lord Jesus Christ, as a reference that will

31

help mortal man achieve insight into his physical nature here on Earth:

"Be silent that I may guide your words. Be still that I may guide your steps. Be serene that I may reside in you. "

Athanasios Voreakos

PREFACE BY SOCRATES

As far as I, Ioannis, am concerned, the most serious Position (entity) that passed through Earth as a common mortal was Socrates of ancient times in the locality of Athens. I quote here his evaluation given to me at a meeting-communication I had with him at the Spiritual level, during which I asked for his opinion with regard to this book.

SOCRATES

"In this book people snigger in the back of their hearts at their own doings. A stranger in a strange land, Man tries to secure his fate following the strict commands of his predecessors. Thus, he is inexorably bound to arrive at the same precipice as they did, suffering a failure he is then reluctant to abandon, since he has already espoused it and given it vows of eternal faith.

Ioannis of the Nations[10] of the Universe, Lord of the Heavenly

---

[10] The term Nations refers to the different populations of the Universe, such as the human race.

33

Temples, leans confidentially over the world and reveals it, smiling and unperturbed. Do not fail to frown upon him, if you want to remain faithful to your inner traditions... For whoever touches him undergoes a shock from the electricity generated by the onrush of his all-encompassing revelation and becomes overcharged, embarking on an eternal interplanetary race in order to consume a minimum of the uningestable dose of truthfulness he has received. And it amuses me to watch you already racing with such vanity of purpose. Because I do not think that any of you wants to bring to light the innermost contents of his Soul and shed their weight, as good sense dictates. And then to hasten to appear as an apprentice of himself and of his Universal creations.

I see you from my *Nucleus here on high and I wonder what made you deserve such good fortune as that which God has let appear among you, and I wait to see how much you have changed since olden times, my good friends and accusers ... of your Souls!

May there be good times for you beneath the shroud of darkness you have drawn across your heavens, so that it will transmit to you with such force as to leave me speechless before the intelligence, dexterity and diligence of the human race as it becomes the creator of a spectacular downfall of the animate individualities that have the supreme good fortune (!) to be embodied in your planetary space.

May God protect me against the punishment of such falls, and I ask the ruling Orders to be lenient with me and not to push me once more on the path leading toward the capital of sin, Earth!

I am thankful that I stand as an observer and not a functionary and if at some time the Gods-Laws of the Universe bring me back among you, then again it will not be necessary for me to write, since all that you are or are not entitled to know with regard to Man, his mind and his Soul, is written here. As for what comes afterward, do not ask about it. For your glands have not yet learned to hear the pulse of the Soul that gives them life and will therefore never be able to synchronize thought and revelation into a functional harmony of superior evolution. For now, receive this, and after a few millennia, if you do well in the field of universal learning, through diligent work, perhaps then you will discern the basic particle of the principle of all things and, if you see this, you can then see EVERYTHING, as all the avenues of the heavens rush open before you...

Socrates

the independent visitor"

Devout invocation by Ioannis for the true life-giving treasure, the acquisition of self-knowledge

"O Divine Positions of the Universe, with your perfect behavior toward the higher Powers, we ask you to enable us to cooperate with the higher and lower Elements of our selves, to shape our entire individual nature harmoniously so that we may function in an ever higher vibrational state in creative Peace."

INTRODUCTION TO THE INNER BOOK

As I begin putting this book into writing, my Position of knowledge summons me to begin at the creation of the entity **Man**. According to what has been written up to the present, none of those seeking to fully understand his mysterious inner-emotive Position have received the grace to fathom the biological composition of his organic Order and gain access to the motivating forces of his possessive impulses in their bio-kinetic state, which emerges as emotive desire and gives expression to his Position. The true essence of the bio-energetic state of his emotions remains shrouded in mystery. It has become evident that those who have tried —and are still trying— to do this, have not reached the state of magnetic perceptive awareness that will provide entrance into the animate domain of this entire organic system in its individual molecular state and its central glandular structure.

Thus I enter inductively into the Position **Man**, as formed, which functions within most everyday experience on two communicational planes: the expressive outer plane and the inner emotive one. The principal aim of the latter is to hide deficiencies, but it is unable to rid itself of them. Then these deficiencies, entangled in psychological complexes, create internal pressure on the individual, who is obliged to have recourse to his outer expressivity in order to hide his own unhealthy pathology. He does this mainly by fabricating fictitious thoughts and events, and setting himself up as a hero somewhere within them.

In this way he charts a two-fold course, which leads him unimpeded along the functional course of his life. And because of this, I, in my awareness of these creations, am here to depict in writing this cosmogonic principle through the revelation of the biosynthetic composition of the individual in its three *hypostases: Body, Soul and Spirit, as they appear, according to the strictest of absolute principles. These hypostases or planes of substantive existence have been positioned in such a way within the preordained Order by the Law of Creation of the planet Earth, and also of other planets belonging to the Intermediate Universe, that each of these hypostases exists within the dimension of its own individuality, but is also completely dependent upon the others. This is why the Law of Creation ordained that they co-exist one inside the other, and that biologically the Position of each be recognized as a Nucleus for the presence of the other two Positions in their nominal ordinations Body, Soul and Spirit. But always on condition that they achieve unification hierarchically[11] toward the formation of the integrated individuality as an evolving Element in the Intermediate Universe.

And, as the Intermediate Universe is pervaded by a great amount of Anti-Lawfulness (negativity), the powers that be,

---

[11] In progressive stages, first the Body with the Soul and then the Soul with the Spirit.

40

the great Fathers of Eternal Light who hold authority to order and reorder the Universes, receive an encoded command from the inner Order of the Universal Creator to send a special Position (emissary), who will always be under their surveillance, and they will progressively and biologically transform and re-order his perceptions regarding the natural composition of the *atmosphere of the planet to which he has been sent. For it is a strict Rule applying to every planetary biology, that each planet's biological functions are distinct and autonomous. And so if the emissary sent by the divine Orders does not receive the guidance and Offers of the Fathers of Light in his biological state, he can not possibly enter into the hypersonic and subsonic states that will lead him into a special heightened awareness of the meaning of the nature of the planet he has entered, exactly as determined by the Law of Human Life.

During such times they also send certain other luminous Souls who belong to the *Psycho-Spiritual Universe. These other Positions (Souls) are sent to carry out individual missionary work, which implies the evolution of their Position to a higher level, but they have also been empowered, because of their individual mission, to produce the required positive energy necessary to keep the balance of the planet in check. They will have strong peripheral protection and the Archangelical Orders will relay messages to them so they can form an idea of what they must seek out. Extreme care must also be taken so that the messages are received in their entire interpretation, and it will be their particular concern to seek out, mentally, the specially sent Position mentioned above and join themselves to its Nucleus, so as to be able to bring their mission to completion. Because on their own they are **completely powerless** to carry out the work preordained for them, as the Negative Order has a way of entrapping them... Only he who was sent by the Pan-nuclear Universal Authority, center of all authority, was biologically endowed so that he could know how the Negative functions.

A Rule (...) has also appointed me, in my animate presence, to be in charge of this work, which I bring to light and which is being performed for the first time in the vast annals of life on the planet Earth. And as I feel responsible in my state of heightened consciousness, I am writing this book for you, in which the greatest revelation made concerns first my immediate communications with Positions and Super-positions of the Universe, which I feel the need to present to you, since I also function biologically here on Earth, and then the exposition and analysis of the Bio-Psycho-Spiritual wholeness of the individuals on Earth, as much as is permitted me by my personal Rule and the level of biological perception of human societies on this planet.

I begin with the analysis of **Body**, **Soul** and **Spirit** as Positions pre-ordained by the Laws of Nature and Creation in their presence here on Earth. Only for the one who is inducted into these noetic states of awareness will the gates of the Heavens of light open in warm embrace...

Chapter 1

ON BODY, SOUL AND SPIRIT

A dmitting the actual state of existence of the human individual in his presence here on Earth, as well as the breadth and depth of his perceptual capacity, it is obvious that a special undertaking is necessary, at this present critical Age, for the future of mankind on Earth. The inner depth of my awareness commands me, as an imperative of my individual presence here on Earth, to reveal all that the understanding of organized societies permits me and I am able to articulate of my perception of the individual *Elementation and organic functionality of Man.

Man is composed of three main Elements in their substantive existence and dimension, on which the creation of the integrated individuality of his physical presence on planet Earth is based. According to the natural human urge to define and distinguish every subject and object, visible or invisible, that presents itself to normal human awareness, a name is given to them in order for a common framework of communication to exist for the social community at large, facilitating a specific form of cooperation. Thus these three Elements have been nominally identified by the terms I believe we all know as **Body**, **Soul** and **Spirit**.

In my view, all three of these Elements are placed within the Lawfully-ordained, perfect functional Universal Order, so that each may exist, develop and consummate its Position. Thus it will find itself in its aligned individual state, in order to be able to appear as individually integrated in its consummate development —as an absolute natural Position— and then it will emit magnetic waves of attraction, and so create a space in which the merging of the two Elements, Body and Soul, will first take place. For, as I know from the Law of Universal Creation, the Soul emanates from the Primordial Nucleus of Creation, as an initial movement out of the All-Universal Soul, on the basis of Laws and Orders regarding the totality of universal domains, for the creation of the manifest Individuality in its missionary courses. And it is determined by the Law of Mysterious Order in what solar, and subsequently planetary, Position the individuality is placed, so that it will be assigned to the planet whose physical *atmospheric organicity is endowed with the appropriate atmospheric and magnetic fields. And there, on the basis of its preordained development, the Soul enters as a central Nucleus, which magnetically attracts the Elements of the animate Order of the planet that have been determined, again by the Law of All-Universal Creation, to move toward interaction, distribution and Elementation with the assistance of magnetic fields, and to be formed according to the Rules of configuration, as we see in the fully-defined bodily Positions of individuals here on Earth. Following partial implementation of interactive functional cooperation, as related Elements in their newly created interdependent Position within the human body, the *Nuclear Soul, in its immaterial Offer, again begins progressively acting as a supply center and sets up communication among all the composite Elements, known as glands; first among them the Gland of *Sensory Attunement incorporates the appropriate Elements into its formative individuality and assumes as a primary function the Elementation of all the other glands, of the nervous system, and of the rest of the body. As the Law determines, all these are attuned within the predetermined Order, to achieve complete cooperation, in order for the *functionality of the organic body to commence. And thence the individual enters into a new state in which, through the development of the emotional system, he develops as an Individual-Body in his mental Position in the form of an instinctive awareness, again supplied by the Nuclear Soul, for his protection. This is, of course, a primordial Rule of Creation, which is specified and placed from the beginning in the domain of re-production, so that the life of this component, the animate Body, may be integrated as a beginning and as a continuation.

Following the unification of these Elements (Body and Soul) in exact synchronization and interaction, always functioning under the Universal Natural Order of Life, they are called upon to enter a more advanced state of perception, **in which the Body will recognize the Soul and the**

Soul will recognize the Body. From this Position people will be able to coexist in an integrated union and to perceive that the aim of their evolution requires them to feel an urgent need to create the proper uplifting conditions in their every inward state, and thus attain a higher level of sensory perception where they can understand their Position in relation to other individuals, and also in relation to their own selves. Then they will feel inside them such a degree of functional harmony that it will produce an emotional urge taking the form of a need to try and create the appropriate Sensory space in which to receive the specific intuition pertaining to such development. This intuition is now able to mobilize, in the appropriately prepared space, the primary Element: the Spirit. As the principal Element needed for complete, integrated creation under the Rule of substantive existence and *dimension in the three-fold state, the Spirit is ordained to enter, in *Etheric bio-synthetic form, into the *Psycho-Somatic (Soul-Body) Position. In this way the Spirit will assume, as prescribed by the Law, the creative functionality of the Psycho-Somatic Position in its essence and form, and shape this Position as an agent of assimilation and Elementation within both the Body and the Soul. Thus this Position does not appear as a distinct entity but expresses itself as a Position at the level where the individual, depending upon the biological composition of the place where he was born and his biological and Etheric connection with his parents, has been nourished and nurtured by the almost unconditional Offer acceptable to them.

Here on Earth the Spirit has not been placed in the Position that was determined for it, but has been transposed by the two previous Positions (Body and Soul) to their own level. It is, however, called upon as a Position, when Body and Soul have achieved perfect communion and fashioned into an evolutionary being, to transpose itself into its natural superior Position and to expand, as has been prescribed during its primordial origins for its evolutionary course toward luminescence, in a complementary whole with the Soul and the Body.

* * *

Again because of the direct and indirect communication that I maintain with a great number of Divine Functionaries and Fathers of the Universe of Light, a super-Spiritual Being of light whose name is **Anemios Deus** —and let me make it clear that it is not Zeus of mythology, who as a Spirit is now in the Anti-universe— enters my frequency and reveals to me explicitly in writing, as you will see below, and in the clearest of language, the Spirit itself, how it arrives here to initiate transformation and activation of its substance within the Body-Soul, and also at what level the Spirit has been trapped by the Body and the Soul and functions within a framework of lower human perception.

The following text is written in the particular scientific expression specified by the Universal Order as a prescribed format for this subject.

ANEMIOS DEUS, code 9.81

"Ioannis, born to all existing animate dimensions, I arrive as the outer crust of your diffuse Spiritual Body and I define: Spirit. A term inspired by Positions of Logos not clouded over by lightning-bolt thoughts. Global logic founded the Order of the word Spirit to express the commencement, the activity and the movement of Logos.

Spirit is the nature of the evolving noetic Element, the formation of the organic complexity of the perceptive frequencies of each and every Being, such as the Etheric atmospheric *Cycle, the Earthly creation, the mental imagery or the Body in its chemical and biological process. The alignment and ordering of these Life axes and conductors into a Position of expression and evolutionary progression is the Spirit. It is the organic pre-existence of the Universal Element in a pre-coded form, its evolution into systematic organization, the intervening natural process linking the site from which the Being emanates to its biological location. And the Spirit, an inconceivable fatherless dimension...

I differentiate between the stages and pre-stages up to the logical installation of the codes around the receptor, the human being. During the preliminary stages of codification into Logos, Thought and Expression, his Spirit is the particular Elements which are biologically formed by means of a vibrational process and exist at the level of his birth as a vibrational womb for the formative arrangement of themes of data perceived by the organic visual sensors, through the partial and total pressure exerted on the being in this space. There are further stages, but for now, only in the first do I perceive activity ... "

EXPLANATION BY IOANNIS: Here, Anemios Deus reveals to us that this super-Etheric Being, the Spirit, — born to the Father and Creator as a Being on His level, where He, as Father, reproduces himself, — is formed and transformed as an infinite Etheric Position-Order which, in its movement, places itself into bio-Etheric Positions coalescing and substantiating into individual Psycho-Somatic (Body-Soul) Positions, at levels appropriate to their biological Position and composition. The biological Position and composition of the individual depends on his origins and the effects of geo-physical conditions plus genetic character, as suppliers, on the individual. In that time and space the Position of the Etheric Element of the Spirit is also established in its active functionality, as the constitutional structuring of the biological state, in order for the initiative to be transferred to the Psycho-Somatic (Body-Soul) Position to seek it out, so that it can progressively offer its gifts at higher levels of awareness and functionality.

ANEMIOS DEUS (continued)

"If Logos is defined as the decoding of internal chains of Thought evinced through multiple levels of vibrational states, internally but also verbally (linguistically), Spirit is the dimension-matter of the organism (organized system) called Logos.[12]

The Spirit is the electro-negative womb of Life, that current which diffuses, through a swarm of electrons—with a tendency to concentrate,— the dimension (the dimensions of individual lives), distributed and emitted in parts from the totality of biological entities, inactive during their productive development, active during the reproductive biological process, under certain inalienable Laws. These electrons extend their vibrational output to the environment, thus formlessly coalescing and centered around their individual code, so as to raise the sensitivity of individual Beings with regard to the exploration of the stimulus. They collect magnetically around the receiver, the receiver being the focus of production and attraction through bio-somatic mechanisms with a drive to develop its biochemical identity. This development takes place through myriad vibrations, rising and falling. The brain center, the receiver and attractive pole of vibrations, transmits to the hypophysis gland, processes forms within its information center, and stimulation is condensed. From then on the process is

---

[12] By this is meant a combination of parts that compose a certain vibratory state expressed through speech.

well known. The organ of human life (the central brain gland) classifies incoming information in its own way and distributes it accordingly. The Spirit is in itself the Universal *Offer of Nature to herself. Fixed points reveal their order and unfixed points grab onto "soaring" ones so that they can proceed through their perpetual Cycles and be determined.

There also exist mysterious Orders of processes of creation, arising over vast intervals of time from supreme centers in the Nucleus of Creation, Age-related classifications, Universal emissions of undiluted frequency, as central solar constituents of the biological formation of spaces from the Creational Order. Such a Cycle has now been disseminated. Those who are able may receive ... Ioannian emission, the dissolution of darkness ...

I depart from the visible, where my Position has no place. Observe how the expression of my Word unites with the spirit of your Logos. Those who have taken in the Word will be set free. The dioxides of the lower forms of Life are incessantly subjected to their burning ... "

The Omniscient Law
the receiver of all

* * *

And let us approach from a different point this glorious Position, the Spirit, as my individual need compels me to present to you the Elements of its biological attunement, called upon by the Rule to incorporate a functional organism in its Etheric substantive existence and dimension, in the plus and the minus (Positive and Negative), exactly as was explained to me by the great Position of functional knowledge named **Ekel O N 1/5**, who functions, toils and creates in the worlds of the Higher and Lower Universe, during one of our meetings in the level of Etheric substantive existence and dimension.

EKEL O N code I/5

"Ioannis, I will reveal to you something unknown. The Element that takes root in and revitalizes cerebral bio-existence into the manifest expression of the Spirit is Iodine of the Earth and the air. Within it there exists a hydrogenic combination of energy transformation that cleanses everything that has been distorted in its frequency dimension, repairs its vibratory expressiveness and forms receptivity geared toward higher hydrogenic biological stages that exist and will continue to exist on this planet. Thus, the biological characteristics of molecular organic life are distributed among six creative Cycles, and thereafter among an additional three.

Within the first six, Bodily functionality develops biologically with intermittent inherent vibrational expressions of doubt with regard to its Position in the environment. There we also encounter the seven great trials in each Cycle. Bio-iodine enters at various degrees of activity into the hydrogenic Cycle of the organism and the ensuing metabolisms either absorb it, which results in a + (plus), or they reject it, creating an organic resistance to it, resulting in - (minus).

The rain they have sent to you is iodine.[13] The attention given this keeps the organisms in a state of expectancy of the transmutation of their biology into a lighter hydrogenicism, which is the chemical bond that frees these Elements from the burdensome Elements created by magnetic d i s o r g a n i s a t i o n ... "

---

[13] While I, Ioannis, was writing this text, I felt very tired. At that time a heavy rain started. It is this rain that Ekel O N refers to as containing Iodine.

Chapter 2

ON THE APPEARANCE OF THE DIS-UNION OF BODY AND SOUL. THE ROLE OF CONSCIENCE

T he Spirit, liberated from the lower levels of life's functions, as an integral essence and Position, is that supreme and resplendent Element that appears in its biological substantive existence and dimension as an entity born and proceeding out of Our Father The Creator. This Offer has as its Rule to provide from Its own Position a most special, most immaterial Element that will infuse energy into our bio-Etheric state, and it will then merge with our biological Position in order to deliver us reborn and worthy of assuming this God-given supreme knowledge which is, as far as the existence of the human Position is concerned, the greatest Offer. It is the purest and most potent creative reasoning power which, in its advent, creates such clarity of perception that the Offer is realized within the immense space of Vision.

Vision is the developing entity born through the enlightening clarity of the *Spirit. Its principal function is to develop itself as an entity at the functional level of the organic Position of the individual, an entity responsible for foreseeing the results of any impulse activated at every spatio-temporal moment created by negative circumstances or by positive Offers emanating from the Universal Law of the Benevolent Function of the Divine Positions, i.e. their function as keepers and givers of divine gifts. Such circumstances always function within the spatio-temporal progression of Offers and manifest their presence throughout the entire biological space of human existence, where negative biological presence also exists.

It is this very space that is also made peripherally available to the Soul, and it is referred to as the space of **Sensory centers**. These are the product, on the one hand, of the expression of the chromosomal Position of the individual and, on the other hand, of the activation effected by the Natural Law of Opposites (the negative Element on Earth). In response to this union, the Sensory centers develop the *vibrational field* beyond the marginal limit. From the definitive instructions received by the vibrational field, individualized emotions appear in our visceral system and extend to our Bodily surroundings, but also in our expressiveness. Due to intensified activation of chromosomes,[14] these emotions manifest themselves in the desire for concerted action

---

[14] Chromosomes are situated in the nucleus of every cell and are composed of genetic material that is able to identify the species of the organism, to place the cell in functional readiness and to induce reproduc-tion. Chromosomes will be taken up in greater detail in chapter 7. [A.V.]

geared toward achievement of the goal we have set beyond our natural limits.

We believe that, with such a start-up signal, we will soon emerge victorious, deluding our selves through our Senses, which leads us to confrontation with others. In reality, however, we will never win. For has anyone realized that in this space, where so many biological centers have mysteriously come together to assemble the specially formed integral Position we call Man, there is a special Element emanating from the cosmic and universal space of justice that we call **Conscience**? Conscience. The impartial worker, the indefatigable functionary, the infallible judge of decisions of one's subjective Position, which is guided 92% of the time by the unconscious and is always ready to modify the subjective functioning of the individual.

For Conscience is within each of us, occupying a special Position, but at the same time very diffuse within the space of the instinctive centers. From there, it becomes a special observer but also a just arbiter. For this reason, I believe that when we ask God to forgive us for some malfeasance, it is very probable that He will forfeit our punishment; our Conscience, however, will never do so!

As I mentioned earlier, because of the regulatory function of the Positions, certain contrasts co-exist within this organic space, and we call these negative states. These, acting in a privileged manner in material Sensory space, have the power to influence it so greatly that they can lead it wherever they wish. Thus, material desires are built which urge us to conquest and pleasure.

Many have observed that when we seek to gain something, after a while this desire becomes an intolerable need. And when the need is fulfilled, then we think that we feel "absolute" happiness and a sense of uniqueness. However, almost immediately a new desire is born, which incites us once again into an unending cycle. Thus we manage to submit to the dominant influence of the Senses, until we reach the point of entrapment by what we perceive to be material "goods." During the process of this enslaving phenomenon, we transfer our attention initially to individuals in our environment who are close to us, relatives or friends —as tradition would have it— and then to more distant acquaintances in competitive confrontation, while at the same time we develop a Sensory uneasiness, manifesting itself in mysterious behavior, which we call *jealousy*.

Jealousy is a nucleus of emotive sensations which form various centers that produce emotional impulses, and it has as its principal mission to eradicate conscious volition in the individual and subjugate him to the lowest levels of subjective judgements. These in turn incite him to action, leading him to scheme to turn against one or more individuals. And he always gives the excuse that God has treated him unfairly and has given another individual —or individuals— the "good things in life." Then an emotion develops within him with regard to others leading to the perception that they scorn and despise him. For instance, for a large percentage of the population, because of the many experiences they have progressively undergone, and without knowing the true meaning of life here on Earth, the first thing they examine and dislike is their own self, misled by comparing the image of others to their own. They fashion a false image of their own self as inferior and they reject the form it takes because they find it defective. And there develops within them a strong negative reaction toward others. Thereafter, they are jealous of the positions others hold at work or within social groups or relationships —positions they themselves do not hold— and they are jealous of what they like to call material "goods" that may be bought with so-called wealth. These three Elements (jealousy, demandingness and self-deprecation) have many peripheral secondary manifestations and many ways of dragging us down to the lower emotional world.

Jealousy evolves into envy and ingratitude and to me, this is a very serious disease, rarely cured. Because whoever reaches this point can never feel tranquil, but lives in a state of anguish, in an effort to surpass another person or persons in material gains, so as to appear superior, albeit in his material identity. He will never understand that he has fallen into the trap of material desires without any hope of escape, except in rare cases. The Law is always there to reveal to all of us this Position which, as a defining principle of the level of Life on Earth, creates these conditions so that jealousy will enter our lives. And if we, in our turn, are able to perceive its true Position, we must try to rid ourselves of it. We must begin by trying to control it, becoming aware of its calculated ends, which aim to pollute the meaning of our life. For the biological principle of Elemental formation of the individual, as defined by the Law of classification of the planet Earth with respect to Elemental material of pure quality, contains a high percentage of contamination within the endo-cellular Elemental composition of the chromosomal molecule. Acting as observers and researchers, we must therefore try to pinpoint in ourselves the lower emotional impulses that lead us to make certain decisions, and we must take care to free ourselves from jealousy's grip, or else it will take us over as an emotional state in which we see injustice to ourselves. This state induces us to become preoccupied with it, raising it to the level of some great tragedy, which is soon forgotten so we may begin all over again. And we do not realize that after the advent of life, death will follow...

The other side of the biological Order of jealousy defines it as the *bio-genetic residue* of the Order of refuse animate Elements contained within the internal individuality of pure Elements, which aim to provoke confrontation and conflict and to fixate the individual at the level of Earth's waste Elements, which means a gain in harmonious living equal to ZERO!

For this reason I shall try to enter into the visible and invisible functioning of Man, in as much as this is possible, and present to you descriptively, or through examples, the causes that almost always bring us to this position of weakness and, without our realizing it, lead us to almost certain Decline. Because, I see that each individual must try to function in a Position of equilibrium. It is this Position that, as we know, permits the Soul to function as a special catalytic agent. The functioning of the Soul activates life in the individual, and it is in the nature of things that the Soul must be nourished, just like the Body, in order to develop. Only in this way will it evince its Position within us in its natural state. I believe that whoever disputes this Nucleus called Soul and maintains, as do certain people at lower perceptual levels, that everything functions from the flesh, must be tragically naive. Each of us must understand that, since there are many reasons that have lead us to this most difficult position, the way we perceive our presence here on Earth is not correct for many of us. If we do not have an integrated and proper presence in all sectors, then we do not function normally. And if we do not function normally then we can neither feel this life nor genuinely live it. If, in addition, we have not managed to know it as it really is, then we have failed both as individuals and in our functional Offer to the cycle of the natural state leading to functional harmony of the organism. I am referring, of course, to the knowledge we acquire as experience during the course of our lives, when we are placed as observers of ourselves and of others in social and cooperative relationships, which we undertake as a partnership or an occupation in order to earn a living, but I am also referring to how we present ourselves to others, especially when we follow vocations such as that of the priest, teacher, psychologist, psychotherapist, doctor, judge, politician or others, where we undertake to serve the Truth as integrated individuals.

And the most sensitive and responsible vocation is that of the priest, which has to do with the most delicate part of the individual, that is, the *Position of his Soul.* The priest in particular must develop a sense of Offer and devotion, as his frock demands, and must not aspire to Earthly favors that aim at so-called material goods, because his apostolic Position DOES NOT permit it. However, if he becomes permeated by these lower emotions, they will consume him, and then the individual-priest, apart from the initial conflict he will sustain with the All-encompassing Law called Conscience, will sustain a secondary, perhaps stronger, conflict related to his vocation, since he is now bound by the Rule of the Promise he has made during his ordination, which is subject to two states: The first creates a bio-Etheric presence in emotional space, and if the priest is not completely given to his promise, as this Position decrees within the harmony of Light and Love, an unwholesome atmosphere is formed. Now, because of our respectful emotions toward him, this creates a disturbance in us irrespective of the state we are in, and in response a disturbance to our nervous system. From that moment on, the individual allows his Bodily self to become vulnerable to any number of illness-causing states, including all forms of lower Earthly bondage. And second, and even more important with regard to negative consequences —and unfortunately this has not been presented and analyzed in its precise semantic Position by any mortal on Earth— is that which brings the individual-priest to the special judgment of the Laws of Justice under Universal functionality which, as I know very well, can sentence him —with moderate leniency —to over 130 years of punishment, measured by Earth's Rule. Of course, due to the ignorance in which many of you find yourselves, you will consider this a joke. But when that moment comes, then you will remember and you will accept this punishment, in accordance with the Law that will determine its duration, which is 130 years minimum, and conscience will bring vividly to your memory the Revelation of Ioannis...

For this reason, each of us should first know himself well enough to be in a position to decide if he is capable of fulfilling the demands that his promise has created and that summon him to the realization of the potential of his organic and individual existence, and also to decide if he is capable of carrying out the task that society calls upon him to complete as a promissory debt.

Chapter 3

INITIAL ACTIVATION
OF THE HUMAN POSITION

I must try, in as much as the present Age shaping the human condition allows this, to reach your perceptive space, to be understood and disclose the very first beginnings of the formation of the human Position up to its activation within society, from the beginning of its creation up to the time of its manifestation.

Now, let us take the case of a man and a woman, whose biological and magnetic fields have determined the time and place for their meeting and who, having met through invisible attraction, each of them having settled on the other as the right person for the fulfillment of his/her desires, decide to consummate their union legally through the sanctity of marriage. We see here that their outward actions are conducted with an instinctive sense of desire, based on the natural needs of the male and the female, and marriage takes place to legalize the position of each with respect to the other and to society and the State. After the consummation of the marriage and the fulfillment of the desire, the true obligations of each party with regard to their common path become apparent.

However, here both the man and the woman must know that the path is not strewn only with pleasure, nor is that pleasure what they understand and envisage it to be. This path becomes part of a new, biological, everyday functional state, and for this reason they must know that the Laws of Nature call upon them to perpetuate Life. If they accept this position, they must also accept the difficult responsibilities of the mission they have undertaken. And they must avoid indulging in egotistical behavior, since such behavior functions as a denial of their roles. For as you must know, the unmindful enthusiasm of that particular time of life gives rise to impulsive thinking, expressed in a multitude of colorful images most readily illustrated by the utterance: "We will have a child so as to make our happiness complete." From that moment on, for each of them begins the great judgment by the invisible observers, the Laws of Justice, with regard to their true mission.

From the time of conception of the embryo in the female organism, a new Position of creative development begins functioning in a mysterious manner, and it is natural that this will be reflected in each of them by the development of a new and more rapid vibrational state. For this reason we should know that, from that moment on, the organic Position of the woman must always function within a very tranquil Bodily and family atmosphere. And in order for this atmosphere to exist within this small social unit, we must know the true meaning of the life we are living. Because the bio-genetic residue I refer to earlier stemming from the woman's past experiences and mental conditioning, along with the genetic characteristics of the individual, will, in accordance with the time rules governing them, bring about reactionary disturbances to the tranquillity required by *Psychic consciousness in its serene functionality. It will also attempt to re-create various states of the past, often distorted by time either into something pleasant, in an effort to create a more attractive image than the one being lived at present, or into something unpleasant. The latter gives rise to the rationalization that we have been "wronged" by everyone, and in this instance the self is sidetracked from its natural state in the present and enters other temporal periods, which results in an unwholesome state of organic functionality, especially for the woman, who thus leaves her state of tranquillity, and consequently that of natural behavior with regard to her child-bearing mission.

Every impetuous action, big or small, on our part, opens a doorway for some minor causality, an accumulation of which activates some greater causality that will manifest itself in some way. However, by the time of its manifestation it may be so altered in form as to become unrecognizable and may not even be detected as the cause of a particular effect. It is possible that at a certain point in time, in all ignorance, we may create a very unwholesome situation that we will live through much later in the future as a pathological condition. At that time, in the throes of a reaction we will be unable to control, we will create such problems that it will be almost impossible for us to solve them.

The child-bearing period is very crucial with regard to the acceptance of the role of spouse and future parent. But often, a very unwholesome atmosphere develops, full of nostalgia for life before marriage, which we consider a "lost paradise," and sadness ensues, resulting in the creation of certain desires that demand fulfillment. If a desire is within ethical bound-aries permissible for both partners, then there is no problem. However, if it exceeds these boundaries, then internal distur-bance occurs, amplified by nostalgia for the past, and we undergo something very unpleasant. This unpleasantness overwhelms us, without our possessing the means to control it and discern its cause, and so rid ourselves of it. Inevitably, then, as an escape, we attribute it to our partner's bad behav-ior toward us, and we demand restitution for behavior that is not actually bad. At that moment an inadvertent gulf devel-ops between us, along with confrontation leading to dishar-mony both in our external common environment and within ourselves, which results in a disturbance of the vibrational field of the inner organs. This disturbance is unavoidably transmitted to the developing embryo and leaves its imprint. If something similar also happens later on, then more imprints are accumulated and create hotbeds of disharmony just waiting for the right stimulus and moment to manifest themselves.

* * *

In my attempt to present these situations in actual terms, my recourse to the Saints and to other Knowledgeable Beings

and Fathers of the Universe provides me with these knowledgeable opinions representing reality, regarding what can
happen during the period of child-bearing. And I will now
present to you two special cases that make a substantial
contribution and provide complete information with regard
to events that may occur during the period of child-bearing,
a presentation made by the Position (entity) **St. Paraskevi**,
code 5, **6**, carrying out its missionary function as a Divine
Position, and more specifically as a special expert on the bio-
Psychic and biological state of Man, providing us with a complete diagnosis concerning the individuals involved.

The first is the case of two siblings, D. and M., children of
mother S., who displayed various somatic symptoms whose
causes were unknown —to the doctors at least— and were
therefore incurable.

SAINT PARASKEVI code 5, 6

*"Ioannis, I salute you in your Spiritual passage and the myri-
ad dimensions you traverse; I observe you as a student of intellectual restructuring, in which I have been irrevocably
ordained.*

*I bow down and I state that the somatic disharmonies in the
two individuals have, up to a certain biological point, a common
genetic origin. The extremely disturbed neurotic frequencies created by fears in the mother, especially during the fifth month of
pregnancy, created a maladjustment in the genes with respect to
certain Sensory environmental data. This was transmitted as an*

inherent vibrational agent that stealthily entered and affected each of their basic individual metabolisms when they first encountered social confrontation and the fear of rejection in its irrational form... "

* * *

The second diagnosis concerns K, the child of mother G, who exhibited disease in the organic Position of its collagen tissue, with incurable ramifications, according to the doctors.

SAINT PARASKEVI

"Here within the realm of activity of the weak conscience, move and reproduce the seven Elements of Life, which decays and is born."

In the woman there is a disturbance in the secondary glands, originating in and emanating from a central primary gland, and this disturbance of regular hormonal secretions is situated in the thyroid, with other glands as co-conspirators. The thyroid gives the order for fragmentation of a productive organic function, resulting in a shortage of substances of primary importance for the functionality and quality of matter in the Sensory organs and the myoskeletal Order. The cause can be located in a past life and first became evident through an inner disturbance in the individual's mother during the fourth month of pregnancy, and later through the interruption of the essential, harmonious working of the nervous system of the individual, which affected the predisposed fine cerebral neurons responsible for the normal functioning of multi-frequency emissions from the strong but delicate cerebral gland... The knowledge of specialists will come nowhere near the cause or the cure, because they lack knowledge of the workings of basic glands of the human Body and the appropriate Psycho-biological culture acquired through Spiritual integrity and correct thinking.

I submit my respects as the apple of Your all-seeing and all-giving eyes.

Created by Your Spiritual Grandeur"

* * *

When we arrive at the great moment of the sacrament of marriage, we must realize that various events marking our path, be they overt or covert, must necessarily be set apart from the great desire formed in the individual for a new direction, and for living a different life. It is the past that puts us in such a disagreeable position, where conflicting states and illusory desires create disharmony. And the pressure is such that it leads us to blame the other person. I repeat that any desire that manifests itself and makes us its willing servants will leave its mark not only on us but also on the embryo. I want to emphasize at this point that any kind of unwholesome sexuality may leave an unhealthy imprint on the newly formed life, since every thought arising from desire produces energy that transforms our vibrational field, but also the field of the embryo. Unexposed as yet to outside life, it absorbs Elements from its surrounding *Microcosm. These Elements create imprints on the embryo, so that when it is born it will carry with it the signs of the disturbance, which builds up into a state of *fear* out of an effort to correlate its own Position with the atmosphere in which it lives, and the unavoidable conflict this entails.

Every woman who decides to become a mother ought to know herself well enough to erase every emotional state from her past. Whatever has been offered to her (according to her own perception) under whatever circumstances, and whatever she has been deprived of at various times and for various reasons, must all be confronted eye to eye and she must make a strong voluntary effort to reject it before she embarks on the supreme mission of perpetuating the species, as ordained by the Law of the Creator for the perpetuation of Life. For almost 36 weeks the woman nourishes the embryo, on the one hand with energized Elements from the invisible Position, and on the other hand she offers it the proper nutritional substances though her Body protein, so as to successfully instill a positive expression of its human nature. In this material space the woman is endowed with visible and invisible Elements, in order to bring to completion the creation of Mother Will, elevated by the Creator to the status of co-creator and acclaimed by Mother Nature as one of her special members. I believe that for a society to develop according to the natural Laws, the woman must first be educated at the higher ethical levels of her Psychic state, since it is her role to be the first tutor in the process of Life. Correct educational instruction eliminates the danger of the child finding itself in the weak position of being deprived of his mother's Offer or care. However, the father also has the same obligations since he is in the same creational space and owes the same participation.

It is clear that when the newborn child arrives into our physical world, having passed through the mysterious corridors of animation, it finds itself in an unknown world and, armed with its natural inclinations and guided by its instinct, it attempts by way of various reactions (such as crying or laughing) to reveal its needs, so as to acquire the means that will permit it to continue living. And the only comforting and social aspects of the child's world are interactions with immaterial visitors and passers-by who observe him, but also often talk to him in a language he can understand, so as to shape his chronological development, which is inconceivable to people dominated by their Senses. But the laws of Nature lead him to carry on the great struggle to learn how to communicate with those he depends on. And thus driven by need, he makes every effort to understand the import and necessity of communicating with his so-called "parents." If the parents have developed their Psycho-Somatic (Soul-Body) awareness and not only Bodily awareness, as is usually the case, then the newborn will be greatly facilitated on the conscious level in communicating with them, and will learn all the exemplary lessons they are trying to teach him. He will therefore progressively develop hierarchic harmonious functionality within his emotional space.

However, if the parents are emotionally enslaved by the idolization of the flesh, then there exists in them a disharmonious functionality situated outside the natural Laws, having as its principal result the binding of the newborn individual to the physical form of his Body and the creation within him of biological conditions that perpetuate themselves within his chromosomal biology. These will consequently hinder his development into his natural state as an individual having a sense of social behavior and human cooperation, creating in him a binding dependency that will deprive him of any integral personal will. All this can be referred to as the "Oedipus complex."

We see that the newborn is governed by two great dependencies that forbid him to act of his own free will, yet with great effort he expresses, as best he can, the need that he has for help. These dependencies are, first of all, on Mother Nature, who renders him unable to activate his will at any given moment, and second on us, as he patiently reaps whatever we offer him because of our own desires. Thus he develops and experiences human support in his own world, where he lives within his own solitude, using crying as his main channel of communication. Crying, to me, indicates that there is a serious cause we are unaware of, and also that we are unable to support him exactly as we should. Throughout his development, although the Rules place the infant in a state of reaction, he possesses an elevated sense of receptivity, so that every happy or unhappy event is recorded as an imprint and expressed in such a manner that even minute disharmonies will create a hotbed of pathological pressure.

The Natural Law prescribes that about every seven years a cellular organic metabolic transmutation will occur within our bodies, something akin to a definitive massive restructuring of the characteristic individual elements that transpose the state of equilibrium or non-equilibrium into a new Position. During that time the individual is susceptible to disturbances, even to the possibility of invisible injury to his health, because the nervous system is greatly affected by this metabolic transmutation, with severe consequences to vital organic harmony.

* * *

And I hereby present an exposition of the bio-energetic transmutational state of Man from the original starting point of his conception, the stage of pregnancy, up to the span of his subsequent life here on Earth. This was made available by the great Position (entity) who passed through this Earth as a doctor and is now up above on a high functional mission, and who goes by the well-known name of **Asclepius**.

ON SPECIAL AND GENERAL METABOLIC CHANGES OF THE ORGANIC BIOLOGICAL POSITION OF MAN

FROM
ASCLEPIUS code 13 106

INVOCATION BY IOANNIS

As the Rules emanating from our Father the Creator have decreed concerning the life process in its biochemical foundation, development and *Metacyclic restructuring, which in everyday language we call "biology," I consider it imperative, because of the book I have written entitled *The Revelation After Ioannis*, to ask you, **Asclepius 13 106**, for a subtitle, and having conveyed to you Ioannis's greetings, I extend my hand in brotherly love and ask you for a complete presentation-analysis with regard to the biological and Elemental Bodily Position of Man, from the time of his conception to birth and from the time of his birth to the time of his departure again from this Earth. How many important special metabolic changes take place within his bio-functional Body, how many secondary ones and which glands undergo the most such changes? I ask for an explanation concerning the number of stages the individual

goes through to develop his perceptive awareness from the time of his birth up until he is
able to function autonomously (e.g. to make
subjective or objective decisions that are
acceptable to his immediate environment, to
society and to the State). And anything else you
consider of value for this book.

I salute you, awaiting your answer,

Ioannis

ASCLEPIUS code 13 106

*"Ioannis, I sing your praises. I am aligned to the Order of
development prescribed by the consonance of your code, at a
frequency that acts as an enzyme of the Heavenly Organism,
and causes all Elements to rise upwards through the catalytic action of beneficial chemical process. The symbol of this
configuration is 7+´.*

*"LIFE ORIENTATION FOR UPWARD EVOLUTION" is one
possible title for this book...*

*I bow to your presence in our space, you who are composed
of all the Elements in the Universe, whose Position Man is
unable to perceive, and I beg you, grant me the privilege of
seeing, there on Earth, your chromosomal fields, whose con-
figuring thought no one has as yet managed to perceive, in
spite of their many colorful manifestations.*

*We have, then, three Cycles, each within one quarter of the
time period whose Cycle is completed with the removal and*

departure of the Soul from its Bodily fields to other heavens and sources of a different Order of Life.

The third and fifth months of pregnancy are steady periods of somatic metabolic restructuring of the embryo's organic Position. Conception is the first metabolic change of enormous scope. The Being is progressively established in its Position as the sperm and the ovum actualize and consummate their union, as the attracted individual, in a state of readiness, gradually approaches his Bodily formation. With regard to his consciousness, he is in a phase of frozen immobility, his instinctive Position has been fixed in the Body and the Body attracts him biologically into the Somatic Position so that he can be genetically established in it. There, the 30 metabolic changes, erupting one after the other at very high speeds, swiftly order the biological life of the individual, while the Earth's field contributes decisively to the completion of the Cycles of pregnancy through appropriate magnetic Rules, so that the Position-Soul will be totally incorporated into the biology of the new Body. And its state of expectancy is followed by genesis. In the third month! Here the intermediate phases of organic connectivity are created out of hydrogenic Elements of the order 10. These are characterized by their condensation of the cerebral Order which, as a magnet, a receiver and transmitter, is redeveloped and shaped into its final form during the fifth month of pregnancy. During that time the mystery of the shaping of the brain as well as of the individual himself is carried out. The mother's fears during the fourth month have an essential and irrevocable influence during this next stage of condensation and consolidation, and this organic attempt at disengagement of the being from the compactness[15] of its previous Position, within the mother's confused[16] organic magnetism, does not resemble any other stage of life. Here also we have the advent of the baptism of the Mind... As you know...

This second metabolic process is followed by thousands more during life in the womb. With regard to the Cycles following pregnancy, I deem basic the adjustments during the sixth month after birth as well as earlier, during the third month. And then comes the great Cycle of one year.

During the third month the child is awed by his environment and he will try to adjust its biological Cycle to his vibrational temperament, but will end by adjusting his temperament to the Cycle of surrounding Life.

There the Etheric central points of the Body are also formed, to be completed shortly afterward during the ensuing phase of the 6th month (after birth), a phase marked by disturbances. Here, the genesis of the Senses is consolidated, a metabolic genesis of mental stimuli from the individuals in the immediate vicinity transmitted to the Sensory Order of the

---

[15] The Universal Law causes the being to be contracted relative to his previous expanded Universal Position, so that it can be attracted by the magnetic fields of the planet's biology.

[16] The biological position of the mother is affected by the turbulent atmosphere of the planet, as determined by its biology.

child as primary and unique receiver of emissions of Elements in his environment.

How many countless instances of metabolic genesis are conceived within the individual by the time he reaches 10 years of age! One momentous metabolic change every month! His glands, resilient and ready for training in the ways of the world, become the clay on which every sound, every vibration in every frequency, the faintest whisper and the loudest noise, are imprinted. The glands are synchronized to the emissions surrounding the human Body on the basis of the child's age and create a normalized identity, which becomes apparent at the ages of 9 and 12 years. Let me differentiate: the glands below the sternum are most receptive to environmental stimuli; the glands of the cranium to cerebral stimuli and the process of learning and freedom; those of the throat to memory.

For purposes of brevity I define the most important metabolic changes of Sensory development as those of the fourth year of life; of intellectual faculties, those beginning from the fifth year with their apex at the sixth; of readjustment to mental-image data, those of the seventh year, during which period important stabilizations and differentiations with regard to the child's visceral position also occur. At the stage of seven years, the great Law of Organic Creation completes its biological Cycle. And there certain decisive organic systems, primarily the anti-body and thermo-productive ones, are established and able to take their final shape. The possibilities for differentiation following this stage are usually very few. Only through **educationally induced biological changes** *can this be altered.*[17]

The crucial period at nine and at twelve years of age, is followed in its turn by the consolidation of the genetic glands in the Order of the animate organic environment, so as to establish the Body of the individual within the reproductive Order. During these years there is a glandular dilation in the magnetism of the environment, which has at that time the greatest opportunity to imprint its speeds,[18] *tendencies and propensities in the child's Body.*

And, behold the Revelation: During these periods (nine and twelve years of age) the important metabolic changes that are to follow are also defined, that is: when exactly they will occur and what possibility they will have for differentiation

---

[17] During the 7th year of age and thereafter the sense of sexuality begins to develop and, slowly, the strong pull in this direction begins to appear, leading the child in the wrong direction and disrupting harmonious visceral function. This is why "the possibilities for differentiation ... are few".

Because of all the difficult processes encountered by the child at this stage of growing up, it is neces-sary for the parents to make every effort to eradicate their egos and to create a bond with the child on the level of children, as friends, but also as protectors and guides.

Only in this way will the child be able to differentiate and develop well-adjusted visceral function of his emotional system so as to reach a point of development where he has adequate perception of the world and the way things function within it.

[18] Vibrational frequencies and biological metabolic rhythms.

from the established Order of the entity "INDIVIDUAL." In other words, the possible extent of any subsequent metabolic change, the readiness of the Body to accept and recover from it, as well as its duration, are defined at this stage. The nature of further metabolic changes is also determined, i.e. what they will consist of: Systolic disturbances and clogging of the endocrine glands or dilation of these glands and trans-mutation...

However, the most momentous metabolic changes, as a general rule, according to widespread observation, occur at the ages of 17, 21, 28 and 35 years and then at the ages of 45 or 40 for the female and thereafter every five or seven years. Or rather every five and seven years.

You may be interested to know that the most intense metabolic changes occur in the glands of the heart, the greatest number in the pancreas, with the most Cycles in the thyroid, and the fewest in the epiphysis and the suprarenal glands. The suprarenal glands, of course, are susceptible to a great number of transmutations, depend-ing on the circumstances. The epiphysis is not. The hypophysis (pituitary gland), the mysterious Position of the Body's Brain, is the purest with regard to metabolic changes. It receives all the disturbances, but in spite of the ease with which it functions logically, nothing affects it. Why?...

The secret Order of knowledge is the only key to the organic transmutations called metabolic changes. It also contains the differentiation between male and female within the framework of the magnetism to which, through the Natural Laws of the planet, all biological organs are subjected.

Please call me

AsclePio"[19]

SUPPLEMENTARY QUESTION BY IOANNIS ON THE DIFFERENCES OF MALE–FEMALE METABOLISMS

Yet again I seek you out for a supplementary revelation with regard to man and woman in their biological Position: How is their metabolic state differentiated in terms of their gender? Does it occur at the same prescribed times or do the times also differ due to their dissimilar composition? As we know, development of the individual also occurs with regard to Bodily structure. Up to what age does the individual develop Intellectually and Spiritually? And if by that age he has not developed into the human being that his nature demands, by which Rules is his bio-intellectual Position bound, remaining constant or entering an orbit of Decline? At what age will he

---

[19] This name is a combination of the initials "ASC" (Authority of Soul Cultivation) and "Pio" (from the Greek poio = to create).

begin having difficulties in the cellular renewal needed to maintain muscular vigor?

ASCLEPIUS code 13 106

"Ioannis, all-pervasive brain and creator of glory, become the intellectual perceptive vessel and create the Order of the invulnerable. The period of somatic metabolic changes in individualities on Earth becomes parallel for both sexes after the 24th year of age. Up to that age time and speeds differ slightly, with Nature giving precedence to the female, so that there is time to prepare certain tissues and glands and to shape their functional regularity. However, this behavior in cellular synthesis is what creates the differences of organic activity and inactivity in the two sexes. The female receptivity and dilation in response to the most delicate physical, chemical and biological codes, increases the intensity of metabolic changes and the physical alertness of the female. The difference in stamina depends on one's gender. In the female, the upheaval of the nervous system during periods of metabolic change may be diffused into other channels of energy and into other activity. In the male it is usually concentrated. The compact nature of his cellular composition calls for extremely pervasive action within his environment if he is to maximize the natural capacities of his metabolism. The female's Position is meant to be accepted into and to expand within the vibrations of her natural surroundings.

As far as his *Intellectual-Spiritual Position is concerned, each Being is called upon at every moment to act and to develop through its intellect and Body on the basis of this activity. The **Femino-Masculine Position**[20] *of the Law of the Spirit both permits and demands that the being be both dilated and diffuse to the Rules that surround it, as a female, and pervasive and inquisitively active, as a male. Glandular metabolic changes that allow the possibility of learning, the expansion or contraction of the being within its environment, always possess the ability to adjust themselves, but cellular response is amenable to dilation only up to the 49th year of life.*

This number is variable and does not apply to one and all, but is accurate in general. Prior apprenticeship in intellect- and Spirit-engendered developments and changes brings cerebral functionality to a state of readiness, able to support the individual toward further intellectual development. The Spirit does not succumb to Bodily Decline. The Body succumbs to Intellectual-Spiritual old age.

Cellular physical regeneration is metabolized at slower rates after the age of 24-25 years in Man. The obvious signs of this retardation were created in order to stir the still waters of the conventional Intellectual-Spiritual ways of the young and to propel them upward.

Intellectual indolence or involvement in monotonous trivial

---

[20] Containing both the male and the female (= neutral).

activity on Earth deprives Man of the view of wider horizons and, as he grows older, he enters the domains of pain, degradation and disease. Here, pain is not the joyful symptom of a regenerating metabolism, but the inhibitor and the prohibitor of all Intellectual-Spiritual expansion.

Nevertheless, Bodily cells have their prescribed time of decay, whereas Psycho-noetic cells, if they do not follow the fate of the former, tend toward immortality and evolution.

Let them be free."

Chapter 4

STAGES OF DEVELOPMENT

Nature swiftly puts the child through many trials in order to increase his spirit of endeavor, so as to endow him with the ability to confront all situations in life, while at the same time his mother and father, through their ignorance, transfer to this already heavily-burdened[21] individual unwholesome states that will exact their toll later on. For instance, an unfulfilled desire that, for whatever the reason, seems to be related at a given moment to certain individuals in the immediate environment, has, as I know, its true cause elsewhere. Any time we feel indisposed toward someone, want nothing to do with him or have other similar impulses, this leads to inner anxiety that expresses itself in some concrete form, often giving rise to negative social characteristics. This impels us to become aggressive in order to gain what our hidden thoughts consider to be profitable, and we thus begin exhibiting pathological behavior.

---

[21] Each individual carries in his Soul and chromosomes the encumberance or "burden" of his previous deeds.

Now, however, we have a child, attached to us and dependent on us, who is forced to bear the consequences of situations we create, as we lack the proper perceptive abilities required for the completion of our mission, and we therefore assume the passive role of a helpless observer. Inevitably, the child thus witnesses and absorbs unsuitable situations and conflicts. At the same time, because of our ignorance, we are unable to control our behavior either in time or in space, and so we expose the newly arrived individual to unwholesome states that will leave their imprint on him. And depending on his **natural *physiognomic constitution** (his inherent character structure), each individual will exhibit, in future, his own particular set of complexes and manifest them accordingly.

As Hippocrates revealed, it appears that Man is initially shaped according to a *constitution dictated by the Laws of Nature, through which he develops a particular awareness with regard to things surrounding him. Hippocrates describes four types of character and constitution, with many subdivisions, which come under the following names: Sanguine, Choleric, Melancholic and Phlegmatic. And these types of constitution determine the degree of rejection and acceptance of future developments, and resistance or openness of the individual with regard to his relationships.

The child will at first want to demonstrate his presence to his parents and then to all others, and to take his place in life and be recognized with the respect he deserves. His on-going experiences, his strongly developed **sense of loss**[22] and the

---

[22] This refers to the child's feeling of powerlessness to contol his own life.

aforementioned natural process (instinctive centers - autonomic nervous system - visceral centers - volitional nervous
system) intervene in his vibrational field, resulting in a certain
local or diffuse disharmony. His young age does not permit the
imposition of his wishes —latent or not— and he therefore
succumbs to the will of the parents, which has been formed on
the basis of their own binding socio-ethical conditioning. His
inability to assert himself thereby imposes a specific image
with regard to the person identified as Mother or as Father and
he strives in a most intimate way to win them over, in the hope
that this will be rewarding. Thus at times he conducts himself
actively by reacting and at times passively by withdrawing,
stimulating on each occasion the Sensory perception of the
parents so as to attract their attention. Their response will
sometimes be a reprimand, sometimes moral or material punishment and sometimes quiet and affectionate explanations.
Normally, however, our impulse as parents is to present, in an
authoritarian way, the rules of proper behavior that our own
imperfect perceptive abilities have accepted as correct, imposing and presenting ourselves as the sole experts in everything.

Soon the child goes to school and a new dependency
appears, as the teacher now exerts an influence, through
new and mostly erroneous projections and concepts. Our
own ignorance and false perceptions often put the child in a
position where injustice is inflicted upon him.

I would now like to briefly discuss the ***sense of loss*** referred
to above. Many instinctive Positions are not yet developed in the
child, or rather they remain in a latent state, so that he is not
able to fully and precisely comprehend events as they occur at

any given moment. Thus an incorrect sense of reality is created, individualized and seen from the point of view of the needs and desires of each child. Under these circumstances the sense of loss easily and quickly flares up, as the child, in his attempt to define the boundaries of his individual space by seeking to possess things, is often faced with loss of ground that sweeps along even the most vital characteristics of his psyche.

The sense of loss develops according to individual constitution, which has a very special Position in every boy or girl. We must realize that every Sensory feeling is entirely different in a boy than it is in a girl. However, here we are merely referring to Sensory feelings without proceeding to a detailed analysis. Perhaps in some other book I will deal in detail with this so that the reader may have the opportunity of recognizing many aspects of himself as they really are, which is very difficult, seeing as every dependency that binds us creates an impression that remains within us as an imprint. Depending on the time period and the physical state of the individual, this imprint constantly reproduces the image of this binding dependency and leads the individual, through the Senses, to a perception of things that makes him demand from the environment things that illusions have mistakenly led him to decide he must acquire and transmute into a means of relaxation. Only then will the binding desire be quelled and revert to the state of a "dormant imprint."

At this point I wish to refer briefly to the essential differences between the male and the female, as a central point of his or her missionary course here on Earth. In the female, the basic natural constitution organizes Sensory functions activated to manifest the Order of her Natural Position through the implementation of the Primordial Task of perpetuation of the species according to the Law that defined it, triggered by a particular attraction. In the male, nature arranges the organic cells of action in such a manner that particular stimuli arising from Sensory Positions excite the corresponding vibrational field in the viscera, so that the nervous system, responding to orders initiated in the hypophysis (pituitary gland), causes an emission that completes the interaction and the provision of special Elements which, received by the female, are transformed into an Offer to Mother Nature; and the Female is recognized as a co-creator.[23]

But we have here another function at work in the Sensory space of every individual, regardless of gender. This Position

---

[23] Medicine has dealt specifically with the development of the embryo, but also more generally with the development of the individual. It seems that everyone agrees that this process is governed by stages and by rules. Let us look at them more closely.

Following insemination of the ovum, rapid cell reproduction begins into 2, 4, 8, 16, and 32 new cells. More or less up to this point the entire formation lacks shape and differentiation. Slowly it becomes oblong, while on about the 40th day the first function develops as the heart and blood flow appear. The step immediately following is the formation of five small sacks from which all the organs and tissues of the organism will emerge. The one that is formed first and begins to function is the cerebral sack, primarily in the sense of the spinal cord. Thus, by the end of the first three months, the beginnings of all organs and tissues have appeared.

The second trimester is characterized by the rapid development of the organs, and, by the end of the 6th month, the embryo has acquired its own mobility. It is believed that it can hear sounds, feel and develop emotions, and interact with those of the mother.

The last trimester has to do primarily with the adaptability of the embryo to the new conditions it will be called upon to face. The last organ to develop is the lungs, through which the embryo will receive its first traumatic experience, the first breath.

acts on the process of our life course and always manages to exert its influence on us, leading us to a place where its functional space exists. If those above us, that is the Mother, Father and other authority figures, as described earlier, could not offer the appropriate services to us as young individuals with less sensitized awareness, then this Position acts on our entire Sensory space. First it acts on secondary Sensory centers, stimulating them to activation of the Senses to a dominant manifest role, so that the Position, which hap-

---

It is also interesting that until the 3rd month the embryo is of undetermined sex as far as the observer can determine. In the beginning there are common sexual characteristics, up to the point at which chromosome Y changes the development to male and bestows not only a different body type but a different functional development in general.

Referring now to the development of the infant we could say many things that are more or less common knowledge and passed on in classrooms round the world. Many schools of psychological research have studied the infant in order to discover the formation of the individual's personality. They all agree that the first three years critically influence development. It is during these years that dependencies, fixations and traumatic experiences take place, but also progression to higher stages of development in a way that reminds one more of leaps than steps.

It is important to see how medicine has shrouded the infant in a holistic viewpoint. That is, it speaks of psycho-somatic development, of psycho-somatic disease, with great ease. As if it considers that Body and Soul coexist in the infant, something that is immediately forgotten during analytical investigation of adult pathology, leaving psychology to deal with the so-called "psychic organ." Through the analytical process gender differences are oftentimes forgotten or become the object of statistical reference, whereas there is widespread indication of immense differences in the approaches of a man or a woman, not only psychologically but also somatically.

Besides, Ioannis's teachings stipulate: Men act first on a sensory-organic level, then muscularly and finally viscerally. Women act first viscerally, then sensory-organically and finally muscularly. [A.V.]

pens to be the biological state of the unconscious, will complete its task. Our socio-ethical conditioning may, however, reject this and hide it as disagreeable. Then, in a second phase, the activity of the Position compels us to conceal within us those events that diminish us in the social world, and we therefore create hidden recesses of complexes. The third phase of the Position's activity gives rise to repetitive occurrences of the act we wish to avoid, yet succumb to, in order to emphasize our inability to escape it and to justify it inwardly. Thus the constant repetition of the complex-induced concealment created by these circumstances "mollifies" it, for us at least, into a beneficial Position, and we now repeat something pleasant and legitimate. The trouble is that these pathological yearnings place under their control not only the Senses but also our progression through life, altering the task we have to accomplish in our mission. And if these hidden complexes are found out at some point, then the judgment of the people who have trusted us will be merciless. And even if they are not found out, the functioning of the Position continues in the future in a latent state, transposed during various time periods onto the functional Sensory space, so that a nebulous desire is created in the individual to seek the experience-encounter with the feeling that had once taken hold inside him.[24]

---

[24] Here, the Position exposed reminds one somewhat of the analysis by Adler, the German pioneer of psychoanalysis, who speaks of the inferiority complex, that is, the propensity of man to experience the world and events around him through a perception of inferiority, in his attempt to make his Position creative.

Let us now return to the child at the time he first goes to school. There he will meet the teacher for the first time and, from that point on, he will enter a new atmosphere, in which the presence of the teacher takes shape and begins to infiltrate him as a third dependency. Then a new struggle begins in the new world he encounters to satisfy the emotion-rooted demand of his parents that he become an educated individual. Rightly so, since the function of people of all nations is to cultivate the individual, so he can acquire knowledge through his initial perceptions, which will become the proper springboard for *correct perception* in any walk of life he may eventually follow. However, the child is not able to feel that this is beneficial, but often takes it wrongly, as if it were a command given by the parents, and since he depends on them, he succumbs to their demands out of pure need. The child thus makes an attempt to communicate with the teacher, in order to receive his Offer, which for the child is proof.

Now, if the teacher has not been liberated from everything we mentioned above, then he cannot make a conscious Offer or cooperate with the child in order to make him feel that the world is his own, and that this same world demands that he acquire the knowledge that will provide him with the ability to become a member of it in good standing, according to the stan-

---

It also brings to mind the bleak Position, described by the psychoanalyst Melanie Klein, that the individual assumes during the early stages of development in order to live through the loss and deprivation of enjoyment from the mother, something that is often repeated at later times.

However, as the creator of this book reveals, this Position is the unconscious. [A.V.]

dards of society in any given Age. Here the Teacher must be extensively educated in child psychology, or at least have access to whatever knowledge is currently available with regard to the functional development of the child, so as to be familiar with the particular behavior exhibited by the child and to have the necessary patience to reveal to him through mutual cooperation the process of progressive conscious perceptions. However, as far as this communication is concerned, there can be considerable negative influence on the child by the teacher who has no adequate functional knowledge about him, and thus the child finds himself in a situation of rule enforcement, with the result that the third dependency is established.

We see that every individual, at the starting point of his life, is bound by these three dependencies, each more demanding than the other. In this complex-ridden situation he cries out in agony for liberation. This manifests itself in the frequent occurrence of characteristically childish reactions. Yet when the child finds himself in a place he controls, the symbolic freedom makes him create things around him according to his own perception, mimicking our influence on him. Thus, play is the only area in which the child can realize his symbolic liberation at any given time, and thereby gain confidence in his functional participation in his social environment.

The years go by, however, and soon comes that special age at which nature demands a new adjustment of the organic biological Position with a new function. Depending on the environment and the child's constitutional formation, a new Position will begin to evolve within the individual. This Position is, in fact, also a dependency, although it takes the form of an outlet toward fulfillment of a particular desire. If we pay close attention we will see that Nature always creates realignments in the organic functionality of the individual. During this phase of development, a new energetic push is created that first leads the individual toward liberation from his initial fixation and dependency, that is, from the primary need for care by his parents in order to survive, and then toward differentiation in his emotional awareness.

Thus, natural influences on the one hand and established society on the other, with its complex interdependencies and interactions, lead parents and teachers to perceptions of Life that they apply to children from their own egocentric view-point. This is perceived by the child as the imposition of a life plan, leading to a need for disengagement from the parental and educational environment.

The parental saying: "Let the child not suffer what I suffered," is dictated by the need to demonstrate a correct parental role, and its authenticity is challenged by the child, who is unable to make comparisons between different periods of time or to foresee his Position in the future. The child, existing in a present colored by dependency and reaction to any form of subjugation, and whose sense of loss is not yet developed to a logical degree permiting him to understand such things as parents' admonitions from a different and more secure standpoint, is living through his own inner social turmoil which manifests itself in rebellious behavior toward the family and also toward society. However, as we know how precious is the child's time in terms of the knowledge that he must now acquire, lest he be deprived of it forever, we have the obligation to put ourselves in his position and understand the inner realignments that nature imposes on him so that he will be able to proceed to the second stage of life.

During this second stage, Mother Nature creates in the child new centers of attraction for outer images, and also the desire for him to be near them, to experience them and to develop provisional perceptive awareness of them. However, organic nature, as a Rule of evolution, must at the same time remove all pathological states that the parents, in their ignorance have passed on to him without realizing it, before these states manifest themselves and take control of his will and impose a sense of injustice on him. And since all this and more is going on inside the child, we must always be close to him, and be aware of how he perceives various situations. We must look on with attention and patience, so as to become suitable counselors for him through our own proper conduct. His path to learning and increasing his knowledge necessitates the recognition of his abilities. We must let the child know that what we are asking of him or suggesting to him is not all that difficult, that he can accomplish it because he has the abilities. At first he may not perceive the meaning of the words and he may react unfavorably. However, in the face of our persistence and through various pathways of understanding, the child will see our proposition as a compromise, having also discerned our great inner desire to assist him. The effort that he will make in a given field of learning will also be confirmation that we are close to and stand by him, and this will give him such satisfaction that he will want to increase his attention, not only to please us, but also himself, through the recognition of his individuality.

When the child follows parental suggestions, the inner satisfaction stemming from this also leads to confidence in his superior abilities and effectiveness in still other fields of competition, where the opponents are not the parents and the teachers, but sometimes people at the highest levels of knowledge. Often, the child, because of his constitution, identifies himself and his goals with some real-life, famous person, who is accepted into his emotional space and is also seen as a model for emulation. For this reason the child needs delicate guidance and attention to realize that he is no longer in a position of subservience to us, but that we acknowledge and respect his individuality. *We must approach the child as comrades, as friends and then as parents*, so as to help him develop sound character, even if his constitution is such that it hinders the development of the accurate perception needed to help him achieve the goals he has set for himself.

I refer to the constitution of the individual because Nature has created us with a variety of characteristics which cause differences in individual perceptions of subjectively or objectively similar things, and therefore give rise to differing reactions in each person, depending on the life-stage of organic transmutations he is undergoing. For example, a basic transmutation occurs in the girl at the age of four years, when a new biological state is formed within her organism, developing through the years in the way Nature intended until it is brought to completion in the mature woman, who assumes special new duties in the service of Mother Nature for the perpetuation of Life. In this space-time interval of realignments, many sensitivities are created that emanate from latent fears stemming from hotbeds originating at the starting point of life and progressively consolidated up until about four years of age. Under the pressure of these realignments, and in light of the above, it is only natural that the girl is confronted by difficulties in her development. At the same time additional hotbeds are being created and progressively produce disturbances whose causes are so latent in form that we are prevented from recognizing their origin in some hidden fear and reacting to it appropriately. Thus, parents and various specialists are unable to obtain information and, as a result, the hotbeds do not remain quiescent but are transformed into special signals to the autonomic nervous system, which then acts on the viscera and disturbs the harmony of their function, resulting in an integrated pathological field of disharmony. Such fields erect a mysteriousness around the inner voices and attractions experienced by the girl. These qualities are now created not by inner serenity but by fields of confrontation. Thus, she is seized by distress and begins exhibiting various, mainly irrational, types of behavior.

Nature has the same influence on boys, with an important difference regarding age. The boy begins, at about the age of seven, to enter a new organic functionality, into which nature leads him in her own mysterious way of realignments. Thus, while on the one hand we have the removal of already inactive organic cells that at one time shaped special Positions of the child, on the other hand we have the addition of new cells that activate semi-latent Positions so that, within this Metacycling, the same stirrings as in girls are awakened, with similar uncontrollable reactions. At the age of 11 to 16 years, during which time the aforementioned massive addition and removal of Elements occurs, the boy is led to a new perceptive awareness of life in a mysterious way, not through tangible consciousness — something I may not elaborate on here. Through this redefinition of Life the individual is, at this stage of life, a prey to inner impulses that cause him to outwardly conform to the characteristics prevalent during a given Era. Since these images have established their presence in him in a singularly attractive manner, they influence his biochemical state through magnetic activity. Thus the individual almost always finds himself in a complex-ridden latent space that he tries to assimilate within the interrelated circumstances of the past and the future, amidst the Positions striving to enforce their presence.

Thus the physiognomic presence (inherent character) of the present is formed, as the sum of two components: On the one hand, there is the newly-attracted perception of the future, creating an impulsive state of restlessness, spurring the development of the capacity to acquire whatever knowledge will offer the personal acknowledgement and social recognition so greatly valued by the culturally accepted Rules of our times. On the other hand, the past asserts its presence by way of a retrogressive attraction presenting those special moments that have occurred sporadically during the periods of the great dependencies and created invisible pathogenic hotbeds, so that for each obstacle confronted, they act almost as a catalyst to weaken the will. This results in a pathological reaction that sends a signal to these hotbeds to function unconsciously, with resultant consequences both for the Psycho-social behavior of the individual and for his health, in the broadest sense of the term. At such moments, if the individual is not assisted constructively by the parents —and this is difficult as they are unfamiliar with the natural history of the functional Rules of the first years of the life of the child who, of course, cannot express his inner needs and conflicts as they really are— then he finds an outlet for his impulses by attributing blame to others, at the same time retreating to the past in order to experience an illusive sense of power and protection, while he is in conflict with others in the present.

So we see that, whereas nature gradually leads the individual through time into the future, supplying him with all the tools necessary to help him create a true purpose for his life here on Earth and assert his presence by developing into an individual united in Body and Soul, at the same time, under the enslavement of particular images encountered along his path, he is forced to carry within Nature's special gland (the thyroid) all the liabilities of his past, resulting in the creation of a complex-ridden state in his inner functionality. This state creates the impulse to propel himself into a space where an emerging desire for an outlet through assimilation of "paragon" Elements of other individuals is created. Modeling himself on such "paragons" diverts perception outside the individual toward goals with complex-related roots in latent productive Positions. In this way, self-perpetuating situations are created that structure personalities into erroneous activation around a central productive Nucleus of complex emotional disturbance, a condition that we call confusion. And this confusion is the result of the carrying over of certain charac-teristics of the individual which were conceived during some other time period for some specific purpose in order to ensure his passage through Life on Earth and the successful perfor-mance of his particular missionary function; but somewhere along the way he was misled away from the route of purity and serenity and followed the road of agitation and instability, for which his payment in the present is: Disharmony and the resultant semi-chaos, or complete chaos.[25]

---

[25] This description will certainly remind one of the Old Testament and original sin, with specific nominal reference to Adam and Eve as repre-sentative elements of the personality molded "in Paradise" through conflict and interaction.

We must also say a few words here concerning the thyroid gland referred to above: The thyroid is located in the throat, in front of the tra-chea, that is, at the level midway between Heaven (the head) and Earth (the body). It derives its name from its shape, which resembles an escutcheon (in Greek, "thyreos"), the emblem, that is, of a dynasty (imme-diate unconscious correlation with the role that Ioannis's teach-ings assign to it). It is controlled through the hypothalamus-hypophysis axis (the "Essential Visual" field of Ioannis's teachings discussed in Chapter 11) and produces thyroxine: a hormone with many functions at multiple lev-els (from the control of temperature and metabolism to the control of development and emotional and intellectual stability).

The basis of the molecule thyroxine is iodine, an element awarded a prominent position in Ioannis's teachings, and also the element that leads us to the sea, to the water of life. [A.V.]

Chapter 5

REGARDING THE INNER WORKINGS OF THE INDIVIDUAL

I t would be only correct for me to make a great effort to trace these matters from their beginning and slowly follow their entire course, keeping an exact record of the manner in which they are produced, attracted and reproduced until they reach a stage of development in which their presence occupies the entire space of the instinctive centers. These matters, these conditions, chart in Man an *invisible path*, which runs parallel to his *natural conscious path*, two routes that control and are mutually controlled, that influence and are mutually influenced, that coexist and bring about life in its active dimension. The invisible path has two aspects: the harmonious aspect, which is lived under ideal non-toxic conditions, and the illusory aspect, which is produced as follows: since conditioning resulting from our experiences occupies the entire space of the instinctive centers, vitalized by the viscera, every image arising in this space activates this conditioning through invisible magnetism and drives it to create illusions that become fixated as primary Elements in key Positions within us, toward which our Sensory centers are already internally oriented. Thus, internal productiveness has a definite direction, according to which the illusory aspect animates and creates latent Positions that slowly occupy more and more vital space, transforming it into a disharmonious state, which in turn dominates and composes an invisible "individuality," to whose existence we submit, surrendering to this "individuality" the governing of our self. From that moment on we are guided by something that has been called "Ego."[26]

Thus, schematically, the Ego is created from Etheric molecular Elements of pathogenic systems[27] which, combining at a certain period of time for each individual, acquire functional characteristics and define a very strong individuality that shapes our entire emotional world and leads us to absolute submission of our perception along the route that it charts. The various expressions of the will of the Ego are revealed to our perception and can be described by the common phrase "our emotional world." This emotional world occupies 92% of the individual biological entity. This per-

---

[26] Referring to the "Ego" of Psychiatry, we can say in a few words that we are talking about the center of consciousness of the self, which shares and controls reality. Through this our senses are experienced and thoughts are expressed. It is situated ("topographically" for the sake of psychological research) at the center of the "psychic organ," in front of the Id of the instincts and the Superego of the judges of Conscience. [A.V.]

[27] The Sensory Ego consists of a lower Etheric molecular system that always leads the organism into pathological manifestations (diseases) that attack the self and others.

centage is given on the basis of the functionality of the unconscious which, as a biochemical emission belonging to the Order of the negative, on a scale of 100%, occupies an area of 92% unconscious (negative) and 8% conscious (positive). And let no one think that 8% is a small percentage. Because though Life may also appear to be a nebulous and uncertain presence, it is nevertheless responsible for the propagation of many acts, and gives proof of this through its presence. However, the individual is influenced more by the negative, because it coexists within his vital nourishment produced for him by the planet. This planet is said to be pathological, in the sense that it extends a net that almost always prevents anyone from escaping from the field in which he is entrapped.

Thus, it is extremely difficult for him to surmount this obstacle and enter the space of Spiritual evolution, which is the space of freedom, peace, joy and absolute respect for Man and Life. Only after the individual has experienced this space will he find himself at some point in time in such a special Position — one where new Elements, invisible up to now during his progression through life, are reproduced, activated and attracted by his Bodily existence, and provide the special Offer of Universal production. This results in a new and different activation of the same instinctive centers, which leads the individuality to function under a concrete plan of "aim and acquisition." Within this activated individuality, the Guide of conscience-based thought evinces its presence, ensuring that this Spiritual evolution will furnish the individual with super-strong characteristics that will upgrade him to special states of being, place him under his Creator and show him the special and vacant Position that He has allotted him for the fulfillment of his function. At the same time it offers him the great opportunity to try to perceive the Position of the Creator and to place his will under His, acquiring the ability always to direct his thoughts toward the beneficial side and further his Spiritual evolution. In addition, he will be able to create an Offer to other individuals so that they may acquire the perceptive awareness necessary for knowledge of Life. Such an Offer will lead the individual to absolute objectivity, as it is defined here on Earth, in the sense of a capacity for correct evaluation of every kind of manifest or imagined occurrence or appearance of unfulfilled desires remaining fixated within us and exerting conscious pressure —at least as we perceive it— or creating impulsive attempts at fulfillment, thus hindering our Elevation.

Egocentric thinking in Man, produced by the biological Position of the unconscious, has the ability to take away, from the special organic center we have just analyzed, all those functions that shape inner awareness, and it thus replaces true expression with sensual desire, which turns us into instruments of its will. Such thoughts are always ready to lead us off on a quest for Elements belonging to Woman or Man, having first persuaded ourselves that our Position here on Earth is not complete (in the sense of complete happiness). Such a perception leads to a feeling of great inner impotence in the throes of an emotional state we ourselves create called "loneliness," which leads us to the pursuit of happiness. Thus our thinking creates, as a counterbalance, the necessary desire to undertake action in order to find the individual *who will complement this extensive lack we have already created within ourselves.*

Here we must take under serious consideration the Law of Natural Evolution and the Law of Negative Decline, which shapes the constitution of the individual so that it becomes susceptible to the attractive magnetic influences of internal states manifested by various chromosomal Cycles. Every chromosomal emission that is the result of a particular Cycle leads to the development of a pulsative tremor at the special organic center called the thyroid, in the form of an action on the Law by the Anti-law. This pulsation will be transmitted to other centers and also to the thymus gland. If these centers do not possess prior functional stability, they will be influenced, and at the same time will develop a disharmonious functionality in visceral space. This unpleasant feeling creates a need for an outlet, which will be developed in our minds into something we experience as so beautiful and so cathartic that we are overwhelmed by desire and magnetized by an indefinite attraction. Thus, without realizing it, we become bound to states of attraction that occurred at certain points in our lives.[28]

---

[28] The thymus gland is situated behind the sternum and in front of the lungs and the heart. Its main function is the development of the immune system (in cooperation with other formations). Here the lymphocytes of the new organism mature, and request the creation of a "memory" of every "intruder," so as to be ready the next time to act even faster. Here also the "memory" of the identity of cells and of substances of the organism itself is acquired, so they will be recognized as friendly and not be attacked by the immune system.

For this reason every individual brought to life must strive to cultivate his perceptive awareness in the midst of the conditions and events which appear at different stages of life and fill us with such enthusiasm that we believe we have gained something important, until it is shattered, often with the same degree of intensity that it first took hold of us. And then a sense of futility takes over, crushing many vital functions. It is precisely at this point that we must live calmly through the disappointment and *consciously accept the errors that have led to this.* Then it will be easy to discern, in individuals around us, similar assimilated desires in which they have invested a lot of themselves, leading them to feel their hidden aggressiveness as a need to achieve what they have set up as their ideal. Thus the trap of "the difficult struggle for survival," into which they so easily and covertly translate everything, is experienced as an anxious need for further conquests. This causes upheaval in our inner world —the visceral vibrational field— which loses its controlling capacity and malfunctions to the point where circulation in

---

The thymus gland, having completed its mission, slowly atrophies and degenerates after the 15th year of age.

The teachings of Ioannis also connect this function to the memory of intruders other than microbes.

It is "strange" that the name thymus makes us think of "affect" (in Greek thymic), which defines the tendency of emotion to exist and to dominate. On the other hand, the Greek word thymos (anger) denotes the emotion that presupposes a memory of non-fulfillment or abstention from a desire.

Once again Knowledge has preceded research in the laboratory and the moment when the latter eventually deduced the "truth" through instrumental demonstrations. [A.V.]

the organism (*blood — oxygen — chemical-hormones — messages*) is altered, causing an immediate reaction of restorative circuits (*in the brain, the limbic system and the reticular formation which act on the hypothalamus-hypophysis, and also through the autonomic nervous system, on the thyroid-suprarenal and kidneys as a support center of the suprarenal glands, and through these peripheral centers the action is eventually diffused throughout the organism*). In this way arise all the well-known symptoms of what is known as stress, which constitutes the curse of the century. [29]

---

[29] It is well known in medicine that the endocrine glands, such as the hypophysis, the thyroid and the suprarenal glands, secrete hormones that act as transmitters of more central messages. Experiments have demonstrated their immediate action on visceral functions of homeostasis or defensive reaction. It has, of course, become apparent that they relate to the mood of the individual, from which it is logical to connect them to cerebral centers "darker" in function. However, we are attempting here to get away from the analytic way of thinking, to read between the lines, so that True Individuality may be revealed within the framework of threefold Creation, something that medicine demonstrates either through its accomplishments or its mysteries. But medicine itself refuses to see this. [A.V.]

Chapter 6

MARRIAGE

I t would be greatly beneficial if we had knowledge, or if some specialist in these areas could fill us in, concerning what I am about to present below. For if we were able to apply this knowledge, we could put a stop to the misleading factors that subjugate us and lead us, without our realizing it, to self-destruction. And I mean **self-destruction**, and I insist on this, because I know what Life is and how the vital characteristics of its biological and Etheric existence and dimension are constructed, whereas you still remain within the perception of condensed matter afforded to you by your Reflective Visual system, itself having its own biological composition, and functioning according to its biochemical condition. Whereas we do not know Etheric nature, even though it is used by Man and it is what creates us.

Since we will not be able to find ourselves in a state of full understanding of the absolute principle, so as to discern the exact primary origin of things, I will try to present this through a certain secondary principle, which I believe to be the meeting of a man and a woman. And how could things be otherwise, since, as we well know, states that are perpetuated are always transferred by the two sexes?

Let us then come to the point where nature pulls us and leads us to the demonstration and realization of rituals of attraction[30] involving the presentation of our sex, but also involving the perpetuation of the species. At the time of their meeting, the two individuals find themselves in a state of perceived desire for total unification, believing that they will solve all the problems created by their behavior up to now, problems that have consumed and therefore fixated their thinking, so that they seek an outlet through the acquisition of a new social relationship leading to beauty and serenity. During such times, it is "easy" to circumvent insurmountable difficulties, to realize impossible things and to acquire those features which, when complemented, will lead us to that most beautiful state we call "happiness." And we therefore find ourselves in this new state filled with happy thoughts for a future shaped into bright images, offered to us as a great gift for our own gratification only. And this false scenario brings us to such a position that we overestimate the opposite sex (naturally, there are some cases where the evaluation is correct), accepting this and following the path leading to confirmation of this union before God and society through the holy ritual of marriage; and when the marriage has taken place, then our Position in Life is made official in

---

[30] Actions that exert a certain magnetism toward their ritualistic completion.

an aura of solemnity. Because we then assume the responsibility, as has been ordained, for carrying out our duties toward each other and together fulfilling the natural human calling, as the Law of Creation ordains. But we have just seen that marital relationships, for the most part, are seen through a filter of overestimation within the world of actual human values. And since we have created such an illusion in our minds, we put forward our needs accordingly, and we demand their complete fulfillment, to justify ourselves and arrive at the desired state of beauty we have chosen, trying to experience infinitude in the domain of human life.

Formed and operating within our sensitive emotional world, such imagery imposes its presence as a magnetic predominance that we ourselves have permitted by accepting the erroneous functionality of things, leading us to false images that we create in our minds and mistake for the happiness of eternal life. Because of these illusions that we cultivate without realizing it, we find ourselves bound by circumstances, deprived of true perceptive awareness of our space-time position, which would correspond to our true Position on Earth. Time tries to demonstrate this true Position in its own everyday manner within the history of any life form, and especially that of a Human Being, by pinpointing right there within us THE OUTCOME of every life process here on Earth. If, through such perceptive awareness, we could become conscious of all, or at least part, of the illusions we mentioned above, I believe that the conditions of extreme disharmony hindering natural vibrations would not have such an influence on the nature of organic functionality of the individual. It is this very lack of vibrational harmony that impels thoughts formed in the past to manifest themselves in the present, leading the individual into his own malleable world, as we try to "reanimate" thoughts into offering us the beautiful things magnified by the illusions emanating from our unconscious.[31]

After the marriage has taken place for what we would like to think are natural reasons, but are often psychological reasons, we believe that during our marriage we can re-examine every bad experience we had in the past and overcome or rectify it. Here I can say with great certainty that whatever crosses our path in life and is experienced emotionally leaves an imprint on us that is very difficult to erase. If a man cannot control his every inner thought and locate the negative and positive aspects of the past without trying to justify his mistakes, and if he does not infuse true substance into his desire so he may very easily ask forgiveness for any irrational act he might commit, then he is not able to function in harmony. It is harmony that will bring about serenity, a necessary condition for the acquisition of self-knowledge, which contains the power to analyze any experience undergone in

---

[31] In the classical view of the school of psychoanalysis, regressive fixations invested with emotional material deriving from the early stages of personality development are responsible for the specific structure of everyone's character, so that the individual is led, through various unconscious mechanisms, to emotionally similar situations diverting the intellect from all logical connection with the primary material, whose purpose is to help the individual attain the security or the emotional fulfillment that he seeks. This is called an anxiety or neurosis-producing relationship with residual emotions from past experiences... [A.V.]

the past and the capacity to accept, as power symbols, the positive as action-based satisfaction and the negative as experience, while relegating to oblivion the extent of their hold on us. Because, if such perceptive awareness does not exist, every unconscious projection of the past will be transformed into a mutated conscious Position sending the autonomic nervous system out of control, and resulting in a disturbance of the central nervous system in its productive functional space, which will be invaded by stress-producing factors. However, since the individual is not able to perceive the source of stress, he transfers the blame to external factors. Thus, the immediate environment, and the marital partner in particular, is heaped with blame, in the form of accusations that he or she is not behaving correctly toward the other, or that he or she cannot meet the demands of his or her natural Position, which means, when translated, the fulfillment of needs. From that moment begin the visible and under-the-surface confrontations that shatter the initial underlying unity of marriage.

On this foundation, given the natural impulse of the sexual Position of man and woman, at a certain moment conception of an embryo will occur, completing its bodily formation during the nine months of pregnancy, so that all the functional centers develop according to their predetermined biological substantive existence and dimension and mature sufficiently to respond to the demands of external atmospheric conditions. Such preparation is indispensable in order for every center of the new individual to develop its Position, attuned to the atmosphere and offer its services to the individual so that he in turn may develop in full those characteristics representing the Human Position.

Let us pause for a while as the embryo takes shape. We must realize that, since it develops inside another individual (the woman), whom nature shapes in such a fashion that she can offer the appropriate conditions and the necessary substances for survival, there exists an absolute unifying process. This tells us that, since the woman has accepted this mission, she must be fully aware of her own importance and rid herself of the false imagery of past situations and of all other thoughts that might produce vibrational imbalance. Any such disturbance has an effect on the developing organism, and will be received and assimilated as its own, because proper development demands, both in quality and in quantity, appropriately selected elements of nourishment (environmental sustenance).[32]

Thus the embryo will satisfactorily form its own centers, which will lead to the harmony called for by its own vibrations. Only then will development be correct and the new life have the constitution that will give it the capacity to acquire comprehensive awareness of its course, understanding any situation that might arise and activating the appropriate responses to protect its moral-intellectual health. Because, if the individual is not offered the proper motherly "nourishment" during

---

[32] The meaning of the term used here has to do not only with structural and nourishing elements, but also with hormonal messages and neural impulses that control the flow, normalcy and quality of interaction, that is to say, what we call "environment." [A.V.]

the period in which its organic state is forming its Position, a partial or total dysfunction will develop, resulting in a corresponding constitution, which will not permit the individual to develop his perception on the wide scale needed to recognize every space-time situation he will encounter or create during his lifetime.[33]

I pass this on to you with absolute certainty, since I possess special knowledge about *physiognomics*.[34]

And as the Creator created the individual in his complete Elementation and formation, his initial nourishment is Etheric matter. He receives this from a special center, but at the same time from the peripheral Positions of this center whose primary purpose is to configure his constitution in the form that will establish his emotional state at a speed that some will be able to control and some will not. Those who can will be without complexes. Others whose constitutional state will not allow them to control these speeds will be dominated by the magnetic attractions of external factors shaped by the atmosphere or by people whose paths, for whatever reasons, will cross their own. And on the basis of the internal emotional behavior

---

[33] First trimester of pregnancy: Stage of creation of the organs. It is considered the critical stage for the organic integrity of the embryo. Embryonic deficiencies "of unknown cause," well known to doctors. Here, teaching proceeds to sub-clinical stages of "diseases" or "syndromes," that is, dysfunctions, without apparent signs, something the proponents of preventive medicine would very much like to know. [A.V.]

[34] By the term *physiognomics* we mean the science of analysis of characteristic signals of the individual's constitution, through elements of his physiognomy, or assimilation with the model to which he is attached and which functions within him. [A.V.]

of their Elemental Bodily composition they exhibit an Etheric chromosomal emission often expressed as an explosion of sound, while other individuals, depending on their constitutional Elemental composition, become receptors or rejecters of these emissions. Individuals who project pathological emissions when others reject them feel an internal pressure and are therefore ready to explode, some with impetuous aggressiveness, while others, with passive perseverance, seek the right moment to attack. Or even to destroy themselves.

The types of constitutional Elementation based on the principles of crime, stealing, violence and suicide are classified according to four main points, each of which is composed of three main elements that form a complex, and this prevents the conscience from imposing its Position to stop the individual from committing an act whose result will be overly painful for him. And we get 4 X 3 = 12, the Twelve Gates of the Heavenly vaults, from which the **dodecapus complex**[35] derives, under whose influence toxic states are situated and act. It is upon this base that the foci or hotbeds of the negative Position in Universal creation —about which we all know— are formed, so as to enslave the individual under their influence. This is why we see petty disputes and arguments developing between people, leading to minor conflicts, or even to major confrontations, which eventually trap people in the erroneous perception that "I'm always right, whereas everyone else is always wrong."

---

[35] See Chapter 12.

118

For three years I conducted research on this subject at all social levels, in order to determine whether there are really people who are wrong. Finally, it was found that all of them are right!... This is true because each of us functions according to his own subjective perceptions and, on the basis of his perceptivity, formulates his demands on people with whom he has some kind of relationship.

In human organic structure, the productive transmitter is the Subconscious, from which two frequencies are emitted that modulate two Orders in Man: the Conscious objective, 8%; and the Unconscious subjective, 92%, where subjective means uncontrollable, i.e., 92% of things are wrong in the scale between the two extremes of emission from the Subconscious. Because, as has been formulated within the biological state of the planet Earth, as well as within that of other planets belonging to the same Intermediate Universe between the Higher and Lower Universes, the scale of the biological state rises to 92% in the negative and to 8% in its positive potentiality. Since the biological state of the planet is in this proportion of positive-negative and Man is biologically aligned with this atmosphere, he will consequently have the same scale as a Bodily biological Position, because it is impossible for Man to differ biologically from the very nature that provided the Elements for his composition...

It is possible that upon hearing this great difference of proportion between positive and negative you will be disappointed. However, it is not at all disappointing. For you should know that on this planet, as well as on others like it, the negative has a dynamic Position in life, one of influence, but conditionally; it has rights only on those whom it influences. The positive is a self-reproducing Order with very strong dynamics which gives Man the opportunity to seek it and invoke its presence, thereby activating its 8% to progress toward domination of the 92%. And in this way he is elevated into a Spiritual relationship with himself and distinguishes himself in the luminous Heavens. Besides, there is a thought that people often express: "This man had or took advantage of the opportunity to succeed in life... " And here I assure you that the Spiritual evolution of Man is the result of only one opportunity presented to him. And this belongs to the 8% of his positive side here on Earth.

And be advised that the number 8, in the creation of the Universe, comes first, followed on the same level by 7 and 9.

This particular point is very important and for this reason we must pay particular attention and try to observe the existing conditions around us, toward whose formation we most certainly contribute in a completely irrational way! Then calmly and with a cool head, which ensures the objective judgment through which we will be able to recognize the space-time point at which a given situation first took root, we will be appropriately activated to achieve what for us is the most beneficial outcome, as prescribed by our human and ethical social Position. Only in this way will we be able to offer what the Universal Law of Evolution demands.

Initiation of the process of acquisition of such perceptive awareness leads, according to the Law of the Creator, in two directions, either of which we may freely follow. They take the following form and expression: One leads to a process of Decline all the way to catastrophic destruction difficult for Man to conceive, even through what scholars call metaphysical awareness. From such a dire Position the individual must do many things and go through many stages in order to return to a Psychic state that will permit his re-ascension. It is the other direction that leads the individual to higher levels of Psycho-Somatic (Soul-Body) Position, where he will be granted the facility of correct perceptivity at all times, so that he can go forward in his mission. For the road to Decline does not fulfill the purpose of our existence in this world, since it deludes the individual in such a way that, bound to his past, he consumes himself around what Plato would call *thoughtforms (fictitious images in the mind), and what I would call "ghosts." These come to us when called up by uncontrolled thinking subjugated to our subjective desire, which deprives us of the will to evolve and liberate ourselves from the Earthly weaknesses that entrap us.

It may be quite difficult to understand how we become bound by every event that occurs, even from our initial state of inception, that is, from the moment the male sperm induces fertilization up to the moment when the broadest perceptive awareness is attained during our actual life. It is true, however, that this initial activation and the events that occur in the environment during the moment of fertilization are extremely important!

We spoke earlier of the relationship between the woman and the embryo, but we should not overlook the Position of the man, who through invisible atmospheric contact "intrudes" upon the functionality of the embryo. Thus every event that works against the harmonious functionality of the parents leaves a mark on the embryo, through vibrational waves emanating primarily from the mother, but also from the father, through interaction with his spouse.

Because of this fact, each of us must follow a new emotional course after marriage with regard to his entire inner character, and proceed humbly and enthusiastically into the new life he has chosen, realizing that he has taken a great mission upon himself and that he must carry it out extremely well. Only then will he be able to sever his bonds with the false ghosts he created in the past. Then he will attain such a degree of purity that he will be able to control every point in time and space, and also to familiarize himself completely with his mission, so that he can offer his presence correctly to the new individual that he himself has decided to bring into the world, through his developing sense of satisfaction with the course on which he has successfully embarked in the space of productive creation.

The Law of Productive Creation also ordains the following for those who decide to participate in it: *What one offers regarding the creation and consummation of the new individual is given with no expectation of reward from him or from anyone else.* But here we observe, both through traditional adages and through the special parent-child relationship, that it is often stated that this act of creation by the man and the woman constitutes a great Offer to the child. And that because of this they have the right to refer to all their hard work as being a great gift to the new individual. And this legitimizes the thought: "I did this or that for your own good, therefore you are greatly indebted, first of all to do as I tell you and second to be of service to us." Such subjugating emotional motives create weaknesses and always lead to the egocentric demand for a disproportionate amount of recognition from the child in this new Position within the family space.

Such demands, great or small, have their origins in well hidden impulses stemming from latent states rooted in the past, whose purpose is to muddle our thinking, especially when it is in a quiescent, or inactive state, through projection onto its control center of those emotions that preclude the differentiation and classification of logical and just facts. Thus a demand is put forth without our being able to realize its true origin, having inner or outer gain as its goal. The gain we may initially achieve is an illusion, since we do not receive any objective benefits with regard to our Somatic (Body) or Psychic (Soul) Position. It may well be that the flesh has found temporary serenity, but for the Soul, if it remains hungry, there will be no such true serenity.

For this reason the individual must never seek to remain in a quiescent state when past memories put him in a state of nostalgic reminiscence, as this leads to the presence of magnetic attractions that occupy the entire functional organic space. In this way he again lives out these memories, trying through imaginary additions of emotional material either to embellish or reject them. In either case we should know that by looking back we end up becoming fixated on illusory, unreal worlds, and we will most certainly end up unable to function within the framework of our mission here on Earth.[36]

Let us, however, look at this from a different viewpoint, that of metaphysical physiology. This field of study deals with all human dimensions and especially the fourth one, which is the path of the individual after life here on Earth, a Position Man refuses to "discover." And it is a pity, because on the basis of this Position he could immensely develop his perceptive awareness of every visible or invisible Position of functional space. According to the Law of Creation, the visible and invisible Positions are determined by the activation of different directions: These create an indefinite magnetism and, in order to reach their destination and meet with other molecular Elements, go through inverse states. These Elements will be organized so that each will function in its own Microcosm from its own Position, as a unit in complete harmony with other functional units constituting aggregates of representative Positions coexisting during the Sensory

---

[36] Some scientists refer to these situations of loss of harmony as regressive fixations at previous stages of psychosomatic development or as character-induced "stress-causing" factors due either to guilt feelings or to unfulfilled desires. There exist many views and schools of thought. The gist, however, is that these unresolved conflicts, exactly as described above, lie at the core of man's inability to free himself from the narrow confines of the Somatic Being and to associate himself with the psychic beginnings and directions through which he can achieve well-being, but also good health in every sense of the word, as is prescribed in an almost utopian fashion by the World Health Organization (WHO). [A.V.]

activation of human organic space. Every constitutional group of the visible and invisible Microcosms thus formed produces both a hypersonic and subsonic vibrational frequency, whose constituents will eventually make up the vibrational state of the individual. And this happens because, in this individualized state, two Positions co-exist and work together to modulate the process, plus a third one, which I shall call **X**. The first is the purified Etheric biological Position, which is forever unchanging, and the second is the organic Elemental composition prescribed by the biological state of every planet where the individual, as a Nucleus-center, will be destined to exist. Now, depending on the vibrational frequency on which every organic cell finds itself, it will transmit particular messages to the appropriate glandular center, which will produce corresponding vibrations. These in turn will produce or cause corresponding secretions, with varying results.[37]

We should know that the results of human actions will lead either to Elevation or to Decline, the latter being the easiest to arrive at. For when the functional edifice of our selves is marked by negative manifestations due to a distorted perception of things, each of our thoughts or acts is taken as correct, up to a point. This results in the continuing produc-

---

[37] Here we have an analysis with a different view of organicity, which assumes the role of expression of energy data. Thus the anatomic description of the body loses its value in the face of this new approach with regard to the interdependence of the cell and the gland on the one hand and the cell and the invisible Positions on the other. This brings to mind holistic medicine (acupuncture, homeopathy), but also Hippocrates. [A.V.]

tion of emotional illusions based on the senses, which creates the need to cover our intrinsic errors. These errors in their turn, because of their own Position, do not allow us to see. This always creates in us the propensity not only to justify, but also to impulsively displace our mistakes and unjust acts onto others, perhaps due to a need to cover things up as well as to refuse to see things objectively, out of fear of exposure, lest others realize that our inner selves are not functioning according to the rules of harmonious balance.

Even when a man and a woman promise to share each other's life in soulful unity, after the magnetic attraction is actually consummated, for visible and invisible motives, each tries to fulfill through the other already existing fantasies, created either by the nature of lower Elements or by the individuals themselves. These fantasies have insinuated themselves into their lives in the past, associated either with acquired behavior influenced by persons in their environment upon whom they were once dependent, or, as often happens, with persons they chanced to meet at some particular time. These two individuals are usually at some difficult turning point in their lives and seek some sort of organic emotional communication in order to find a way round an existing problem by which they feel trapped. Its hidden influence activates them so that their Sensory centers produce a state of mind where they are prone to transfer their mistakes to others, and to mistakenly believe in the correctness of their own thoughts, so that they feel prey to the envy and machinations of "bad people." However, at the same time they try, having internalized their belief in their own supposedly "good" intentions, to keep what has happened to them an absolute secret so as not to be disparaged by others, and simultaneously to become counselors to others, not in the sense of real protectors from the pitfalls of life, but because their own experience is magnified within the framework of their subjective knowledge. Thus they strive to protect themselves and, based on their own situation, to lead others to a path filled with pitfalls.

In this way we become creators of an invisible world that forms and consolidates itself in our everyday space and uses up the greatest part of our functionality. This is unfortunate, because we are the primary agents responsible for the development of its acquired features, those images that finally become incorporated into the sensation-producing center of our individual world, having grown in substance and influence. In this way the unequal union of the two Positions, the Acquired and the Genuine, where the Acquired is predominant, issues its commands through over-sensitivity toward satisfaction of the Sensory centers, and we are unable to perceive that these commands originate in a different world which attempts, consciously or unconsciously, to establish its spurious reality inside our selves. Then, if we are not able to control the situation at an early stage —of course special abilities are needed because of the disruption these commands will inflict on our vital space— it will be easy for us to be trapped and led into Psycho-Spiritual Decline, which will result in not only our own Bodily Decline but also that of our children and of the even broader family circle we influence.

We have just spoken of the influence of "acquired" behavior on the individual, which can lead him into Decline. There exists, however, the inherent influence we receive from foci (hotbeds) that define our presence and derive from our own tradition, created at certain times by those who influence our various social units from the family to the State. Such foci lead our hidden sensibility to feed the fictitious personality, which attracts the fields of the Sensory centers at the level of the chromose-rooted emotive atmosphere, producing satisfaction that is not a representative of the present or of actuality in its objective of creating the future, but aims instead at the absolute subjugation of the Senses, slyly drawing the individual away from his true space-time trajectory, and leading him to the past to entrap him there. This comprises, as far as man's true Position is concerned, a dead zone, and he must never try to "revive the dead" because he does not possess this ability. The only ability he possesses is to become bound to fictitious or even real ghosts and to carry them inside himself without realizing it. Thus he shapes his own future life, as well as his future Psycho-Spiritual development, in a world of ghosts, so that his coming into life here on Earth is no more than a disastrous failure.

For this reason there is, for me, a great need for every individual, from the moment he makes that sacred decision to enter into the relationship of marriage, to erase everything from the past, be it beautiful (according to his own judgment, which is mostly subjective) or ugly. He must always operate in the present, with his purpose being to behave and function in a manner appropriate to the creation of a better future, and to perceive the past as an objective counselor.

Chapter 7

CHROMOSOMES

W e humans perceive only the visible functional Elements that represent the various Positions in life, without knowing that many invisible Elements have to be mobilized in order for them to function. The Rule is that the visible functions on the basis of the invisible. Since the Creator of life has ordained that Life is a synthesis of the two Positions, the visible and the invisible, we must direct our attention toward them both in order to see precisely what each represents in the totality of Life.

As we examine these Positions more closely, beyond the almost non-existent human capacity to perceive, and investigate their functioning mechanism, we see that they draw sufficient vital energy from their birth through the Universal Womb to animate and direct them in their mission of Offer to the offspring of Creation. There they are activated to perform their intermediary Offer, which creates all organic transmutations at every spatio-temporal point at which Nature disposes her catalytic presence so that the Cycles of Positions and Anti-positions can be completed. This intermediary Offer has been termed vibrational energy[38] by those who first discovered it in the hypersonic biochemical energy of the organic system. External factors always play an important role in the functioning of the organism, entering and affecting groups of cells whose responsive vibration stimulates the instinctual centers, which affects the control center, often causing uncontrolled and erroneous behavior. During the formation of the constitution of the individual, these external factors enter the Positions that science calls chromosomes.[39]

---

[38] The energy of biological speed in its natural rhythm, where *biological speed* means the particular frequency at which a biological unit functions as well as its characteristic biological time, which determines the duration of its life. The biological time is different for each part of an organism so that its metabolic changes are carried out in a balanced way and not as erruptive explosions.

[39] According to medicine, chromosomes are a kind of coded messages which, when decoded, will organize the development of a given organism. During conception, 23 male chromosomes meet with 23 corresponding female chromosomes and combine. One of these chromosomes, called phylogenic, when it originates in the woman, always gives rise to a female organism, whereas when it originates in the man, it gives rise to either a male or a female organism. During the progressive decoding of the way that the genes (constituents of the chromosomes) combine, groups of cells are formed with independent function and complex control from other groups. In this way the organism is constructed, but also reconstructed, since in its mature form each cell possesses the inherent dynamics for multiplication into identical cells. The control center of the cell's functionality, and consequently of the whole organism is, however, in the chromosomes.

When they are at work, these chromosomes are in a sparsely unfolded state (for this reason the nucleus of the cell in which they reside appears almost transparent), and through special cell formations they transmit instructions resulting in the production of substances characteristic of the cell (be it adrenal, neural, stereome or mixed, always in close contact with the immediate environment but also with "distant" control centers). However, when it is in a quiescent phase, at which time the cell is "inactive," then it

Here I feel a strong obligation to explain the notion of the CHROMOSOME, as I see it in its organic Elemental genesis, and exactly as reported to me in the hypersonic scripture by that higher Position of the Hierarchy of the Universe presiding ex officio as a great God, coded under the name **Anemios Deus 9.81**. The womb of chromosome's origin is formed by the atmosphere of the planet, the region and the space in

---

is amply folded, dense and the nucleus appears dark. Even this "non-activity" constitutes a function in the sense that it has been ordered by a control center to spur increased activity in a different group around some particular need, on the basis of the organism's principal Order.

The chromosome itself is X-shaped and is composed of a number of substances, ingeniously placed in a series of four bases (organic compounds), which encode specific messages and are called genes. Many of the genes have been mapped out in numerous scientific studies, and scientists have also discovered a perfect control system for their proper functioning, called operon. Nevertheless, there are still many aspects (perhaps most aspects) of chromosomes that remain unknown with regard to their function, which we call dark areas and which are considered to be additional control mechanisms.

For further interesting details on the ingenuity of chromosomes, one can consult specialized books on biology or on biochemistry.

At this point I would like to mention that science recognizes that the genes transmit hereditary characteristics upon which the organism builds itself. If we generalize this tenet and realize that the entire external world in which the individual moves is "transported" through the sensory as well as the emotional mechanisms of specialized message reception, we see clearly how close we are to the new concept introduced in this treatise concerning the external factors that invade a given structure and modify its response (even biochemically), depending on the hereditary states of sensitivity. In medicine, we are always confronted with unsolved questions, dark areas, insufficient knowledge, which direct us toward notions of "the mystery of life" or, as it has been more precisely put up to now, toward the "invisible element," the element which is analyzed here and to a certain extent identified below. [A.V.]

which the individual has been ordained to exist. This revelation compels me to record it solely according to those Rules of exposition set down below:

ANEMIOS DEUS 9.81

"A narrow chain creates a channel for the genetic Order of the stellar system from the outer to the inner sphere of the planet where life is formed and concentrated through thermal processing on the individual being, assuming its form as an organic entity. The genic Order (chromosome), originating as a creational specification for each individual according to the Lawful Precept which applies to all Elements of organic individuality in its primary and autonomously reproducing Position, is Etheric[40] and, as the Rule prescribes for the proportional and fully integrated distribution of this organicity, the magnetic field of the planet's space attracts and binds it, placing it as a peripheral zone around the individual's head Position. From there the epiphysis gland magnetically assimilates these Etheric Elements. It subsequently places them in the hypothalamic juncture of the control center (or critical gland). Then the thyroid and the adrenal glands are called upon to transmit the appropriate biochemical hormone, which combines with a bio-Etheric hormone and configures gene

---

[40] The genic Order of the body is always generated and formed from the Etheric genic Order, as a Life Rule.

groups that implement chromosome-linked functions within the cell. The chromosome[41] is the mastermind and organic instructor of the organism when it comes to the order that must be followed within the environment of the stellar system in which the Body exists, i.e. on the planet Earth.[42] It is also an indicator. Along with the information on "how" it is formed, made out of nitrogen,[43] —that is to say this information is invariable— it possesses **Hydrogenic Lineability**,[44] *which is an indicator of its development as a singular property in each body. Hydrogenic Lineability is transmuted and altered slowly with regard to its chromaticity (the chromatic expression of its biological composition) on the basis of the Law of well-*

---

[41] Chromosome refers to the radiance of color that compels the other parts of the body to adapt to it and determine on this basis the functionality of the organism through hormonal secretions. The chromatic configuration of the chromosome (see appendix: the transcription of the "Symbol of Ioannis") is formed on the basis of the behavior the individual has been induced by various factors to adopt. The chromosome in its organic state and shape consists of coils of constituent Elements, whose function is to transform its chromatic state to various manifestations.

[42] The chromosome, as a primary Position in its Etheric existence and dimension, is the Element borne by the Soul as a peripheral Bodily garb. And this generates (inseminates) the material chromosome of the organism, which contains innumerable codes with regard to the organic Position of the human Body.

[43] This Element (Nitrogen), which is an invariable Etheric substance, is recruited by the Law of Creation to enter as a special worker into the individual's organism so as to create an Etheric and biological protective mantle around every individual Element that exists as part and parcel of the organism.

[44] Hydrogenic Lineability refers to the schematic distribution of hydrogen in the Body: a channel of Hydrogen surrounded by nitrogen.

attuned functionality and correct alignment with the entire organism. The Bio-Etheric combination of Nitrogen and Hydrogen within the hormonal environment creates accelerations in the energy chain of phosphorus in the chromosome, and this chain evinces its own forms, named genetic.

The chromosome constitutes the organic Order of communication of the parts of the Universal Body of an individuality: the productive parts (Soul) and the kinetic parts (Body). It is the smallest cellule which, as a biological principle, diffused as geometric biology in the Ether, generates production systems within the Laws of the Sun, the planet and the origin of the Soul. The central organic positioning of this ability is located within its neural figurine, which is an energy "trap" (a concentration point) defined in the periclonium, i.e. in the four corners of the schematic chromosomal coils. This is a carbon oxide base acting autonomously in the organism that polarizes electro-chemical reactions through phosphorus and draws into and out of the Nucleus low vibrational energies, in combinations dictated by gonal cells[45] that "inform" the chromosomes about the organism's state. The hormone termed **Pyea**, deriving from the local contractional secretions of the peripheral cells of the gonads (near the genitals), incorporates electro-positive currents within the body of the Tetracydes, otherwise known as chromosomes. Each Tetracyde, in re-

---

[45] These are cells that incubate Elements for carrying messages within the organism.

sponse, determines electrically the speed of transmission of chromosomal production and incorporates potentials. The echo-vibration that is transported to the system of the Tetracyde in a charged state will produce the specific individual self-identity of the system to which it belongs,[46] and the genetic cells will be transformed or will be retained in the order dictated by their relative distribution through heredity from one Body to the next.

Finally, here is how the temporal sequence, as a schema leading to the birth of the chromosome in the Body, is defined:

Nitrogen O X 80 H-C-OO9

*Oxygen-based Rule, Cydetic (animate chromosomal) Position, that is a combined atmospheric Position that enters the individual Body through the brain, initially as a special creative Element, then as a catalyst within, through the center **A-las** in the Kymba hemispheral lobe, on the left side of the brain.*

A-las is the "transformer" gland which absorbs external and internal energies from the Ether (or Etheric medium) and transforms them into intra-Somatic biological forms of a higher density.

The gap is interconnected through the transposition caused by molecular fermentation, and the chromosomes are immediately generated at the nosterolic position (= the 4th spermatic phase). This is the way it happens! "

---

[46] This will happen in accordance with the system's own biological-natural expression of heredity, on the basis of which it will produce a particular chromosomal state.

Turning my attention to the initial act of Life, ordained as the placement of individual sperm within the womb, I see that after the onset of spermatic formation leading to fetal development, the first gland formed is the Sensory Attunement Gland, whose mission is fetal Bodily formation; and, as the great Fathers of the Universe have revealed to me, it is also referred to by the name "**Connector gland,**"[47] And as a Rule of Evolution, the *Sensory Attunement Gland takes its form as the established beginning and manifestation of Sensory ideo-mobility[48] leading to the development of Higher Sensory Attunement (the highest level of Sensory Attunement),[49] whose main creative focus is the shaping of the magnetic field between the Positions of Sensory Attunement and of Higher (harmonious) Sensory Attunement. And this field's mission is to emit hypersonic magnetic frequencies, so that it can unite in its totality with the internal atmospheric state where the Etheric chromosomal system is located, where-

---

[47] The gland which connects external atmospheric conditions to the inner organic-biological state.

[48] An axial factor in the process of human thinking that transmits messages through biochemical energy of the organism to the Senses. Schematically:

Idea in the mind ⟶ Message ⟶ Senses

[49] Higher Sensory Attunement = the harmonic functioning of the Senses. After the corresponding natural characteristics have been incorporated and implanted into Man's nature, Sensory Attunement develops to a certain level, depending on how detrimental or beneficial the individual's background has been. There are twelve levels of Sensory Attunement, including main, central intermediary levels, composing a scale with "Higher Sensory Attunement" at the top and "Sensory Decline" at the bottom.

upon this union is effected the same way in the corresponding entities within the bio-material space of the Body.[50]

The chromosomes begin functioning in the Body's inner space, following their activation based on their acquired speed,[51] which determines the density of their response. This is carried to the various centers and, depending on the stimulus, initiates the appropriate secretion, which results in a specific biochemical energy. Then, if the control center [52] is able to handle it correctly (i.e., is in the proper state of equilibrium), it will provide efficient service, so that the individual will not be thrown into confusion and be led to erroneous perception of every conceptual event leaving its imprint upon him. When the activation of the chromosome is violent, then the density of its response will be great. When it enters the individual space of the centers in this fashion, it is unable to become transparent, on the basis of its biochemical phosphoric Position, and consequently creates a dark spot, whose interaction with the center which controls the clarity of impressions in the region of the hypophysis, through contact with Etheric and biochemical Elements, stimulates the control center there to produce insufficient Elements.

---

[50] This may be given schematically as:

Atmospheric Element - Nature ◄──► {intercourse and insemination of human nature into Man} ◄──► Man

[51] The functional behavior of Nature on Man —who is supplied by Nature— takes place at a speed X which is specified for each individual as "acquired."

[52] This is the brain's most central control gland, and its purpose is to control the specific (but also other) amounts of hormonal secretions of the glands, through pulsory motion taking the form of contraction and expansion.

We will thus have a decline in the full potential of the organic capabilities for enhancing transparency and consequently a consolidation of the dark spots within the instinctive centers. These centers therefore relegate the individual to a chaotic gap formed and surrounded by magnetic fluids contained in the atmospheric space and create in him the feeling of fear which, on a scale of 1 to 10, begins at 4 and ascends to the dangerous zone of 6, after which he is seized by panic. Now, depending on the degree of **marginal power**[53] he is offered by the Universal Powers, this will create a corresponding reaction, which will either lead to his liberation from these impulses or will entrap him somewhere where the result will be proportional to his own state of Decline, and events will be such that they will lead him to a complete annihilation of his individual Position, and various other lower instincts will make their way inside him. These will dominate him and the fictitious coloration (false picture) of the negative[54] will form in him the illusion that he has been fortunate enough to taste the nectar of life.[55]

---

[53] Extra-normal protection given to most people on Earth by the Universal Positions of Light.

[54] The creation of lower Sensory emotions attracts negative residue from the atmosphere, and its influence is shaped according to the individual's wishes in such a way as to bring him to a state of dissolution, without his being able to see his own destruction.

[55] We should explain here that the phosphoric Position of the chromosome is the gene, since the sequentially-arranged bases from which it is composed contain phosphorus as a basic element. We can see the connection between the dark regions of chromosomes and poor functionality of organs, which translates into pathogenic susceptibility, in the sense that under certain circumstances sub-clinical and clinical stages of organic or psycho-pathological states develop. [A.V.]

This is a very concise revelational account of this Element (chromosome), with its special basic Position within the functionality of the organism, having as its main mission to transmute into its seven main chromosomal Positions,[56] and into many other secondary manifestations. And because of its chromatic (colorful) nature, it has been named —and rightly so— "chromosome" by the enlightened scientific community.

And as always I am called from my super-Etheric Position to enter into the special axial domains of the corporal Elemental composition of the individual, and through the presence and contribution of my Supreme special Counselor **Deus 9.81**, who makes the most complete revelations to me, Ioannis, I feel the obligation to present to you these main substructures of Bodily development toward the integration of individual organic life — substructures having as their function to serve the entity called Man who, defining them for communicational purposes, has given them the names DNA and RNA.[57]

ANEMIOS DEUS code 9.8I
ON DNA

The chromosome genesis within an organism during the division of cells, initially formed through genetic transferal of

---

[56] See the Transcription of the Symbol of Ioannis in the Appendix.
[57] These are acronyms for two difficult biochemical compounds, that is to say for deoxyribonucleic acid (DNA) and for ribonucleic acid (RNA).

*parental Elements to the embryo, has its functional reference point primarily in the acidic domain under the name of DNA, which I would call **Nouovogonia**. As a Nucleus (the central core) of heredity, this is nothing more than the **Nistasic substance**[58] that oxidizes the nucleic derivatives inside the cellular organelles, which then isolate their genetic nature to protect it from external influences and reproduce it.[59] This entity is a preliminary biochemical phase of chromosomal formation, and it is an acidic protein, that is to say a very special kind of protein whose nitric trivalency permits the continuously recycled conservation of a genetic code that remains constant under transformation within the cell, i.e., remains unchanged. The Nistasic substance is produced by the cerebral Etheric assignor of the space and of the parents of the unborn child and is a combination of Etheric magnetism and currents that compose and order the Elements in the new space of the newly emerging human being.*

DNA is the convergence point of factors acting as Nuclei of Creation in the space of their biological activation. These factors acquired concrete existence during the conception of the individual, whereas up to that point they were unindividualized and diffuse within his internal *atmosphere.

---

[58] The basic chromosomal substance.

[59] They isolate their organic nature against change caused by any intruding element or influence, and thus are always reproduced as identical entities, with the same protein chain constituting a continuous reproductive cycle.

This dimension (DNA) springs from the productive Position of the brain and has two states: the variable and the uncoupled or invariable. The invariable is protected by nitric Elements, 6 for every 4, that is, 24 in all, and is regenerated during conception, when the development of a new life is in a pre-stage of creation, i.e. during the process of Union.

The Rule that determines the invariable Position of DNA is planet-specific[60] and is under the control of variable factors pertaining to biophysics, geophysics and the time of birth. These factors, although probably unknown to the peoples of the planet Earth, have primary initiative, a faculty that remains dormant in the depths of the cell's nucleus. There is a biological code —a biological instruction executed by all the glands in unison that combines the biological speeds of the productiveness of all organs and glands up to the pump of the vertebral marrow— which volitionally commands the brain to generate and send an electrochemically produced stimulus all the way to the nuclei of basic cells. These will then order the transmission of changes to the variable rate of cellular vibrations. Then the gonadal cells will transmit to their nuclei the order of transmutation through a centrosome. Thus, the invariable four-fold nitric sequence will create an electrochemical

---

[60] It pertains exclusively to the specific planet and the specific place considered.

process[61] through the electric fields produced by the said instruction. This electrochemical process will alter the rate of transmission of instructions for the production of DNA as a sequence, which will modify the Etheric expression of its hereditary structure, and finally this mutation will permeate all the cells of the organism via an echo-protein[62] formed in the lower axis-bond of the DNA by the etherization of three genic acids with reproductive properties. These acids support this transmission (or mutation) and bolster the vibrational chemistry of the cells, so that they will now reproduce mutated protein composition in the Body, named **Ylasa**. *Ylasa is all animate matter born and adapted to the variability of the Laws of the planet. It is a Position of matter that may undergo mutations. It is formed biologically under the Laws of the planet, having received beforehand the invariable nitric Position of acetic DNA. Now Ylasa is slowly engendered through transmissions of Elements and conditions in the environment and consolidates a new Position, creating new genetic products substantially different in their genetic base as contained in the cellular nuclei.*

DNA = Indisruptable, oxy-protein biochemical com-

---

[61] The interaction of two or more Elements creates electricity, which is followed by the production of a new chemical Element.

[62] This Element is an Etheric and material protein that, through its two components (matter and ether), shapes sounds, which activates vibrations.

pound, whose structural configuration is transmitted to the individual through the brain. Through electrochemical vibrations, they connect charges that are trivalent with regard to their neutrality (plus, minus and amyn). These sustain a chain order of nitro-phosphoric formation that initializes the reproduction of a protein base, which is Etheric. Being Etheric it breaks the Law of DNA's domain in regard to the conservation of initial principle. Its initial principle is Gonasi, which is the origin of the instruction for somatotype formation under the Law of Heredity. If this Body type affects and is affected by the chemical-vibrational metabolisms of the cerebral ordering gland, it can regulate its vibrations to transform the activity of its nitric inner Position toward a functional realignment of its receptive Elements, which are sulfuric proteins. These activate the metabolisms, are stabilized by the invariable nitric bonds, and manifest themselves in a myriad of ways from their phosphoric Position. The twenty-four nitric gates are at once called upon to conserve this oxyproteinic Law,[63] while at the same time they also transmit its mutations, finally mutating themselves as well, depending on the type of protein required, six for every two...

The functional center that gestates, composes and disposes the edicts of DNA under the schema of the Tetra-

---

[63] The Law according to which the power of oxygen gives biological speed to the protein.

cydes (chromosomes), is the phosphoric offspring of DNA, which for the sake of brevity is called RNA.

The function that defines these acids and reveals them at their birth is self-containment which can be explained as follows: RNA is not a different type of entity from DNA, but is simply its own (DNA's) body. The creative nature of DNA determines the transmission of its products (RNA) within the cellular Order at all times, thus determining the organism's potential for change, as well as for self-conservation around its defining pillars (chromosomes), the axes of its gradual effort to adapt according to the Laws of its space.

In its temporal Position, DNA has four phases, and during the fourth phase, consummating its physical autonomy, it re-creates one of its dominant parts and "delivers" it to its environment in order to mobilize the inner instruction it has formulated inside the cell and from there to all types of tissue. This sequence is the regular regeneration characteristic of every manifestation of nitrogen within the nature of the planet's system, and is expressed as follows: Auto-genesis of the nitrogen-based Element, as the product of planetary Rules (Rules of Life), whose purpose is the translocation of Life, otherwise called "Perpetuation." There is no exception. Nitrogen, in its multifarious activity and behavior, replicates itself and its nature at regular intervals. In this way the "Conservation of Life sequence" is carried out.

*The Rule governing **Nitrogen F**[64] (the nitrogen being generated) contained in such formations as DNA, is dormant within the particular type of nitrogen and is implemented as soon as this Rule is reflected in the mirror of a matching Nitrogen F of a different type. There its inherent intelligence, as it penetrates other spaces, is integrated and realized at a level of neutrality. Then it splits and, one by one, its derivatives leave to define domains of creation in the organism they inhabit.*

The purpose of the newborn RNA is to upgrade the organism's Elements metabolically in response to organic demands. RNA focuses on the general order that the organism must assume under the specific categorization (with respect to the overall organization of the individual) and the interactive relationship of the proteins, and the haematic enzymes, which bring about the organization of tissues, glands and the Etheric Element of the Body by transmitting instructions from one to the other. DNA is therefore the backbone of the process of life maintenance and development of all the Elements inside the human Body. Its Etheric support is what maintains this specifically assigned Position and disposition in unchanging stability. For any change whatsoever a signal must be sent by the Etheric center-axis of the brain to the corresponding Etheric chromosomal region. If DNA's phosphoric colors are the basic axes of cerebral functionality, RNA is the self-generated ser-

---

[64] Each material element has different types, belonging to different levels. One of the types of Nitrogen is called here Nitrogen F.

vant stemming from DNA's body: deriving from, living in, and resembling it."

And here the question arises: What is the relationship between RNA and DNA? Is it possible that RNA is the spermatic Position of DNA? ... [65]

* * *

And taking matters relating to Man's organic state from the beginning, let us enter into **the manifestation of the Life Cycles of the two Positions, male and female**, as elabo-

---

[65] What is described here is the discovery, well known to medicine, of the "nucleus of life." DNA (this is the acronym of a complex biochemical compound, namely the deoxyribonucleic acid) is the building block of the chromosome. When it was discovered in the laboratory that the code of its structure was characteristic of every type of organism, a revolution occurred in science, and the fields of genetics and molecular biology were developed.

Many hopes are "attached" to DNA, in the sense that one can intervene on bad or faulty parts of it in order to "eradicate" hereditary diseases, or create "smart" antibiotics or cytostatic medicines that will attack only ailing cells. For some people, there is even the hope of understanding and creating life in the laboratory (!)

We are now familiar with and can reproduce DNA in the laboratory. We can distinguish regions (genes) which code organs, functions, controls or development, as we also know the process of its transcription by the cell (during cellular division or reproduction), or its translation through RNA, which is the vehicle carrying the instruction from the nucleus to the cell (more precisely to the ribosomes). Through RNA the execution of the instruction of the cell's nucleus is made possible, which usually involves the production of a protein that has a specific role either inside or outside of the cell. [A.V.]

rated for us in a most important revelation by the Position *Gya Iypera 28 18*, set in place by our Father the Creator long before Man, and whose creative function on planet Earth —a female planet— is to serve as the model for the Etheric nature and form of people on Earth, but also to be a participant there as part of an immaterial Spiritual Order of observers of the logical and biological progress of Man.

THE SUBSTANTIALITY OF THE MATERIAL BODY DIFFERENCES BETWEEN MAN AND WOMAN DIFFERENCES BETWEEN HUMAN AND ANIMAL

INVOCATION BY IOANNIS

The Rules have prescribed that I now be here on Earth, and that I reveal the way they operate, in my capacity as a Position perceiving the course of things, starting in the past, proceeding through the present and, through scripture and language, describing the future course into eternity in order to implement the Rules that determined the creation, formation and shaping of the Human Order, both present and future, amidst the new realignment of biology and of biochemistry during the perpetuation of Nature's creation. This grants the supreme Offer but also the supreme Responsibility for human existence in this space that we call Earth. And you, **Gya Iypera 28 18**, as the Life principle of this planet, created the internal affinity between a Human Being and Nature leading to the genesis and evolution of the Positions *woman and man* by the maternal principle.

And I, Ioannis, now of the Earth, as you well know, since you have communicated with me and revealed to me the Elements of Earth during conception, birth, development and in their myriad expressions, bow down in the face of your divine knowledge and humbly salute you. And I ask you to reveal to me, through physics, chemistry and biology, the density of the Bodily matter of man and of woman. As far as their biochemical Elementation (characteristics) and their chromosomal Positions are concerned, are they on the same scale? Also, with regard to their biological classification as organisms, are there differences, and if so, what are they?

What is the difference in Bodily matter, with regard to density, between Man and animal, and what is the difference between animals? Also, what is the difference in Bodily matter between Man and fish, and what is it between fish and other terrestrial animals?

Is eating animal meat and fish beneficial to Man? Are there Elements in animals and fish that have ill effects on human health?

Also, the science known as biological and biochemical therapeutic medicine, as part of its research to create therapeutic elements (medications), has designed and carried out experiments on animals for every medication it is developing against a particular disease. In order to test certain perceptive notions regarding Man, the science referred to as psychiatry places animals under conditions of distress to observe their reactions and perception to see what actions they will take to escape from or endure these conditions, and by conjecture they believe that Man functions in the same way. Is it right for them to act in this manner, and can they derive correct results from this or are they committing irreparable mistakes?

Please, reveal to me all of this in the greatest detail. Expressing my infinite gratitude and my life's salutations I, Ioannis of the Earth of the Sun KARYA, bow down to you.

GYA IYPERA code 28 18

"Initiation and induction into the Order of the organism is accomplished through knowledge of the composition of Life's Order. But it is also a diaphragm that prevents the intermediate Delta time, the time elapsed between the time of creation of evolving Elements and that of the Bodily incorporation of their codes, from being seen.

Ioannis, the gate of the vibrations of the Universe did not open for the knowledge of the sameness of the Earth's Order here and the Order of the whole, which is a cosmic condensation of unifying matter that unites, positions and is itself positioned in parts throughout the universes of molecular entities existing in the places where they were engendered.

Have you now opened these gates? The configuration of forms of the biologies has been released from its code network and emerges enlarged, through the hand of Ioannis, as at the hand of its Creator.

Following the creation of plant life, a Rule of creation ordained the formation of the female Body to create, unify and condense a human torso as a basis-framework for action, with high molecular density, more dense in man than in woman.

The nature of cellular Orders in the human Body in the male and in the female evinces primarily a technical similarity, generally with regard to structure, with particular points of differentiation in their functional distribution and location. However, their cellular nature as a unit of animate creation belonging to an Order of biophysical process, functions and is governed by a different Rule for each of the two organisms, the male and the female. The primary factor that divides and delineates cellular birth within the Body has different Etheric receptors in the gono-occipital system[66] of the woman. The female apprehends more delicate vibrational codes, which are able to traverse an enormous vibrational space and locate themselves in spaces of action which are directed toward and away from a Pole[67] and suitable for the archetypal formation of the somatic cellular organization defining them. There is a

---

[66] The system that produces and receives special substances for the creation of the biological behavior of the female.

[67] A pole is the central point of processing for the creation of emission from the Element.

clear difference between what determines the initial shaping of the individual during conception and what completes this shaping at birth. The molecule of the female Order, apprehending the clear sounds of the Nature in which it is placed, resonates with and is determined by them. It diffuses within the glow of phyletic animate vibrations, and actuates biological diffuseness and multiplicity of action during the production of substances that will organize and manifest the Body's organic life.

The chromosome configuration in the female, defined as such by a phyletic (gender-determined) planetary code,[68] *shows levels of qualitative gradation in relation to the chromosome core in the male. The female chromosome may be defined by means of an additional four variable factors in excess of those for the male, where each of these factors delineates a fourteen-fold group of multifaceted vibrational biology. These factors are electro-vibrational in nature and establish their functionality in the chromocellule, depending on its receptive infrastructure and capacity. This functionality thereby penetrates the walls of the Bodily molecules, consolidating their Order within the natural Bodily distribution, so that it determines the operation of the centers and their function. Then these centers assume further structuring of the organic*

---

[68] Chromosomes are of a neutral biological nature but may function both as male or female. Their primary Position is neutral and, for this reason, they may undergo transmutation into male or female.

Position and productivity, within the bounds of its Rules, which are strictly different and separate from the male Order (in other words, organic physiology), which is structured by cellular receptors of a different thermal resistance to the elec-tro-vibrational environment and of a different sensitivity, more concise in its options.

The male individual natural unit is formed by a genetically organized center that apprehends inwardly various levels of fields and atmospheres, differing with respect to their intensity at their point of origin and the extent of their functional presence in space. Its chromosomal Order, as created, apprehends the dimensions of space and supports their expression as an implacable structural pillar in its strong variables. Its receptive axis moves between two Positions (Orders), emanating from the Body and its environment.

The Cellular structure of the male, built around the basic (rather than the local) quality and nature of his particular space, does not fluctuate between the vibrational forms of the bio-genetic[69] waves it receives, but defines its organic life as it is received in its genetic form, completely supporting and reproducing it unchanged within its organic system. Its two Orders are those of support and intrusion (penetration), the latter possessing two functional loci, reproduction of its genet-ic type and its total destruction.

What is commonly perceived as the Chromosome manifests

---

[69] Pertaining to biological origin.

152

through the two genders the differences of an entire planetary bi-polarity denoting the female as biologically diffuse in her genetic nature, and the male as penetrating and solid within the surrounding female vibrational expressions of Nature. The female is Earth's surrounding nature. And the male the wanderer, transmitter and traveler...".

THE BODILY POSITION
OF HUMANS AND ANIMALS

"In contrast to the composition of the human Body, the Body of animals differs in the density and the quality of its Elemental cellular matter. The Elemental organization of the Body of animals is based on Rules of diverse organization of plant life, with the additional participation of Rules of condensed vibrational resistance, in reception and also in action, which is called living. Here we have systems in groups of six that regulate chromo-cellular nature, so that its field of logical reference can only organize sound groups of Sensory reception, classified solely according to instinctive Orders, without the possibility of organization of these biochemical receptions into Logos, as the previously mentioned Order suffices for survival. The number of chromosomes in the cells of every species of animal defines a level of genetic variability in which it can display its phyletic (species-defined) dimension, strictly confined to its own expressive organic and physio-kinetic characteristics. This number, known with regard to its density by species, is a locked code forbidding metabolic mutation or evo-

lution of the species into something else. This contrasts with the human genetic code, where Nature and conditions of logic permit a renewed metabolization of its capacity for vibratory receptivity, through slow evolutionary process, which is nevertheless stable in the primary basic cycles to which it returns when evolutionary mutation does not lead on to further renewed biochemical metabolization. While the human genetic code is also locked, the genetic intrusiveness of the male nature in every human being fosters the ability to detect and break through this locked genetic gate toward transformation.

The fish, organized as a Body inside its aquatic space, possesses a finer transparency in its cellular receptivity, which defines for it a one-dimensional, but more diffuse, chromosomal configuration.

The Elemental composition of the fish may soften Bodily vibrations that are stronger than its own, enhancing the inherent capability of the fish for multiple exits from its biological poles —a capability that other Bodies, such as the human and the animal, do not possess.

Existing in spaces that Man cannot approach electro-biologically or chemo-vibrationally, fish and animals may provide him with Elements in the form of nutrition that will make him more multifaceted and enduring within the natural environment of the planet, serving the needs of his biological inquisitiveness. He enters into inner states of consciousness within his Bodily dimension that he could not have reached before, and is consummated vibrationally in his animate Order, hav-

ing acquired a natural basis for his mind to soar to infinite heights of perception."

ON EXPERIMENTS WITH ANIMALS

"The consequences of widespread animal servitude in Man-made spaces in the present day and Age have become apparent. The animal Order may indeed offer its natural methods for healing, but its vibrational resistance and its organic form, in connection with the absence of intelligence capable of enhancing logical Sensory perception in the visceral centers, preclude any comparison with animal Orders such as Man undergoing evolution with regard to their Bodily formation on Earth. Falsification of conclusions is the primary result, and its consequence is an endless genetic assault upon cellular brain structures in Man, causing changes in their phyletic support systems, often to the point of degeneration. The gland centers, whose mandate is to instill Life and ensure Man's survival, adapt their secretions to pharmaceutical products and transform the **organism into an organic subversive agent targeting its own physical Order,** *secretly killing off systems of cerebral organizations, slowly or precipitously causing the appearance of diseases in mutating organs. Organic death is the lesser evil... You know the ensuing Order, Ioannis.*

In response to your question as to your own perceptive abilities, I appoint you in my thoughts as Iasonas (healer). May human conscience seek out its true therapy through the infi-nite variety of your cerebral creations.

I return to my creative Position, with infinite thanks..."

IYPERA

* * *

Because of the keen desire of my Nucleus, as Ioannis, and my own particular feeling regarding the completion of my writings, by necessity partial, I hereby cite for you yet another revealing written communication from an Ioannian friend of mine. with whom it was once determined by the Law-ordained Creation of my Authorities and Functions that I be in close contact. This closeness enables the performance of a multifold and most special type of work within the created Universes.

It is a pleasure for me to now present to you the most eminent **Igmios 7**, who will shed much light through his revelation for all the seekers of knowledge in the domain of genetic research.

Introduction of **Igmios 7** by the Position **IN Δ** of the sun **Lambadias**

Igmios of the many revelations, whose thinking can reach and access stellar systems, who was once, long ago, an attendant colonel next to Ioannis, in spaces where new Laws ought to be enacted and established[70], around the

---

[70] The systems of life in the Universes are not similar to one another. There is an infinite number of different kinds.

mid-point of a 10,000-year period in a previous Cycle.

He made his appearance in order to connect Ioannis to a new set of powerful fighters who will support him infinitely during the coming months and who will transmit and set up portals of magnetic fields around him to attract the right people.

Igmios 7 *was also at Ioannis's side during other critical moments in his course, not on Earth but elsewhere. And it is he who activates chromosomal eruptions induced by the usual mental representation evoked by Ioannis's presence and deep changes brought about by the reflection of Ioannis's image in human beings.*

There is great understanding and love sent from Igmios to Ioannis, but he is also a Position who acts independently upon Ioannis, since at some point in the past Ioannis himself has deemed him worthy of that right.

I bow down in respect.

INVOCATION BY IOANNIS

With my Ioannian respects, **Igmios 7**, I arrive at your Position, which is akin to mine. I extend my Ioannian greetings and express to you my great joy at your coming to find me here on this journey that is truly one of the most difficult I have made.

I now ask you to work for me, which is something you are accustomed to doing, but this time, by virtue of your particular abilities, you will make a revelation concerning your own multifaceted functionality within the biological synthesis and disruption of chromosomes that shape the rarefaction and density of atmospheric conditions surrounding human beings on their course.

How is the individual integrity of the biological synthesis of DNA maintained, so that its productive activity remains constantly in tune with the regenerated and restructured chromosomal Order?

Does DNA have its source of supply in the central Nucleus of bio-energetic DNA of the planet that structures Somatic life?

What is the Position of RNA within DNA and the continuously reordered chromosomal emission? Is RNA the Nucleus of relationship to the Nucleus of the atmosphere of the planet?

And how do you arrive amidst all this and bring about the re-ordering of semi-stability into stability?

How long does it take for your Position to effect its function of disruption and individuation?

With infinite reverential friendship I take my leave of you,

Ioannis

IGMIOS 7

"Yes, certainly I will speak to you of the Order of disorder, Ioannis. The Earthly realm, moreover, has always aroused your curiosity as a place whose conditions of torment you wished to test yourself in. Now of course you speak of diffi-

culties. But, remember, I told you this when you were enacting the Laws and rights of the Law systems applying to Earth. By what divine decision did you descend there? A god unauthorized and ungoverned, you decided to sacrifice yourself, and this you did. And Earthlings received you as they always do people of merit: with repugnance!

With great emotion I came and spread the chromosomal beams of my authority round you, and I took hold of you by the lower right part of your brain so that you would recognize me. A Nucleus of yours, born and crowned by a mixture of Logos and Mercy, I came to bow down before you and quietly perform my activity of insubordination, an ability I acquired during my years under your tutelage. First, you found and reveal the very universe you sanctioned with your Logos, and then you are continually disloyal to it. Such presumption requires daring and knowledge. Otherwise, it is pure suicide...

Propelled by the beams of your Mind, which sweeps me on to unprecedented sights and contacts, an innovator in the field of natural Laws giving life to world systems, I come to alternate action with inaction, mobility with immobility, appearance with disappearance, precisely within that genetic system that evinces form, mass and functional stability under the government of the Order of instability.

The stable identity of DNA, its inalterable genetic nexus and the interlacing of transformations at work within the closed chromosomal system, are derivations of and the result of a defense mounted by their Nuclear code against the strong-ly changing and variable atmosphere of this planet.

In other Universal domains, where the fluctuations of cen-tral Nuclei that stabilize the identities of Elements and beings are more steady and harmonious, the genetic Nuclei are more easily changed.

I mean that the individualities, the Positions and the intelli-gent beings in these Universes possess the attributes of flexi-bility and changeability, placed in a broader scale of trans-mutations, which provide them freedom of Psycho-Spiritual movement and evolutionary entry into other sets of levels and harmonies. But here we are talking of free worlds.

The Nucleus that locks and secures the similarity of the species of life on this planet is an almost inviolable code, genetically created so that it is not amenable to a great deal of metabolic restructuring. This has been ordained by an invio-lable Law, and only through divine command from the domain beyond the jurisdiction of Universal Laws could this ever be contravened. The Divine Fathers, however, have no desire to modify their creations, because they have a certain signifi-cance for the portal of Creation.

The basic order of the chromosomes of living organisms cannot be altered. But the site of their ability to influence liv-ing space, the body, the atmosphere, other organisms and whatever else they are able to, can be restructured and revi-talized. This site undergoes restructuring because the chang-ing atmosphere surrounding living things is in constant motion and upheaval. If the Earth's system were permeated by absolute harmony chromosomes would not be merely restructured, but would be capable of complete change and transformation. Now, however, the set points of genetic codes are under attack by the perverting force of the toxicity of Earthly Elements and atmosphere, and this makes necessary the unalterable fixedness of genetic combinations as defense.

Moreover, any organism, human or otherwise, having a particular origin expressed in its genetic chain, cannot be set to accept any artificial changes, even if doctors or others wish to impose such changes. Every change to the roots of the genes can cause a rupture between the individuality and its Psychic center of nourishment and supply, as there is a disturbance of the codes — not the codes of the genetic chain but those pertaining to the endurance of the formed Etheric Nucleus ordained to serve as an underpinning of existence to the organism. In such a case, the organism becomes a stranger to its own Psychic environment, that is to its coded Etheric dimension, and this turns it into a victimizer-organism or a victim-organism. And this is something you should remember.

As for the Elemental organic product of the biological cells, called RNA, know that its activity of doubling and of multiplying the code within the cellular domain is by itself indicative of the evolution of the species in every aspect, Bodily, Spiritual, and Psychic. The Elements receive from the Nucleus information about their course. Once they have received it, they themselves become creators of new living identities. The act of reproduction, through copying of the codes, fosters greatly development across each level. In order to create one must act in accordance with what is acceptable in his domain.

In this way, RNA is itself a reflection of the chromosomal agents of gestation within a domain. The Nucleus is reflected in the domain, and the reflection becomes the embryo born and extended into life. Thus RNA has no place within DNA but is itself DNA.

The Law of self-presentation of organic life is what created it. And let he who can, understand this...

As for me, the timing of my action upon the domain varies according to the Nucleus of the system and its capacity for change.

The Earthly domain does not lend itself to brilliant creations. Only to scheming. And so I pass through and take over certain centers of chromo-genetic central Nuclei in those domains where I want to disrupt their false image creation, and in so doing I bring about the disruption I want of the false activity of the negative.

There are, as you know, moreover, Ioannis, idolized, highly enthroned images (idols) in Earthly domains, which have been erected by emissions from organisms and their transmutations under possession by the Element of desire, which also becomes a biological precedent. In other words it acts with the participation of all the endocrine factors and their affects.

My Position comes through these images into the atmospheres and dampens the intensity of their schematic form, thus plac-

ing the unconscious human factor in semi-wavering doubt as to everything it thinks, desires or remembers. With this vacillation, which may last for a short or a long time, the Element keeping the idol intact explodes. Then the idol loses its glamour, and along with it the erroneous judgements and responses of consciences in all their unconscionable behavior.

At such moments, the strongest Element that happens to be in that place is the one that will attract the attention of the organisms, be they material or immaterial.

Do you know of such a person? Because I see one such person this very moment on Earth...

I thank you for accompanying me on this revelation. To be more precise, for guiding me on it. In response, and as your reward, I too will guide you somewhere that you have never even thought of. The only thing that keeps you safe in this instance is that YOU YOURSELF once gave me this right. And when Ioannis says something, it cannot be unsaid.

My respects. You will see me many times again. Stay well."

Igmis .

Chapter 8

THE MYSTERIOUS FUNCTIONS
OF MAN

L et us proceed to the analysis of the individual's interdependence with external factors and see how he
receives stimuli from the environment. The Universal Law
decrees that the flow of events is governed by the relationship
between cause and effect, action and reaction, so that functional activity may proceed with the best results. When activity
takes place in the environment, we perceive it through our
sense of sight and of touch. This constitutes the visible Position
and gives us sensory proof of the effect of becoming on being.
But if we look a little more carefully we will see that there are
Elements that lead us to the acceptance of a different Position
(the invisible), which has a transparent cosmic composition. Its
purpose is to activate the visible Position, through special cross-
fertilization between the visible and the invisible, and to make
its function manifest.

These two Positions —the visible domain of the Body and
the invisible, Etheric domain of the Soul— coexist initially in

human nature as a presence, and the individual, depending on his degree of Elevation, may even enter the Third Position, that of the Domain of the Spirit. There he may experience the special Offer called *freedom*. As we will see below when we examine the inner world of the individual, Man has not been able to attain a degree of evolution enabling him to enter this higher Spiritual space, although the Three-fold nature of his presence is generally accepted. In order to enter this space we must become acutely aware of the level of perception we must reach in order to be able to reject certain Sensory states that have created hotbeds of disturbance within us, which almost always lead us to a worship of idols that entraps us through an illusory gloss of temporary happiness. In fact, this idol-worship distracts us from reflection on those matters deemed essential for self-realization during the course of our present life through time and space, with its transmutation from a course of Body and Soul to a course of Soul and Body.

Understanding means the sending forth of the intellectual perceptivity into the space and time of events or situations where we become transubstantiated to be identical with that point in time through Etheric, attractive propulsion and as a result we represent two Positions: that of the transubstantiated essential Element and that of the observer with a particular interest. Therefore, as we begin to very roughly understand our Three-fold substantive existence through indications gleaned from our own functioning, we may also be able to understand that, should we attain Spiritual hypostasis (as an actual experience and not as a hope), this would offer us the *visionary Insight* indispensable to our effort to see the result of each of our actions not only on the flesh but on the Soul as well. However, we know very well that, under the influence of illusory perceptions ruling over us, we believe that we will obtain social acceptance and "happiness" by gearing our actions toward amassing so-called material goods as much as possible here on Earth. This is often achieved by our stepping on other people, indifferent to the effect on the course of their Soul and *to the right for respect that the Creator has bestowed upon them*. Because of the subjective attachments that shape our values, the respect we pay to people often has to do with the image they project based on standards of financial prosperity and social status, which unfortunately reveal only a small part of reality.

Thus, through the fixations created by this acquired logic, we transform it into an arbitrary guide on a course I will present as follows: The Third Position (Spiritual hypostasis) resembles a very high mountain at the foot of which Man's two-fold Position is placed, according to the Law of Creation. There stand two paths, each ready to win over the individual:

One, the negative path, leads the individual to the banks of a deep river. Should he follow it and fall into the river, strong currents will drag him down into the abyss, and he will be saved only if a strong vibrational wave throws him back toward the shore, where he may find something to grasp. There is, moreover, a common saying about someone on a path to destruction as "being swallowed up by the river with nothing to save him." The negative path is constructed to present things as easy during the course of the individual's life, creating attractive illusions that will lead him to future "pleasures" and furnish him with a sense of uniqueness. Thus an enthusiasm is built that undermines true judgment, preventing the individual from seeing the path that benefits *both* the flesh *and* the Soul.

The Position of the flesh is mentioned first, because it is here that the functional Elements called Senses reside and, as the magnetic prime mover of the negative, it enters the amplification systems of these central Positions (the Senses), imposing their activated atmospheric state as the primary Position for creating and shaping happiness in Man. However, the Senses constitute the receptive space of the negative path, whose aim is the isolation and removal of the individual from the Spiritual path — the only path that can also provide the Soul with its own sustenance. Nature produces the appropriate protein substances for nourishment of the flesh according to the blueprints of the functional atmosphere of Earth. In order for the extended Position of the Soul, which is called "the Senses," to be united with the protein substances of the Earth, a special part of the Bodily affinity of the Soul expands. This part possesses a special Etheric organic ability to metamorphose with the protein into a substantiated Element within the organic functionality that produces the sense of touch. However the toxic-protein state also enters there, organically incorporated along with the protein and the Senses. The Rule defines this toxic-protein state as a Third Element in order to create a balance in human behavior; but Man, in his ignorance, is misled by false phantoms and conditions,[71] so that the third Element, counterbalancing the other two, acts and usurps, dominantly or not, the functions of the individual. This eliminates the intended state — as the Law of balance has ordained— of the Senses and of Etheric luminous protein and leads the individual to a state of Decline. We may liken this to the manifestation of the Position of an organic condition inside the human Body that destroys it as a living entity — a condition known to us as cancer.

Because, as we should very well know, Man neglects to create the proper conditions for building the foundation that will permit development of the visionary Insight that can distinguish every Sensory Element and control it absolutely, without being influenced by it, as happens when visionary Insight has not been developed. Only then will he be able to make a correct choice, beneficial to the flesh within the limits of its moral development and at the same time allowing the offer of the appropriate proportion of Psychic nourishment, which will give the Soul the capacity to attract the sensual flesh into following it. Then, together, the two Positions (Body and Soul) will create the adjustment that will permit them to move in a direction toward discovery of the third or Spiritual Position, which resides at the summit of the mountain (Psycho-Spiritual awareness). Toward this end the two Positions will follow the narrow path on the east side of the

---

[71] The phantoms in an individual's atmosphere, which produce images that change over time and appear at certain given moments, depending on the binding force they exert on Man.

mountain (as a term of perceptive Intellect) that starts exactly where the individual is originally situated and leads up to the plateau at the summit. There, through contact with the Third Position, the integrated personality is developed, whereby Man acquires the ability to penetrate any past or developing situation that will attempt to disrupt balance. On this path, the difficult part is for the individual to attain a Position of complete unity between Body and Soul, a unity through which the Soul-based sense that we call conscience will purify the lower Elements and prepare their union with the Spirit.

We usually describe as "Intellectually and Spiritually accomplished" those people who have an education and hold important positions, either in the community or in the estimation of other people. However, I believe that formal studies do not lead to, foster or guarantee Spiritual attainment, as we have defined it above, but simply a certain perceptual agility, corresponding to a level of learning (not of KNOWLEDGE) and sufficient to fully carry out the objective of one's studies. Let us repeat here that Man is naturally of a Three-fold nature, but that the hypostasis of the Spirit, although it occupies the appropriate Position inside him, exists in a latent form and its activity cannot be perceived. Only if it is realized consciously, in the manner I referred to above, will the individual arrive at Spiritual perception and follow the ascending path to consummate, integrated individuality and supreme Offer (service) to his fellow man. Unfortunately, however, due to the illusions we normally follow, we offer almost everything to the flesh, aiming at temporary gains, depriving conscience of the pursuit of necessary Psychic nourishment. Thus we try to immortalize the flesh and we condemn the Soul to death in an attempt at inverted creation, very far from the course toward Eternity —the only course that can bestow the beauty of immensity, which is never disrupted by temporal intervention from Elements of negative functionality. Inverted creation leads the individual to a state of Decline and, depending on the gravity of the wrongs he commits, in the hereafter he will enter the space of suspense, which consists of many dimensions. I assure you that it would be much better for each individual to try and channel his organic visceral emotions, towards a strong impulsive desire to acquire the Logos-attuned Offer known as Spiritual evolution and to cultivate this within his all-encompassing thoughts as his supreme duty to himself. And to strive to attain this Offer by fighting the great battle to translate the expression of this word (Spiritual evolution) into a holy duty, no matter what pressure he is under or from how many directions, or how hard the struggle, rather than letting himself be enslaved by one of these dimensions.

It is very hard for Man, to comprehend this situation, as he is by no means prepared to develop the visionary capability of inner Vision that would give him access to the spaces of entities in suspense.[72] These entities are ordained by the universal Laws to manifest their existence and coexist in the dimensions in which they are formed according to the small proportion of condensed matter deservedly allotted to them.

---

[72] Entities with bodies of "thin matter" remaining on the planet, commonly referred to as ghosts.

And this is based on the burden they carry due to actions committed in a state of Decline when they passed through this Earth as existential Positions in human form. These entities can exist only in very few stellar or planetary fields. One of these fields is that of the Earth, which is configured as a parallel horizontal scale containing these coexistent levels in their incorporated atmospheric proportions.

On this basis, as a responsible functionary of his actions and of the Law, Man has been ordained to enter as an individual into this level of atmospheric conditions and be subjected to the Laws of Perfect Universal Justice, thereby creating for his individual being either conditions of liberation that impel him upward to illustrious fields, or conditions of enslavement to lower phantom (illusory) Elements. The latter entrap not only the Sensory state produced by external illusions, but also the internal Sensory state of the viscera, which therefore succumb as a group to phantom dependency (attachment to illusions). Most so enslaved individuals remain on the planet where they traced their downward slide (Decline), which has brought them down into this latent and painful state.

At this point, my missionary perceptivity obliges me to cut short the presentation of these three dimensions. Because this book is not written in order to present the occult Position of other dimensions, but rather, as far as the Supreme Holy Position permits, to enter into those functions of Man that could be called *"mysterious functions of our unknown self."*

To begin with, I would describe as a mystery anything that functions with an invisible power and always produces a result incomprehensible to those whose perceptions have not embarked on the quest that would produce the passion to know which in turn would lead them to cognitive alignment with the mystery's functionality. Everyone's thought process is a power with mysterious functionality. Thought is free to develop into two Positions: the conscious (aligned) and, more often, the latent (subjective-negative). In the latter, the individual is unknowingly in a state of pathological activation, without objectivity in his perceptual field, so that he is unable to discern what actions may be harmful to him, and he extends his dysfunction to close relatives who depend on him, especially to his children. All this, because of his pathological activation, creates disharmony within them. Such disharmony, of course, is not only due to parents, because for each newborn individual there is a previously formed Position of inner characteristics and conditions whose blueprint exists and is incorporated into his Elemental composition from the time of his arrival here on Earth. The individual must exist within all this so that, if he manages to approach these things with self-control and handle them with dexterity, he will be able to transform them into a demonstrable state in which he can discern more clearly the benefit or damage caused by his actions. And this is necessary not only for a sane life for the flesh, but also for the required Offer to the Soul on its path in quest of the Spirit, which fills us with well-being and harmony and instills in us the need to thank the Supreme Position of Conscious Spirit for everything we and others around us have. In this way we arrive at true consciousness of the Position and the value of our presence and mission here on

Earth. Whether this mission is ordained by some special Law or we ourselves have assumed it, according to the Rule of the Laws, we must nevertheless strive to carry it out in order to gain what is truly the Eternity of Light.

We all believe that it is very difficult to rid ourselves of all these ominous conditions and events that appear in our path and manage to sweep us along on their own course, depriving us of our will and leading us into conflict. Sometimes this happens only in thought, and sometimes it extends to a wish to do Bodily damage, which is more harmful still, as it not only leads the Body to self-destruction and premature annihilation, but also creates conflicts with laws of the State. Then the flesh becomes forever reprehensible and is damaged, causing damage to the Soul, a consequence that will be borne later on by the individual, after his separation from the Body. I personally believe, based on my extensive perceptual awareness that very easily unites with Psychic consciousness, that it is more difficult to follow the course of hate, envy, confrontation and mutual destruction, because it demands enormous effort, consuming all of one's healthy energy. Thus in the end one is left without serenity and falls prey to diseases of the Body, because diminished inner energy erodes the viscera, attacks the nervous system and affects vital centers, with consequences ranging from serious to tragic. And one of these tragic diseases is cancer in its various forms, the consequences of which we all know. When it comes to cancer as an organic entity, we can observe that the ability to resist disease has deviated from the level of dynamic equilibrium of the organism in its natural substantive existence and dimension as decreed by the Laws, and this is due to inappropriate activation of Elements assigned to vital Positions to keep their autonomy in equilibrium at the same missionary level.[73]

---

[73] Here, in a few lines, is the holistic theory of pathogenesis, under the special form of carcinogenesis. If we examine the data to date, we will discover that within the human organism two opposing powers are in operation: The power for well-being and the power for self-destruction. The positive power is created by psychic serenity acting on receptive biological centers of the brain (such as the pineal gland, and perhaps others) and is transferred, through the peripheral system, to centers of hormonal control (hypothalamus-hypophysis system) and neural controllers (centers of the autonomic nervous system —hippocampus, parahippocampal gyrus, substantia nigra) and delivered to the target organs and to peripheral neuroreceptors for further treatment. When this route functions ideally, the whole organism enjoys the most appropriate energy conditions and a state of health exists. The negative power develops primarily through the sense of loss described earlier. The lack of psychic serenity, or the existence of entrenched energy deficiencies (hereditary, parental transfer of illusions), creates a vacuum in the acquisition of psychic energy, which is translated into a disturbance of the aforementioned system. The power that develops reactively tries to act on behalf of the deficiency, in accordance with organic homeostasis, and draws on matter endogenous to the cell (peripheral chromosomal protection). However, this causes a new reduction of the energy potential and plunges the organism into a vicious circle (similar vicious circles occur in non-reversible injuries, such as circulatory shock and others). But in this way homeostasis ceases and the target organs, from sub-clinical symptoms, now evince clear symptoms, which become very pronounced in "sensitive" organs or regions, depending on the particular structure of the individual. According to this point of view, the organism, although it has been derailed from its normal state, restricts disease to a certain part of itself, so as to retain on another level its biological integrity, albeit with a diminished functionality. The state of increased readiness (stress) that accompanies the disease leads to an attempt at healing the symptoms (or even the cause, according to classical medicine), with no particular effort made toward restoration of the energy potential. It is, however, logically possible for an ailing man, even if he is not aware of

How different our presence here on Earth would be if we followed the course of serenity, self-restraint and humility, living with self-respect, and with respect for Life as a gift of the Creator, thanking Him for all he has made us worthy of having. We must never forget that our presence here on Earth is like the sun that rises in the morning from the east and sets in the evening in the west, and that no one can escape from this metaphor. And it is eminently reasonable that we see this as being so and do not strive to live with self-destructive illusions.

---

the cause, through primarily unconscious but also conscious mechanisms, to find the road to well-being, even though he forgets it immediately afterward. In the case of psychopathology, the target organ injured is the mental organ, which receives feedback from the peripheral centers through sensory and sensation-producing mechanisms. Since loss of energy leads to alteration of the pieces that compose an image suited to the environment, mental illness ensues and the patient transposes himself inwardly to a familiar environment through images he manages to compose in his attempt to sustain a functionality compatible with survival. In the case of cancer, when the supply of reserve chromosomal energy of certain biological elements is diminished to such a degree that the peripheral control action is unable to restrain injury, then control is assumed by lower centers with a logic opposite to that of an integrated organism. Then, with the development of negative power, the cell acts as a whole, produces a maximum of vitality and uses the organism as a means of survival at the latter's expense. Finally, without a goal or, to put it differently, without the feedback of a control mechanisms, it kills off the organism, at the same time putting an end to its own development. Cancer is this system of uncontrollable cells (or, rather, the neoplasm —the tumor— since cancer is the generating cause, a power inherent in life, but like a form behind a mirror). Besides, we are more than familiar with the experiments of geneticists who have managed to develop "life" in the laboratory from genetic material, without however being able to give any meaning to it, since the cells develop in a mass lacking orientation. But all this demands extended analysis, which may possibly constitute the starting point of a different book. [A.V.]

Chapter 9

PSYCHIC CONSCIOUSNESS

A great number of erroneous things have been said about the invisible functional center that we have already discussed under the name *Psychic consciousness*. It is believed that every desire leading to enjoyment of the flesh has its center in the Soul and its practical expression, i.e. Psychic consciousness. This, of course, is a great mistake since it is simply an illusory image of fulfillment that entraps the individual in carnal desires developed through the Senses. If we look into this more carefully, we will see that these desires come from weaknesses that are based on an *inferiority complex*. This is nothing more than a series of erroneous evaluations concerning certain individuals, ideas and the self, due to *fears* of recent or distant origin. They produce stress, which has become very familiar to us in recent times and has secured a steady following...[74]

---

[74] Psychiatry calls stress the fear of an imminent calamity and classifies it as centered (if it stems from concrete situations of fear) and as free (if a conscious cause does not exist). Adler, a pioneer of psychiatry, has talked about the inferiority complex, which he considered a dominant element in

This entire progressive disharmony in people is produced in its manifest final expression by the mysterious Element called *Thought*.[75] This is why each of us must try hard to understand his functionality and to distinguish those things that benefit both the Elements, Body and Soul, from those that benefit only the Body and do so in appearance only. And if he cannot himself control and become conversant with both, let him try at least to find someone who can help him. You will say, are there such people? Truly I tell you, there are.

As far as I am concerned, the only thing that anyone inclined in this direction need do is bow down in prayer to the Creator with a clear desire and with his whole being. He can then be sure that he will be offered exactly what he needs in energy to begin the quest for intellectual awareness of his intrinsic status within his organic progression toward the discovery of that Holy Light we call "our Holy Spirit," which is ever-expectant of that charitable Offer. And sooner or later the Creator will send someone who will give him the initial start on his particular quest for solutions based on proper conduct of his own, and set him on

---

structuring the personality, and in fact he believes that under positive conditions it is transformed into a tool for healthy personality structure. The psychoanalytic school attributes phobias to fixations during the first stages of psycho-sexual development, whereas others attribute it to separation stress, etc. It is generally admitted that, even in non-pathological situations, erroneous evaluations by an immature personality create phobias and produce stress, and that this creates the need for concealment. This is achieved through internal, irrepressible desires of a disorienting nature which, when fulfilled, diminish the painful sense of stress. [A.V.]

[75] For a definition of the term *Thought* see chapter 11.

his natural course, where he will be able to make the most of this Offer.

I know this because, during my years of following the human condition in all of its manifestations, I have often seen that the impulse to speak about a situation that someone has experienced personally takes the form of advice to whomever he happens to meet. Man needs this expression, because he feels pressured by the small percentage of conscience (8%) residing in the unconscious, and this holds even for the greatest criminal... For this reason, I consider it imperative that we bring ourselves as close as we can to the primary functionality of conscience that resides at the core of the Soul, and that we recognize and enter the gates of Elevation. This process of Elevation is consolidated in a mysterious way that we may describe as follows: At first **it infiltrates all instinctive centers, opening up a great road to realignment of the productive Positions of the organism, in order to reach the first stage of *preparation*. Then it proceeds to the domain of *validation* and thence to the *control center*. There it will receive final approval in order to proceed to the stage of *execution*, which will establish the newly-shaped thoughtform[76] in all the functions of the organic centers. Then the thoughtform, after having been *personalized* in its dimension, attempts to occupy the space of the Senses. There, depending on the direction the individual's goals have taken, it will act on the corresponding Sense (with the participation**

---

[76] The term *thoughtform* is used here to describe a form, or shape, created by and existing only in the mind of the individual.

of vision) and will dominate practically the entire functional space.[77]

When the individual has acquired diffuse Etheric, conscious functionality, time is eliminated and he is endowed with free will, capable of assuming the Position of an objective individual who has a liberated control center as the nucleus of objectivity with modified initial secretion. Then he will be able to discover the underlying cause of every action, be it from the immediate or distant past.

But let us analyze this. If the cause is in the immediate past, he may, with some individual effort or with the help of a psychoanalyst, free himself and find himself able to control any kind of thinking that might cause problems and leave an imprint he will carry throughout his life. It is even possible that these problems will be so intense as to affect his health in the manner we have already mentioned. However, if the cause has its origins in the very distant past, and has been transferred through the father or the mother, who in their turn have received it from their own parents, then it will be very difficult for the individual to become free of it. For what we have here are deeply rooted inherited conditions and events, passed on from generation to generation. Thus only someone with special knowledge might be able to penetrate these conditions — someone with the ability to become a peripatetic explorer of this sound-

---

[77] A similar progression, at a lower functional level, is encountered in the cell during the process of protein synthesis. Anyone studying its stages in a specialized book, from the conditions that create the need for it, to the active participation of chromosomal matter and the mobilization of numerous productive cell units, will understand this relationship and will certainly discern the close affinity between the eternal Cycles of the Universe. [A.V.]

recorded state[78] and discover its links. Only he will be in a position to observe the sequence of inborn phantom Elements that create illusions in the individual and form a distorted organic system. This distortion absorbs us into its domain and shapes our desires for action in such a fashion that we cannot observe them clearly in concrete images, but only through the "mask" it imposes on them in their chromosomal reflection. And it stimulates us organically so that we accept these desires without any critical reflection or resistance. Therefore, only such a specially gifted person could change the course of this chain of events, because as it is transferred from individual to individual, it increases its field of intrusion into functional space until it reaches an intolerable level. Then the individual in question will be unable to withstand it and will be led onto a negative course without ever knowing why. On such a path, under the influence of invisible erroneous desires, people become resistant and aggressive toward anyone attempting to alter their prescribed course. Such people need someone special who is familiar with all the visible and invisible functions of the individual.

The first ability this specially gifted healer must possess is a super-special perceptive awareness and knowledge of what is called physiognomics, in order to reach all the lower peripheral factors and find comprehensive solutions that release the individual from the effects of various time periods that have trapped him in his present Position. With this the healer will be able to recognize the receptive Position of every individual and the frequency at which he functions. Because, the frequency at which the individ-

---

[78] Everything concerning the individual is first recorded in the Etheric state and then propelled, through sound, toward its destination.

ual receives external influences corresponds to the frequency of penetration into his inner states (depending on his constitutional formation) and thus the healer will be in a position to recognize the location of disturbance within the individual. However, we see that, apart from *physiognomics* (knowledge of Man's physical nature), correct knowledge of *meta-physiognosis* (Man's metaphysical nature) is also needed, since in various psychoneurotic or other pathological situations, certain conditions are involved that originated in the distant past and are well hidden from the members of the present generation. The most important thing, however, is that the healer should know how to behave and at which space-time point he should begin probing certain pathogenic hotbeds. It is in these hotbeds that the beginnings of metastatic (easily transferable) Positions are developed, creating various desires in the individual that are difficult to fulfill, since he is not entitled to do so.

Now, because of the metastasis occurring due to lower natural factors such as the inability for fulfillment, the individual becomes caught up in the illusions of an artificial reality without realizing it. And since he is not able to realize that he himself is responsible for his own lack of fulfillment, it is easy for him to blame other people, specifically or generally, whom he perceives to be hindering him in this. When his thoughts turn to situations that he believes were created by other individuals, who appear in his inner visual field in varying transmutations at different time-space junctions, he tries to attribute to those individuals the blame for what they have done to him, according to his own subjective logic. Because of the transmutation, however, he cannot satisfy himself except through exhibiting aggressive behavior. This can take two forms: Either active aggression (violence) or vocal aggression (swearing), which is simply violence restrained due to fear or guilt often causing one to act cowardly for no apparent reason. This is because during his initial break from controlled functional behavior, he is transported to other time periods and regresses to events that have occurred sometime in the past, carrying them into the present or even the future (the ability for prophecy is sometimes acquired in this manner). When such images from a different time and space are charged with considerable but unrealizable needs for fulfillment, the individual reverts to reactive behavior through aggression or withdrawal from the events occurring around him, in an attempt to reject reality This, of course, leads to recurring states of depression, which may even end in suicide.[79]

The specially gifted individuals possessing Three-fold awareness, or knowledge of the Position of the flesh in its constitution and mission, as well as that of the Soul as an activating agent along the path toward the Spirit, are able

---

[79] Here the course of depressive syndrome is in evidence, or rather the syndrome of mood disturbance (manic depression) which, as one school of psychiatry claims, always stems from covert aggressiveness and is directed either at others or at one's self. The futile investiture of psychic material is defined as the essence of the disturbance. The new revelation is the break-down of time and the surrender of the individual to different spaces and times as cause-centers of functional disturbances. It is interesting to see how biological psychiatrists discover, in depressed persons, disturbances in cerebral neurotransmitters (serotonin - dopamine - noradrenaline), that is, in vehicles of message transmission from one cell to the other and from one center to the next. The relationship between the visible and the invisible is thus indirectly proved, with the visible receiving pressure from the invisible and forming its image. [A.V.]

to understand what is happening within the disturbed individual who has been led to this uncontrollable state, and they know how they must work with him, as special healers, to offer him genuine assistance toward the restoration of his health. Having entered the individual's actual perceptive functionality in its disturbed state, the healer develops empathy by drawing on the abnormal vibrations, and embarks upon invisible activity with diffuse penetration into every constitutional Element, unperceived by the Sensory receptors of the individual. Thus, unrolling before the healer's eyes, as in a motion picture, are all the events that the individual has experienced in the past, be it immediate or distant during other sojourns on Earth. Of course, the healer must be very careful to first of all discern the time and place of the events, because these seem to be covered in a kind of fog that hinders easy recognition, and then their special course and the imprints they left on the individual under study. He also has a duty to take care how he directs the pathological individual into these spaces and times, so that through participation as an explorer-observer, the individual (patient) will learn, as he is led back to formative moments, to recognize the events that have influenced his individuality and developed his erroneous perceptive awareness. His goal will be to clearly see true reality and to function free of negative magnetic influences. In this way, a kind of operation is carried out with the healer as the operator and the patient as the co-operator. This is possible because the quantity and quality of the intrusion into the disturbed functional field does not cause negative charge, which could result in rejection through defense mechanisms.[80]

For this reason I believe that anyone wishing to enter into areas of knowledge about the invisible functional Elements must know that these operate all the inner chords of the cellular system, from the single molecule to the entire production center of the vibrational pulsation, with the absolute cooperation of the autonomic nervous system which subsequently influences and activates the major nervous system that operates the entire neural world. I call this a world because every molecule constitutes an individual entity and every cell an organized entity, and similarly every neuron is an individual entity and every neural center an organized entity, all the way up to cerebral centers, which constitute organized groups of organized entities. When I refer to organization, I mean the entity that is set in interactive relationship and aligns itself with another entity or entities, with the purpose of serving both the individual Position and the super-individual Position, which comprise the constitutional Elements of Man, that is, those Elements that serve biological existence, self-sufficiency and homeostasis of the organism. They are called biochemical sub-

---

[80] Here we discern the foundations of a systematic therapeutic approach that brings to mind psycho-analytic models, the only difference being that it increases the scope of investigation of individual fields from early psycho-sexual stages of development studied by psychiatrists to more essential analyzed levels of existence, well hidden in the sub-individuality of man. However, the depth of the healer's operation is also increased, since with the KNOWLEDGE he has been endowed with as his material, and his own energetic Offer as his means, he becomes able to heal the cause before it is discerned by medical doctors. [A.V.]

stances in medical terminology and labeled according to their contribution.[81]

These substances are produced by ten centers in the organism. Seven of these are well known. There is one center, more or less unknown, that has a most important task to perform. I have named this the **Control Center**, and on it depends the well-balanced functionality of every individual. Its efficient operation depends basically on the formation of the constitution of the individual human being (based on Physiognomics). Depending on this constitution, it receives corresponding charges

---

[81] Here the nervous system of the individual is analytically pictured as a miniature of the universe and as a second presentation of the three-fold nature of Man, stating that the world and all that it contains serves its units but also their creator.

In this way we become aware of the existence of the autonomic nervous system, which functions independently of our will, the voluntary (or kinetic) nervous system, which serves our volition, and the interconnecting function of hormones, which are receptors, controllers and regulators of neural messages and, more generally, of the biological functions of the organism. And while the kinetic system is entirely understood, the autonomic and the chemical (hormonal) refer to centers with "dark" homeostatic dynamics but that are also intimately connected to psychic functions that puzzle students analyzing the organism.

We are also aware of the existence of neural cells with extensions (dendrites, axons) that terminate in other neural cells, where certain substances (neurotransmitters) intervene and transfer a message from one cell to the next, but also act as a control center regulating the responsiveness to and variability of the message.

With regard to the constitutional elements, we know that they are basically proteins, fats and hydrocarbons in varying complex chemical composition, the variability of which, in location and functionality, ensures the complexity and effectiveness of biological function.

Further on, hormones will be analyzed with regard to their productive centers and the functionality of the organism. [A.V.]

and manifests accordingly negation or affirmation, at which time it undertakes related control actions. These permit and impel the spinal cord —with the inter-Elemental cooperative participation and productive interventions of the hypophysis (pituitary gland)— to issue the appropriate orders to the nervous system, with the coincident participation of the Sensory functional Element, to do the same, according to the interpretation of the control center. This interpretation was given because of the individual's constitution, which is susceptible to the invisible functional world.[82]

All these invisible and visible, shaped and molded,

---

[82] The seven secretion-producing glands known to medicine are: the hypothalamus, the hypophysis (pituitary), the thyroid, the parathyroid, the suprarenal, the pancreas and the gonads (the ovaries and the testes). If one examines their functions and classifies them within the framework discussed here, he will see a whole new world within the human body. The same glands are described schematically and topographically by students of the occult under various names, on the basis of the energy fields they produce.

Now, following the guidance of the teachings concerning the three unknown glands, we must examine the thymus gland, the system of centers of the autonomic nervous system (substantia nigra, hippocampus, etc.) and stop at the pineal gland, which is referred to as a control center.

According to medicine the pineal gland has no known function. It produces melatonin and is not immediately connected to other cerebral centers. Melatonin has been found in the retina of the eye (where the neural route associated with vision begins, something like the film in a camera) and in the skin, as the producer of melanin (a substance that causes tanning in the summer and protects the skin and the eyes from exposure to light). That is all. Only a few people have talked about primeval connections with the optical route discarded in the course of evolution.

The spinal cord is here referred to in the sense of the kinetic nervous system, whereas by nervous system is meant the visceral part of centrifugal routes. [A.V.]

Elements are activated in order to carry out the task assigned to them — which, because of the individual's constitutional state and relationship to his environment, usually benefit the negative path and deprive the individual of the Spiritual Offer. Only a very limited number benefit the twofold Man and reward him with Spiritual enlightenment. Both these Positions are produced by the Universal Order of Laws defined for each planet. And when we speak of the Universal Order of Laws we must understand the following points of the Rules which, if we accept them as being the authority of Everything, will create in us a super-conscious emotive state,[83] and this is a most essential thing for Man. This will shape for us a perceptive awareness that will carry us, with a motion encountering no resistance, into the atmospheric organicity. The latter, as a Rule of existence, is classified as a primary Organism (organized system) of the infinite dimension instigating proper organic peripheral development and the appearance of organs in their assigned Positions.

The atmospheric organicity further operates as the principal Nucleus (central incubator) in the separation of Elements for coupling, composition and arrangement into their individual organicity as functioning individual entities and in their bio-genesis, with predefined Elemental composition in

---

[83] This is a sensation that does not derive from the Earth's atmosphere but from super-conscious states in the higher part of the Soul. It is created by core Elements sent to the individual to shape the biological functions associated with the brain and the suprarenal glands, so that the proper secretions are produced in the brain and cultivated in the proper proportions. At the same time the negative secretions of the thyroid are suppressed.

relation to their biological functional course toward a balanced Position in the Order prescribed by the Laws within the organic Position of the Universe. The individual thus emerges as a copy of his organic reflection, and based on his acceptance of the Universal-organic Position-individual, is called upon by the Law of Evolutionary Progress to accept these other Elements and enter into mutual functionality with them. This means acceptance and well-intentioned communication with the particular organism (interrelated whole) that constitutes his entire individual entity, so that an interdependent relationship will develop and be consolidated into a Position of cooperation with the organic principles of his Position. From there he may begin developing his individual-mutual functional relationships and seeking out paths for maximum future benefit, which means his Elevation to the illustrious worlds of the Higher Universe.

For this reason each of us must strive, through these Positions, to know his own self. From that moment on he will be magnetically attracted by a desire to do what pleases the "Pure One," as the ancient Greeks used to say. The classical Greeks used to urge everyone to penetrate the motives of his own Sensory functionality so as to become aware of the sub-causes that create causes of disturbance that eventually produce the path leading to failure of Spiritual development. They were trying in this way to help Man to know his own self ("Know thyself").

One of these specially endowed teachers of Self-knowledge was Socrates, who certainly deserves the title of the Great Philosopher. Self-knowledge was analyzed extensively in his lectures, in his attempt to offer everyone the knowledge necessary to become a creative individual, useful to himself and to his fellow men. What I do not know, however, is whether the method used in these teachings was geared to the perceptive level of a large audience or whether the lectures were conducted in closed circles where only a few had the opportunity to listen, so that the meeting may have been permeated by pathological egocentric behavior. Perhaps because of this the students developed a desire to present their own Position in the domain of perceptive dimension, resulting in a distance between themselves and the teacher. It would therefore have been impossible for the teachings of the Great Philosopher to be passed on with accuracy.

Chapter 10

THE POSITION OF THE NEGATIVE

I mages pass by us on a temporal trajectory toward the future, while at the same time they deftly synthesize the history of the past and present to us both the mistakes and the correct actions of people before us. In this spirit of entreaty they call upon us to show us self-knowledge, that is, what we really are and what our purpose is here on Earth.

The Creator of the Universe has initiated certain people into this special knowledge and has sent them here during certain special Eras to teach people to develop to higher levels and give their lives a different meaning and expression. And these chosen ones have spoken according to the dictates of their times. Most of them, however, have failed to carry out this most worthy mandate, for along the way, they allowed more elements of human weakness inside them than was permissible, without realizing it. Thus human weakness has shaped an angel-like individuality, but with an unconscious functionality with the ostensible mission of servant-special counselor, armed with the enticing images of the accomplishments of a successful and unique individual and vested with the soft melodious sounds that the unconscious has the right to orchestrate. Such an individual therefore enjoys the illusory satisfaction of feeling unique, most special, competent, and indispensable in leading mankind on a course of progress toward redemption in his own eyes and in the eyes of the Creator.

With regard to the Creator and the created, I can provide a brief analysis; the Creator is he who shapes the Element composed of micro-Elements that unite and function together on the basis of the Universal Law. The Universal Law itself is nothing more than the Lawfully perfect thoughts of the Creator, within which the plan of Creation places the small entities-individualities that we have mentioned above, under the influence of the Position and the Anti-position, or the Positive and the Negative. This is something like what is expressed in theology as God and the Devil. Naturally, it is hard for me to say that the Devil is a great power, one that can stand against God, who is the Creator of everything, as a power of resistance. I cannot accept this. Because for me only the Creator of everything is the supreme power in the temporal and eternal Universe, and all other existing powers of the Positions and Anti-positions are derivatives of the Super-position, with a mission to initiate functional activity in the Element and to follow it throughout its course. Although the Negative is immensely dominant at the borderline solar and planetary Positions that divide the Higher Universe from the Lower —and our own solar system is among these— the Higher Universe is governed, according to the infinitely Perfect Law, by the principle of functioning in absolute neutrality, and thus the Negative Position has no latitude there to function autonomously. And while the Perfect Law in the Higher Universe relegates the Negative to complete inactivity, its permanent Position remains by right at the borderline, where our planetary Position is also located, and from there it exercises its universal mission as a disturber of human equilibrium, causing Man to experience the confusing and amazingly twisted thought patterns that will lead him to the Lower Universe. As ordained by the primary Law, the Fallen are placed there and, having previously failed to act correctly, are meted appropriate punishment through atmospheric conditions, about which you will read in greater detail and analysis in a book to be published very soon.

* * *

And being who I am, identified by the name of Ioannis, the great and supreme Positions of the Universes reveal to me the nomogram (delineation of the Laws) of Metacycling Creation in its multifaceted Orders and states. And out of my own true desire, without any Law of Creation imposing this as a mandate, solely on the basis of my own volition, I present here along with everything else, as an Offer to enhance your general perceptivity, the subjects revealed to me by the Universal Functionary **Glaumon Edi 1** who governs the sector of the two Positions, the Positive and the Negative in the multifaceted synthesis of Creation, functioning interactively within the atmospheric biological space of any given level in all Universes.

GLAUMON EDI code I

"I turn to your imploring call, Ioannis, basking in your multi-faceted wisdom, and I bow in order to convey my salutations to your rigorous and discerning nature.

My name is Glaumon Edi. I belong to the Universe of borderline Positions of presence possessed of two-fold knowledge of a positive and negative character. I receive from both of these Orders, and my thought bisects the access from one level to the other. I come from a Third and Neutral Order of orientation that places me in a propitiously serene receptivity toward both biological types, that of gravity and that of levitation.

I do not serve anyone in particular; the two atmospheres are equally focused within me and unite only within themselves. They are separate.

I watch and gain precise knowledge of acts of Decline and acts of Elevation at their special points of contact.

I possess elements of both and I act sometimes in the north and sometimes in the south, without exceeding the limits of Isonomy (the Law of Equal Distribution of justice according to what one deserves).

My Position engineers the meeting of two totally opposite

entities in the same space. I bring the Negative in proximity with the Positive, causing the Negative to partake of the Positive and vice versa.

I am not bound to anyone, but I remain, Ioannis, at your service. My rise comes with pleasure, my setting with submission, since you have knowledge of it...

I remain in readiness for your queries. I thank you."

Glaumon Edi 1

INVOCATION BY IOANNIS

I, Ioannis, who am now on Earth, approach your great apostolic Position, **Glaumon Edi 1**, Functionary of the Law. I express my salutations thrice and in my apostolic capacity as a revealer of the mysteries of mysteries, I invoke you to enter my thoughts and describe to me in great detail your mission in the manner that you discharge it.

How do you consolidate the biological state of the negative, as a Rule, and bring it to life within the positive state, and how do you Elementally compose the positive within the negative, so that both these levels —the positive and the negative— may coexist in the same space and each function individually? What is the purpose of the two Positions as to their functionality so that each may achieve its goals?

What is produced by their activity that is beneficial to the Universal Organism?

How many of these levels of activity of the positive and the negative are there?

As we know, the *Lower Universe* is absolutely binding for the course of Man as the place of criminal justice; the *Intermediate Universe*, in which I now reside, contains a great percentage of the negative Element, while still giving Man the free will to choose his path; and the other *Higher Universes*, award a more important Position to the positive and their inhabitants find themselves much more functionally attuned. In view of this division of the Universes, how does life in these levels function as biology and as organic functionality of the individuals?

Also, are there other planets in the Intermediate Universe similar to the one where I now reside (Earth) with the same density of matter and with the same proportion of atmospheric Elements? If there are, how are they defined?

Is the negative Position ordained to dominate and to perpetuate its function as a conqueror? If so, why?

With infinite gratitude I bow seven times
Ioannis

GLAUMON EDI code I

"I apply the central geometric scheme of inter-universal com-munication and I appear to Ioannis. I have made my Position manifest to give to the one and only Ioannis still another dia-gram of the plan of Creation that activated worlds, Nuclei (incubators of Creation), life forms and truth.

Ioannis, I confer from afar my respects for your most estimable work of sowing enlightened revelations on barren soil. My conscious presence, following your strong call, orders me to declare that I serve and represent the system of inter-communication and mediation established from the beginning of the Universes by a Functional Law of All-Universal Order. I bow to the Creations and I continue:

The co-existence of the two worlds that are defined by name as "positive-negative" is the beginning and the end of every biological system.

The Position of biology as actual metabolic activity is gov-erned by the Rules of Creation and Anti-creation. Together these constitute the principle of action that sets in motion the entire Universal Elemental Organism.

The graduation of their communication from lesser to greater, equally or unequally apportioned, and distributed in an infinite number of ways one within the other, yields the result of differentiation of universal systems, into three broad categories (Lower, Intermediate, and Higher Universes), exact-ly as you state. My Position is meant to activate the special magnetism of either the positive or the negative in a particular space in order to impel a particular biological system away from its axis of operation onto an ensuing one of a different functional Position.

The Rule of Motion of All Things governs the interaction of the Positive and the Negative so that biology will evolve through its own temporal Cycles, generating the reproduction, movement and *Metacycling of the Universes in their infinite manifestations of organized Life. Thus my Position is ordered by an inherent Rule to introduce to a given domain whatever is lacking, be it the Negative or the Positive, mobilizing this domain to move beyond the state which it has maintained up to the present time. This is accomplished by the biological acceleration of only a few Elements in the domain, which will escape from the overall frame of reference, augment or trans-form their Position with regard to the entire system, and "force" the system to proceed toward this new organic scheme and perceive its Position. This perception is manifested by two Positions: either the entire system patterns itself after the indi-vidual accelerating Elements, or it increases and improves its natural animate Order, so as to attain the speed of the new one, augmenting and improving itself until finally the system surpasses the new Body in certain fields and reaches a new biological Cycle of different and increased endurance. This is how my work is carried out.

An example in the Intermediate Universe is the positive action of botanical oxygen on the planet Earth when it is in higher than normal concentration, and the contrary activation which yields carbon.

Similarly, in the Bodily cells of Man there is functional equilibrium and suddenly accelerated cellular transmutation. Likewise, there is susceptibility to illness at times of high inner speeds and, at the same time, antibody action, which activates the organism, reinforcing its ability to resist.

Coming now to the domain of systems of individual or collective Thought, in all Universes, I am obliged to counterpoise organic environments with Elements of different speeds so as to arrive at **action** *as an outcome. I do not aim at an absolute choice between positive and negative, but rather at increasing the speed of a few Elements of a particular organic set of thoughts through metabolic actions, so that it will undergo a disturbance in its vital energy and will be drawn into confrontational resistance.*

In the Lower Universes, as on Earth, this is usually accomplished through the Bodily biology of individuals, and in Nature, through the suspension of the mechanisms of quantitative distribution.

In the Higher Universes it is accomplished through atmospheric projection.

The aim is the mobilization of the Universe within the range of its Elements, so that everything dedicates its Position to development, genesis, and new action within the Cycle of eternity.

The levels of production of Negative-Positive are as many as the Elements in existence. Every Element has its Positive and its Negative, defined according to the space in which it exists biologically, because each contains within it action and counter-action.

I accelerate certain of these toward temporal Cycles of change to reach the positive or the negative according to the Law of Attraction of Affinities. That is, I open a channel of acceleration with a third external Element of a different vitality, but which contains within it Elements of our reference organism. These immediately seek union with receptors of the same biological quality and thus reciprocate with the overall organism, due to the small number of Elements attractionally activated and accelerated.

This is, schematically, the way it happens in all Universes. Even in the domain of the Most-sacred Functionaries of the Light of Perception —to cite an example— a negative apex matching in power with their Order emanates from Lower Universes as a concrete mass, and they are called upon to lean downward and resolve this. This is how they render their services.

In Lower Universes, just as on Earth, it is biological functioning itself, in its renewed Cycles, that initiates its Position of rejection of a previous Cycle and is at the same time attracted by it, contrary to its structure, so that it resists its own exit from any of its Cycles. And when it becomes stuck within one of them, then the Cycles of Nature call for its release, evincing continuous change in speed and action during the process.

My Position here on Earth is to induce the extensive release of both the positive and negative Elements, so that the former can develop and the latter can function. In this place I represent interference with an Order, through a different Order, and I am ordained by Law to promote a law within another, revitalizing and promoting Life.

A planet identical to this one, with the same animate presence and Elemental density, is not permitted to exist. There are others of relative similarity, but in this Universe, absolute similarities are forbidden.

The Negative Position has as its purpose to activate but not to dominate the Universe. It dominates the lower levels because there exists a deficiency in biology and Order, but I would say that as a rule its aim is to be "caught like a criminal" and to be dominated.

Revealing entirely to Ioannis an absolute code, I bow in gratitude and again direct myself to my work."

* * *

In principle, Man, in order to develop on a hierarchical course to the level of the Higher Universes of Light, HAS A NEED to enter into the knowledge of the Negative. And I enter this Position so that, through a strong Psychic emotion, I may confer upon you this great Offer, which I consider to be the most important thing for any man desiring to enter the Psycho-Spiritual worlds. It is a worded exposition of infinite value, expounding knowledge with regard to the

Negative from the great Father of divine knowledge **Pa Penedea 13′**, that is, with regard to how the Negative has been ordained to function. I pass it on to you exactly as it was communicated to me in answer to my active request, conveying its knowledge in its own precise terminology and style.

INVOCATION BY IOANNIS

Proceeding as the genuine Ioannis, I, now Ioannis of the Earth, enact my missionary function as the Law of our Father the Creator has ordained, in this Age and in these Times, to present the great revelation of the Laws and Mysteries of the two cosmic Universes, the Higher and the Lower, the Always and the Everywhere, as the sole Apostle of these revelations, who also brings forward the new composition and ordering of the Higher and Lower Orders for the eternal New Age. And therefore, as you, venerable **Pa Penedea 13'**, have also been ordained, I appear before you, bowing before your all-Spiritual knowledge, and I ask you to reveal to me in written form every detail of your divinely-inspired acts and observations.

To begin with, what do *Negative Order and Function* mean with respect to *Positive Progress and Evolution*? What does the word *negative* mean? What is its biological state and in what manner does it function within the biological and electro-chemical Position of Man? What is its ultimate purpose? What should Man know in order to understand the effects of this negative energy, which has as its aim or functional purpose the dissolution of his integral state? How must he determine his movements and his receptivity so as not to find himself under the complex-inducing energy of the negative? And anything else that is useful for the ultimate revelation concerning the mysterious negative state.

I bow with infinite gratitude,
offering my salutations,
Ioannis, now of the Earth.

PA PENEDEA code 13′

"IOANNIS, CREATOR, I present myself and I reveal within your code the code that composes and distinguishes one half and one quarter of the functional awakening of the Universal ideal world. The Negative, as you distinguish it in its assigned functional Position within the other Rules, is the basis of stability of all Rules for the activation of motion and equilibrium in the Pan-Universe. It is the Great Principle of universal biology as a Position that nourishes itself with its self and creates complexity as a function within every animate Spiritual Order.

If we define Spirit as the catalytic synthesis of Logos, then the Negative, due to its nature, is born long before this synthesis. The Principle that justifies it is the ORDER OF ANTINOMY, Anti-Lawfulness, which is the Order that composes, maintains, and recreates LAWFULNESS in its entirety.

The negative is organically neutral and is implanted inside each of the two parts: the Male and the Female. In its neutral state it is inactive.

The type of relationship defining this natural distinctive entity called the "Negative" is the result of a biological space-time placement of matter in an inverse capacity with respect to itself, so that matter may continue to produce matter through its activity. Or, to put it differently, the negative, as a creator of all activity, is a great inseminator of this Universe. It is what differentiates this Universe from the other. The other stays as is. This one functions through activity. Amen to this R e v e – l a t i o n...

The action of this natural stable Position of a type of energy that acts, reacts and is called Negative, varies from place to place. There, on the basis of Rules of mutation, it meets with passivity-induced restrictions that are graduated in magnitude, and impose on it an analogous scope of action. With regard to your question concerning Man of the heavens of this Earth, I reply to you that his actions there are totally reciprocal with every type of life and atmosphere in his environment.

The genesis of an individuality on the level of this planet is, in every way, good training in the knowledge and the influ-

ence of the Order of the Law of the Negative. The aim of the Negative is to function according to its nature in the visceral and Sensory organic Position of Man. It performs, is performed upon and discharges in this way its Strict Rule not only for the maintenance of Orders of equilibrium and evolution of individ-ualities, but primarily for the edification of these individuals concerning the terrible cogwheels of their irrevocable damna-tion.

The Position of the Negative on Earth can be found EVERY-WHERE! There is no living space that has not harbored it. Everything on Earth is permeated by its Anti-life, completely incorporated in biology. All beings breathe the Negative; they breathe it in and they breathe it out. The drama of human exis-tence within the punitive enclaves of the Rule of the Negative is ONLY dissolved through its recognition—an act that does not get rid of the Negative, but fortifies Man as regards his Position, bolstering him with the **Salt of self-knowledge**. The Negative then does not cease to surround him, but it does cease to exercise its influence on him, and then MAN becomes a creator. Being on Earth, his means and materials are always influenced by the Negative, but he places them in such an order that their organic composition yields a state of equilibri-um. And then he may enter into Perceptive Awareness and perhaps into the evolution of his positive electro-genotype, as a biological and Etheric entity.

The apprenticeship begins as follows: Man scrutinizes him-self from his most subtle to his most conspicuous organic

action and mental activity, in order to discern negative forma-
tions within himself. In this dynamic process he is aided by
the acceptance of the existence of negative formations every-
where inside himself. The Negative is not a foreign agent. It is
a body within his Body, an active part of his thinking. It is the
Rule of his life on Earth. And thus it is active incessantly with-
in him. It is not a disease. THE PLANET IS SUBJECT TO INVA-
SION BY THIS DISEASE and calls upon the Being to become
intellectually and spiritually healthy and vigorous.

Individual knowledge about the Negative is achieved as a
process within every living entity, as a universally placed
mechanism that brings forth the antibody activity in all ani-
mate beings. Its Position in the cellular Order of Life as animate
energy is the vibrational contrast and antithesis, which creates
the logical complexity of the organic Whole of every organic
combination. In this way it is INTERNALIZED biologically.

I reveal a basic Position of the Negative at the mental level
of the Earth: the impetus of the subjective desires of Man,
which does not produce relief, as in the lower species of
Nature, but instead is regenerated in this manner. The recep-
tivity of the individual, in order to avoid expansion of the neg-
ative factor throughout his biological Order, must become criti-
cal in judgment. In the beginning, it must also be inwardly
silent and probing, so as to induce the remission of the initial
cellular chromosomal Positions of the Negative in the depths of
his Bodily existence, which is the cradle of Spiritual develop-
ment.

Because I am inside your Mind, I am NEVER deprived of the organic gratification of expression! My Position has been Elementally composed within you, Ioannis. For this reason, the revelation of the Negative is also one of your temporary apostolic missions on Earth for the full enlightenment of those who seek to evolve along a Positive path.

I hold your thoughts within my own inner thoughts."

PA

* * *

AND I, IOANNIS, WARN THOSE WHO BELIEVE THAT THEY KNOW THE POSITION OF THE NEGATIVE THAT THEY MUST ABANDON THIS BELIEF, AND THAT TO DO SO THEY MUST ANNIHILATE THE ALL ENCOMPASSING EGO THEY HAVE STRIVEN SO HARD TO CREATE.

Thus two roads open up before us, the Positive and the Negative, each with its own Offers, which we will receive without being able to resist. We will be transformed by these Positions and we will follow them. In the Positive Position we will have the supreme Offer, which we will experience as a strong sense of protection and an immense serenity and beauty, which we will live out eternally, our only feeling being that we are always at the beginning of the Offer. We will be filled with the impulse and desire to thank the Creator for what he is offering us and for making us, His infinitesimal creations, worthy of gradually ascending all the way to the special Creation singled out in the space of the Universe. Then, all the other levels of Life living out their Cycles and

Metacycles in universal space, will perceive us, depending on the dimension they occupy, as a concentrated mass of light traveling great distances at time intervals very difficult for Man to grasp in his present state of perceptivity. This is because in the human form where we presently find ourselves, we perceive with the apparent animate Elements, of the Soul and the Senses, always through a Position of delusion with respect to the natural Laws that determine the mission of each Element.

We should note that every Element, on the basis of the natural Laws, must trace a path that ultimately leads to its *higher archetype*,[84] so that it will enter the space of *metamorphosis*, and from there will be assimilated by the *higher Psychic Element* in its entirety so that it will become the whole of the higher Element. However, the functional Position of delusion, molded by a certain functional Element, intervenes and has as its mission the creation of *antithesis* (reaction) in the special centers of Man called Senses. Then these engender thoughts of disproportionate magnitude, depending on the constitutional formation of the individual, and because of this magnitude, the corresponding attractive magnetic force is created. This distracts the individual away from his evolutionary path and leads him toward the attainment of the desire taking form within him as the correct activation of Life, but without his having control over the consequences of every such endeavor. Thus, not knowing what he is doing, he struggles to change the Natural Laws in an

---

[84] The original form of the creation of the Soul.

attempt **to immortalize the destructible and destroy the immortal**.

This is why the great Teacher Socrates insisted on "knowing thyself." I believe that this man of unique wisdom, who passed through this Earth and indeed through Greece in 470-399 BC, was meant to appear in Athens among the so-called "great men" of that Age who influenced the laws of the State and led it to oppose anyone attempting to resist their perception of things and their own desires. He alone rose against them, saying that their teachings, which they believed contributed greatly to the success of Man, do not in fact solve any problems for the individual. Through their teachings they were shrewdly using their eloquence as a means of persuasion in order to render others subservient to their own desires.

All this does not lead to Knowledge, and what is clear from the results of our actions is that in the end it offers little satisfaction, with the consequence that we strive continuously for more and are finally trapped in an endless chain of events. Because we have never stopped to reflect on the fact that in the same way that we were trapped by the desire for gain and pleasure, which takes many forms, others have been trapped as well and will use these teachings to attempt to persuade and mislead us in order to achieve their desired goals at our expense. And since we too have been inundated by the same teachings, we will attempt to do the same to them. Thus these "appealing" sophistic teachings lead men to a war at first invisible and later manifest, which always has apparent and non-apparent victims. The latter will claim to be the victors and the former the vanquished, although in reality they have both lost. Because when a battle that creates victims begins, the acquired weakness of revenge flares up, just waiting to be unloosed upon the offender and repay him in kind or with an even costlier fate. Thus the apparent victor remains wary for fear of reprisals, in a higher state of trepidation than the vanquished, since the latter has already tasted the bitter fruits of defeat and been reconciled to it, and his sole aim is now to overthrow his victor. On the other hand the victor is obliged to remain activated simultaneously in three different Soul-destroying states. The first involves savoring his victory, the second staying vigilant against reprisals by the vanquished, and the third fearing loss of what he perceives to be the glory, respect and admiration bestowed upon him by others. And because of this he is excluded from the state of tranquillity and serenity Mother Nature so lavishly offers when she is not waiting in the wings to create a disturbing influence on the harmonious path the Creator has laid out for us and for all His creations on Earth.

And Socrates the Teacher continued: "*The manner in which I describe things makes them seem strange to you, and you wonder how I can speak of them and analyze them in a way different to the one you know. Because, the way you speak, it appears that you are always right, but you have never observed the true result of your actions, whose purpose was the subservience of others to your own desires and Earthly pleasures. But of course you will always observe the external appearance of things, because your abilities have been cultivated only up to that point.*"

And I say to you, however, as Ioannis, that if you had developed the appropriate Spiritual awareness, you would be able to see things exactly as they are without the illusory images that mold a disharmonious inner state. In this sense you are no different from the slave who tends to the insatiable and unending appetites of his master — appetites that stimulate a continuous production of carnal desires as a personalized emotional need along with presumed entitlement to fulfillment. When the desire is thwarted, the presence of continually changing illusory inner images will cause blame —mostly on the basis of subjective opinion— to be laid on others, which leads to a counterbalancing reactive impulse for revenge.

Thus, the Senses of the individual generate conditions that lead us to experience imagery adorned with attractive magnetic colors, whose exciting dazzle deceives us into accepting it as logic central to consciousness. At that moment we become voluntary servants of this illusory consciousness, convinced that we will be led to a historic moment when we will enter another domain of human existence where the Natural Laws do not apply. There, supposedly redeemed by everything that can be seen and touched, we follow the invisible path, free from all the encumbrances of our Senses, and we transform life into a strong fortress we believe no invader will be able to besiege. And just as we are about to rest on our "omnipotence," our besiegers confront us and take away all our rights to the continuation of our one-sided life. In this way the fortress falls, leading either to the last uncertain steps of our existence here on Earth or to our being impelled toward new "conquests," more "powerful" and more "secure."

The tragically absurd thing is that, while we set our sights either directly on money or on its acquisition through high office, academic studies or science, we try to validate our existence within the Law-ordained Perfection of the Universal Creator, stating unequivocally that we belong and function in the Intellectual and Spiritual world. And we offer our knowledge to others with great pleasure, though having first demanded recompense according to desires we deem appropriate. However, we never examine what the fruits of our Intellectual and Spiritual Offers really are. We could perhaps learn by observing the multitude of dramatic events played out daily by individuals who have been officially pronounced "*Intellectually and Spiritually accomplished" by the academic authorities and are legally protected in the performance of their social functions according to the established rules of ethics. But as has often been demonstrated, such individuals, regarded by the State as highly "Intellectually and Spiritually accomplished," have fallen victim to their own ignorance, made mistakes and then, unfortunately, tried, every one of them, to find some viable excuse.[85] This is a grave error because no one will ever be able to escape his responsibilities, and punishment will be inevitable. Woe unto them who believe they possess Knowledge when they have not even approached it. Woe unto them who rush in any way

---

[85] For a fuller discussion of these so-called "Intellectually and Spiritually accomplished" individuals see chapter 14.

they can to acquire offices and worldly honors. And woe unto them who make excuses for their mistakes. What will be their punishment here on Earth and how will it come about? This is very easy to understand if one observes certain characteristic events. Such events sometimes start with the deterioration of mental and Bodily health. Thus the individual is finally afflicted by a malady which will play a major role for the rest of his life, appearing every day as a dark humanoid figure whose expression says, "whatever you do, wherever you go, I will always be with you. And when the moment comes I will bring down your false image or idol and there will be no hope of resurrection. In the end I will encase it in a frigidity so infinite that even those who, like you, have worshipped it, will come to reject it in terror that the same will happen to them. And as for a Life beyond? The conscience will be the witness and the unconscious the avenger.

Off, then, on a tumultuous course, translated within us as chaos and a sense of grave loss concerning the image we have formed with regard to the future, we feel all our visceral centers being strangled, and an undefined pain develops, putting a distance between us and the false image or idol we have created of our self. From that moment on we experience great fear, with the result that many seek out a route to the annihilation of this false image. This happens because all the Sensory Positions that produce desires for Earthly pleasures have previously abandoned the Position they had assumed inside the formation we call the Body, and have followed the unchangeable path that the Universal Law prescribes for every visible and invisible Element, and men cannot modify this regulating function. And if we are not chosen for enlightenment by the clarity of the Holy Spirit in order to understand this path, we will find ourselves in the disagreeable position of maligning the entire Order of these regulating functions of the Positions and Anti-positions, whose mission is to offer absolute justice to the animate entities of all dimensions.

But on the whole, most of us have not been able to reach this special perceptive awareness that I call Three-fold, which would allow us to comprehend the true dimension of the Creator and the way He has placed Man on his path on Earth. Were we to understand that the Creator has bestowed upon us the right to decide ourselves on the path we will follow, we would receive the appropriate Offer. This is what Greek mythology teaches us with the example of Hercules, whose entire history is really the effort of Man, passing through various symbolic obstacles, to perceive the Creator. Thus, at some point, Hercules had to choose between the path that leads to human pleasures and to the worship of idols culminating in the darkness of annihilation, and the path leading to the true struggle, without pagan pleasures, where the reward is the special key that allows him into the space of the famous Immortals. And an Immortal is one who becomes free of all lower biological characteristics so that his Bodily formation is Elementally composed of superior biochemical and electro-chemical Elements embodied in optimum biological manifestation and expression.

It is, however, difficult for us to reach this Position where we have the prerogative of choice, since without hesitation we call ourselves good men, classifying others as bad. This reminds one of what Our Lord Jesus Christ said, that "you do not see the beam in your eye, but you speak of the mote in someone else's." And this is because we have never dealt objectively with ourselves, so as to see what we desire, what we do and what we would do, given the opportunity. Instead, through a prism of subjectivity, we excuse everything in ourselves and readily place the blame on others. For me this is a mistake because very seldom can anyone hurt us if we do not grant him that right. This happens because of a certain factor unknown to us that almost always steers us to seek a solution commensurate with our own subjective sense of right, of logic and of justice with regard to our desires. So we struggle, guided by these desires, without reflecting that we may ultimately emerge not as victors but as vanquished, and to such a degree that cowardice, fear and even the desire for revenge will develop in us. Some people manage quite well, while others are less successful, unable to escape cowardice, and they converse about this with others, relating the injustice done to them with such emotional intensity it is as if they were looking for someone to offer them protection and restitution, hoping to predispose him toward such an Offer of assistance. In such cases the latter will regard them as fools and, considering himself intelligent, will try to take advantage of them at any opportunity, disregarding all human responsibility to adhere to moral laws.

We therefore see that among men there exists a strongly developed desire to subjugate and, if possible, to devour one another, and they initiate war from a field of invisible functional factors originating at certain special moments in time and space that create a reaction in Man impelling him to act all this out. We might examine this with particular attention and sensitivity, after first attempting to focus objectively on things and to look at those moments when certain minor events made us feel something we define as injustice at a certain point in the past. Then a dark gray atmosphere gathers around us, enclosing us in a circle that slowly compresses the respiratory system, causing us to live in discomfort and fall prey to a chaotic condition called loneliness. A continuous inner nervous disturbance then creates a desire in us for others to pay attention to us, along with the demand that they respond with a reaction appropriately satisfying to us. Such people, however, are seldom to be found, and left with unfulfilled desires, we devise plans for revenge against those who have not managed to respond. But if we analyze this, we will see that ultimately we turn against ourselves, because revenge can take two roads toward implementation. One road is to find a way to injure the health or the environment of others, in which case the self-destructive process is in plain view. The other road is to isolate ourselves, our rationale being that since others are responsible for our own impasse we must cut ourselves off from them, and by dint of a childish stance of denial, we gain a certain sense of inner satisfaction. Then we look for people who will listen to our grievances, believing that they will show the compassion and emotional support we deem appropriate for our elevation as personalities and our social gain. Another road to satisfaction is to turn inward, this time leading to rather complex inner activity erupting into a desire to violently take out our anger on others. And since such a thing is not permissible, all this anger is turned toward the self, and culminates in an attempt to commit suicide, in the belief that through this act we will make those we hate suffer so much they will literally be destroyed. This erroneous evaluation brings an intimate sense of redemption.

We see here that such individuals are in a state of utter confusion, in a chaotic wilderness, where there are no more healthy emotions left to generate hope or even the thin ray of optimism we would need to proceed to new creative relations with other people who, behaving as people do on Earth, might just offer us the desired appreciation and communication.[86]

When Our Lord Jesus Christ said "Peace be unto you," he was referring to the peace of our inner Position, which establishes the Position of the Soul. In this way we will discover

---

[86] To continue a previous discussion of the bio-genetic origin of depression, where the dominant element was visible, we have here the downward path of a depressive syndrome in which a life plan (according to Adler) based on small disappointments endowed with great investiture of emotional material is shattered with a consequent disorientation with regard to aims and an agonizing quest for fulfillment of unattainable needs. And since the entire development of the personality has created pain, the individual reverts to primitive forms of expression (that is, a childish desire for immediate gratification, a complete denial of reality, vindictiveness and autistic forms of thinking). If all these defenses are broken down, then no other solution remains except that of ultimate destruction, that is, suicide. Lack of sensuality, lack of emotional vibrations, and self-deprecation become guideposts between the fallen bridges of the divided self, the self still living and the self we kill since it can no longer satisfy us... [A.V.]

most easily our true path within the Universe, reflected in an immense feeling of happiness, an invincible power filling every pore of our being, overflowing in an infinite liveliness of colors displaying themselves before us, and forming the words of our inner response into a crescendo of universal lyricism, its hypersonic tones reaching our inner sense of sound like transcendental voices heralding the absolute expression of Life. Happiness—peace in life—is very rare, because Man conducts such a misguided struggle during his presence here on Earth that he ends up rejecting, through some indeterminate form of resistance, the enormous Offer that has been so lavishly bestowed upon him by the Creator, believing that this will not lead him to happiness and a full life. And he enters into a very intense struggle which, when examined, we will find to be a struggle of the Sensory organs resulting either directly or indirectly in an affliction of the nervous system, depending on the constitutional receptivity of the individual. From this moment on he will be impelled by his biological perceptions to engage in a whole range of activities that will supposedly lead him to success and incite a strong competitive impulse and desire for supremacy over others in acquiring those goods that have been pre-determined as necessary for his ascent up the social ladder. And he finds himself adrift at sea without the guidance of Psycho-Spiritual Three-fold perceptive awareness, the only thing that can protect him from the multitude of dangers. Thus our poor perceptive abilities mistake every wave we encounter on our voyage for loneliness, injustice, cruelty or ingratitude. This takes its toll in pain, while at the same time it induces us to persist in the same behavior, fabricating and then rejecting these waves, as if we were asking the wave to change its behavior toward us, to change course so as not to touch us as it carries out its express functionality. We are unable to comprehend that we are tossing on a sea of myriad waves, one generating the next.

Only when we realize beforehand that we cannot help ourselves in this emerging tortuous situation, whose goal is our destruction, will we seek help from the hierarchy of our Father the Creator, that is, from the Saints, the Angels, the Archayles,[87] and the Fathers of the Universes, whom our Father the Creator himself has established as primary agents of the Rule of Compassion. On the basis of this Rule and of the natural insights appearing to us over time as a result of our actions, we may develop our perceptive awareness with regard to men and things. But He also sends certain people who have well-developed conscious perception and are free of Earthly bonds. They can assist us in learning how to ask for help. If we do not seek help from them, then some wave will surely sink us to the depths of the unconscious, that is, the Negative. And we will not be able to escape, unless someone sent by the Creator is found who understands the twelve special functions of the Universal Law of Anti-lawfulness that impede and confuse the human mind so that the productiveness of the Essential Visual Field finds itself entrapped in the world of animal emotions.

---

[87] From the Greek *Archi* (Primary) and *aylos* (immaterial). The primordial immaterial divine entities.

But it is not merely necessary for some Knowledgeable Being with regard to these functions to be found. Our whole-hearted desire is also required. It is what Our Lord Jesus Christ said to those he healed: "Go now, for you are well. Your faith has saved you." At that time he was trying to infuse into their perceptual potential the ability to focus their attention on their inner self and begin reflecting on the atmosphere created inside them at the exact moment the Lord gave them what they desired. This act, called a miracle, is the result of the elimination of stimuli from external factors that invade our Sensory organic space through Somatic centers that respond to their magnetic emissions. The Sensory organic space acts on the *Reflective Visual system and, through an automatic synchronization, enters the Essential Visual system, from whence it dominates the visceral system, which acts through the Essential Visual system on the spinal cord of the individual. Then the brain requests the appropriate percentage of biochemical energy, which is regulated by a gland (shaped into a left and right pole) and enters the expectant centers of the organism, which are activated and mobilized according to the demand or the desire.[88]

---

[88] The process described here is difficult to explain through the anatomic notions we possess today. Otherwise how could we call this phenomenon a miracle? However, we should stop and reflect on the references to the visual, acoustic and spinal systems as well as on a not easily discernible cerebral gland. What could these signify? Every external stimulus is captured by the sensory centers and, following a certain centripetal route, excites certain cerebral centers that process the new data and initiate a response (or responses), either as an element of memory and identification, or as an emotional response, or as a kinetic response or finally, most

This knowledge, however, concerning the organism in all its greatness, will perhaps be given in greater detail in a different book...

Do we, however, understand why this process of the functional miracle exists? Our Lord Jesus Christ professed that we should travel our path in peace. In saying this He meant to underline and prove that all of this individual functionality exists between two Positions, each with a mission to express its presence, influencing the individual to follow in its direction under its attractive magnetism, which the individual perceives as an emotional sensation shaping an integral impulse and ultimately a composite motive for his present and future dreams. These two Positions exist within human Elemental composition and, according to the Law of Composition-Decomposition, they are termed *Subjectivity* and *Objectivity*. When the individual is in the subjective state, his personality will receive absolutely automatically the influence of the sympathetic nervous system, which acts mainly in visceral space. Within this system *subjective conscience*, as opposed to the conscience of true justice that we analyzed earlier, is organized. It is activated after a particu-

---

usually, as a combination of the above. No matter what happens, however, it is certain that there are also other less apparent responses that activate a demand within the visceral centers (or even cellular centers) for secretion or transformation of function. In addition, cerebral proc-esses, barely known, certainly do not entail one function only, but are multifarious and inaccessible to research.

Through the teachings of the three-fold structure of the individual and the placement of the organism on a different basis of functionality, many centers acquire new dynamics. [A.V.]

lar act of ours has harmed someone else and is projected onto the Essential Visual system, where it is transformed. If we possess enough strength, and indeed much is needed, we try to rectify our error and reinstate our Position with this conscience and with the people we have wronged. However, this is merely an impulse of sensitivity formed in the pneumo-cardiac system, and from there it projects various states to the Essential Visual system, which creates corresponding emotions. These produce the pull of remorse, which steers us toward redress of the injustice.

We see therefore that the motivating force that influences our higher functions in such a case, generated by subjectivity in the visceral system, is the sensitivity produced by weakness and based on fear of reprisal by the wronged party. So we attempt to rectify the wrong that we have done *through fear*. Hence we see that any Offer toward the wronged person is produced by the subjective side of the individual, the side we must know is 92% under the influence of the unconscious and only 8% of the conscious.

Chapter 11

THE SUBCONSCIOUS

I must now present to you, as concisely as possible, exactly what I discovered first hand, through meeting privately with so many people, tens of thousands of them. These meetings took place at their request, and were held mostly in my small office near Constitution Square in Athens, and also in many other cities of Greece and in many other countries.

Through close analysis we see that, depending on the inner functionality of each person due to his constitutional formation, his family and his social environment, appropriate receptors for the corresponding influences of the Subjective and the Objective will be developed. These two Positions are very important in the shaping of Man, because they act directly on human functionality. Whoever can enter the state of perceptive awareness that will enable him to follow the status of these Positions in respect to the Law of Evolution and Decline, will be led either to divinity, or to enslavement in the lower levels of Life with regard to his inner, biological, organic world. In the latter case he will suffer the great pressures of the flesh: stress, pain, loneliness and illness. But on the path to divinity he will be able to slowly learn what the Universe is, what it consists of and why, in its entirety, it manifests an animate functionality differentiated into infinite animate expressions, placed on various levels and dimensions, contributing their individual functions on the basis of the Law of Just Allocation. Thus, through this perceptive awareness, Man will begin to distinguish these two Positions of the Subjective and the Objective, as well as the source from which they derive, that is, the Subconscious.

Now there are many people who have spoken and continue to speak about the Subconscious, believing that they know its Positions and its functionality. I maintain that only a few of them say anything bearing on the truth. Most, however, are unfortunately very far from reality. And I say unfortunately because with their abilities there is much they could learn, not only with regard to the forms taken by false images of illusion, but also with regard to the true essence of things. Instead, they become trapped by the lower sentiment of self-promotion in others' eyes. But even the few who know a part of the truth are not free of great responsibility, because the gaps in their message are sufficient to throw the seekers of knowledge off their prescribed course. The latter still try, however, through books and through attending lectures at organized meetings (at places of worship of different denominations, sects or cultural centers), to glean information to help them attain Elevation, but still lack the necessary first-hand knowledge of the consequences of their actions in time and space. And the only thing they achieve is to transpose the errors of others within themselves, compounding and perpetuating these errors.

I must also tell you, and this is very sad, what I have learned from my observations, in the many countries of the world where I have been invited to offer my healing services and explain the difference between "ego" and "being." It is that for all the conditions created by various societies to date, the particular responsibility lies on those of you and those alone who have hastened, because of your ambition, to present yourselves to the world as enlightened representatives of God, using persuasion to sway other people into following and trusting you because of their own inner need. Some of them might even have had internal messages to seek the truth. They have been led by you into this condition. *Of course they also have their share of responsibility...* If, however, you had true perception concerning Knowledge, you would really know what it is, what it can offer you, what abilities you would acquire so as to free yourselves from all lower dependencies; and how things and Positions work in the functional Universe of the Positive and the Negative — Positions which, according to the Universal Law of Creation, present themselves during every request for aid by the integral Element called "Man." This perceptive ability would endow you with Essential Sight to see further than the lower appetites that enslave Man, whose exertion only serves to land him in the boundless abyss of his personal creations, and to engender the diseased molecular hordes that act on the entire cellular Element, delineating the various illnesses we can so easily discern. But these illnesses are nothing compared to what can happen to us when we carry all the ephemeral things here on Earth along with us forever. For if you could see the other dimension, which can be seen only with the *Essential Visual system, you would be more than willing to be deprived of many things here on Earth and even suffer many diseases, provided that you will be reinstated upon arrival in the communities of the Hereafter.

All this may seem very funny to you, but I possess proof of all this and I know it as well as you know your own name, the city you live in and its laws. I will not try to give details in this book, because this would require many years and thousands of pages. This would be very difficult since my responsibilities as an individual presence here are many; I spend a great part of my available time helping people with various psychological problems which constitute 95% of the true causes of every disease. I say to you only that what I write is the **Truth and nothing but the Truth,** because all the people who have visited me and have asked me to help them have given to me the clearest proof that the things I have perceived both internally and externally in Man, and also beyond the other dimension, are in fact the true reality![89]

---

[89] The reference here to the cause of disease, which has been roughly characterized earlier as emanating 95% from the psyche, needs some further explanation. There is a modern discipline, psycho-somatic medicine, and also to a certain extent homeopathy, that accepts the Body-Soul connection, except that the Soul, psyche, is perceived in the narrow sense of the conceptual organ of unknown origin and location inside the organism. If we broaden our way of thinking and afford the Soul its true substantive dimensions, including its individual history, the family and social environment it carries with it, we will arrive at the cause of diseases of unknown origin that are so troublesome to medicine, which considers them inherent to life and impossible to control. [A.V.]

As I mentioned earlier, a good percentage of the Earth's population has tremendous potential and has already received many messages. Certain people may have made sense of these and become aware of exactly what these messages intend to convey to them and how to understand what their behavior should be toward other people, and toward all creations that are expressions of Life. Then a simple thought within them will be able to foster the desire to knock on the door of Knowledge. And the guard will open the door and will show them the path they must take to complete their quest. Guided and protected by the functional Elements called Angels of Offer, they will be freed from the lower levels of animate Orders delineated and shaped in the functional fields of Earth's dimension, and they will be relocated in the vast undivided fields of Universal space, where they will express their presence as integrated personalities within the brightly colored vastness of the Soul, redeemed in its individual integrity. Then a sense will develop that will activate their entire individual Essential Visual field, through which their Thinking will be guided to correct evaluations, and they will enjoy the vast beauty of creative serenity.

However, for Man to reach this stage, he must first know himself, because, as the great Saint Abbas Isaak the Syrian so correctly writes, "those who can see the Angels and even talk to them have not reached the highest level of evolution toward knowledge with regard to Man and God, but possess only partial knowledge of certain animate and non-animate universal Elements of Creation." Only he who has come to know himself has attained an even higher level.

Of course self-knowledge does not mean discerning some of the shortcomings that create our weaknesses and the tendency to control them, while at the same time we provide excuses for them. If this is all we do, we will be led objectively to the conclusion that all this effort has been expended in order to excuse our erroneous activation with respect to the process of objective functionality above the lower levels of Life. Only true self-knowledge leads to freedom from lower desires stemming from the multifaceted emotions of "Man-the-human subservient to Man-the-animal." For no one can deny that today Man has distanced himself from the natural beauties of his emotional world and, without realizing it, has placed himself in the vast space of loneliness, fragmenting himself into four pieces and scattering them to the four points of the horizon. Now, because of his scattered thoughts he cannot find a way to call back these parts and reunite them, and reshape his genuine self in order to function as a well-integrated individual. If he manages this, then and only then will he have the right to know all levels of beauty and of ugliness, so he can make the correct choices that will allow him to redeem himself during his presence here on Earth. And with his Higher Sensory Attunement adequately sharpened, he will organize and form the Position of his higher emotions, so as to meet the corresponding emotions of other individuals who constitute functioning society. In particular, the higher facility of emotional attraction of the male to the female will be formed at the highest human level, where they will meet in the space of true happiness and will enjoy the consummate radiant beauty we humans know as "paradise."

However, at the level of Man-the-animal, entrapment by lower emotions leads Men to the anguish-ridden need, during their entire presence here on Earth, to change the type of the Positions, that is, to transform the unchangeable into the changeable and the changeable into the unchangeable. Let me now try to explain to you exactly what I mean. Changeable is the human Body, because when an individual arrives here on Earth to follow his path and fulfill his mission, according to the functional Law, he makes use of various Elements originating from the Earth or nearby sources, which are subject to continuous changes, in order to integrate himself as a form within the dimension that we occupy and perceive. Unchangeable is the Soul, which has been created complete and whole by the Creator from materials whose source is the supreme level of material fields whose principal inherent quality is that they can penetrate any material density at all levels of the Lower Universe, which is composed of lower layers that are more condensed and heavier when compared to the Higher Universe. And herein lies the grave error: We try to overthrow what has been created and to shape it within the lower levels of our perception, which functions under the influence of the subjective emotional Element. And when Man is trapped in the world of confused senses, he will find himself in the pathological state of illusions to which he is led by subjective impulses. Thus his doings will always leave a void in his life and this will create stressful conditions, and it is easy to see where they lead. The main restraining factor in the face of this ongoing destructive process is the promotion of objectivity in our perceptive functioning, which is situated in our **Essential Visual Space**.

Here I must analyze in part the notion of the Essential Visual. Inside the brain is a place where a system of specialized centers operates, to which many peripheral centers are connected through special nerves. On the basis of the *decision* made by the Essential Visual, it will demand that another center (gland) right behind it supply the necessary energy for the promotion of the function of other glands, causing them to prepare to send the Elements required to form the *image* in the gland located behind the Essential Visual. When the image is transported there, it will then give a command to a special neural center for stimulating vibrational activity, through which it will form either an entreating, demanding, passive or aggressive (essentially destructive) response. This will first pass through the nervous system of the lungs, then of the heart and will return to the Essential Visual, having passed through the thyroid gland in the throat, where it will be invested with emotional *formations*, which are memories of the immediate or distant past that act on vibrational functionality.

Following the arrival of the message, the Essential Visual forms the image of the thing sought, which automatically activates the acoustic center to participate in the completion of the image, and from there it passes to the Reflective Visual center, through which we finally perceive the image with the instrument of eyes. The mission of the eyes is to become activated within the creations of the Essential Visual and to sweep Man wholly toward *acquisition of the desired object*, creating magnetism within us and enveloping us in the emotional attachment that gives rise to desire, and in turn to the need for fulfillment, restoring the happiness that we judge ourselves to deserve. The mobilization of all this activity (there is, of course, a lot more activity that is difficult to discuss here) forms the entire energy-based functional Element that serves as an inner guide to our life and that we normally call *Thought*.[90]

Thought is the crowning activity of human functionality, with the participation and concurrent action of many special centers which, depending on their functional state, lead human functionality either to Elevation or to destruction. We experience every one of Thought's integral images as a natural formation of the functional conditions of Life. And all of this is contained in the invisible book (which in mysticism and in Sanskrit is called the Akashic Record) of everyone who arrives on Earth. This book contains the entire history of the course he must follow, as well as the obstacles he will

---

[90] The anatomic position of the Essential Visual is in the region of the central brain where the hippocampus, the amygdaloid nucleus and the surrounding gray matter send somatotropic signals to the hypothalamus-hypophysis system. The hypophysis, composed of a variety of cells, secretes hormones that target somatic glands, controlling their activity and, more generally, the level of activity of the organism. It therefore becomes evident how important the role of the hypophysis is in the harmonic "bonding" of the biological order of the body with the spiritual state of the mind. Medicine refers to this cerebral region as the limbic system, without linking it directly to the hypophysis. These teachings manage to unite it with the Essential Visual system, bringing home the point once again that anatomic and neuro-physiological knowledge exists only on the instinctive-sensory level of perception. [A.V.]

encounter because of his past behavior and activities, and which he will experience as misfortunes due to certain defeatist feelings of inferiority or even his own life experiences. All of this is written down and is useful in exhibiting the other side — the side of Offer and good luck in all the things that create unexpected joy. Caution is needed, however, with regard to these "lucky" events. Behind them lurks an outer-environmental and inner-reactive Element whose mission is to negate every correct evaluation and to impose new desires impelling us into a detrimental and destructive struggle that corrupts all the emotions of Higher Sensory Attunement. Thus the value of the Offer is lost and "luck" becomes "bad luck." And so our thinking, through the process originating and completed in the Essential Visual, culminates in a search for what has been created within our selves.

Now there is another factor that occupies a special place in this whole process, called the **constitutional formation** of the individual. This is what we call not only the general formation of the Body but also the delicate formation of the vital centers of the individual that act on his functionality and differentiate the activations, be they positive-beneficial or pathological-detrimental. Perhaps in a different book in the future all this will be analyzed in detail and, in this way, every reader will have a better understanding of it, if, of course, his desire to do so overcomes his fear. And I say this because deep down most of us, out of fear, do not try to correct our pathological states but struggle desperately to justify our errors and place the responsibility on others. This entire "dangerous game" is just waiting to sweep us along in its merciless current, in a sweet, enticing way, and this is perceived by us as succor and reward for our expectations. And the recognition of our personality, as well as its validation, is always considered a success.

The biological and biochemical functionality of the individual is influenced by the environment. By the term environment we mean the mother and the father, the siblings, the relatives, the teachers, the professors and, for men in military service, their superior officers — all those people who, out of necessity or due to special reasons, will cross our path during our life and influence it, raising questions. This results in the first chromosomal formations of our internal atmosphere which is the molecular internal environment according to medicine, and according to metaphysical physics is the Microcosm. During those moments they form a chromosomal expression corresponding to the environmental behavior, and create an interaction with the coiled molecular system of human constitution, the Body. And on the basis of their chromosomal color they influence the corresponding molecular system, and consequently the cellular system which, acting on the organized nervous system, acts upon the Essential Visual system through the special centers we have already mentioned. Thus we will have a fully-shaped Thought which, depending on the degree of its penetration into functional space, will direct all of the Sensory organs into its activation, involuntarily bringing about various results. The process of Thinking, this supreme noetic activity, therefore deprives us of all reaction and fixates us within its demand for attention, following its preordained path. We thus become fellow travelers and fellow workers in its mission, seeing as it has such a predominant presence in the molecular entity of the Body.

However, the primary presence in the Body is not the process of thinking, but a Position created and refined by the Creator of Everything, who has also ordained it within the process of all things, offering it to the Body so as to serve it on its path through time as prescribed by the Law of Justice. And this Position, in its two-fold Order, has been given the name **Sensory Attunement**. And it has been endowed with patience in the face of much pressure and humiliation, with remarkable perseverance, so as to equip the Body with that special Element that activates the world of the Senses. This world, apart from the five known Senses (sight, hearing, smell, taste, touch) on a Reflective and Essential level, contains two more Senses which serve higher and supreme perceptions. The sixth helps us perceive things beyond us, as well as beyond the present time. The seventh liberates our hypersensitive emotions from the lower levels of Life in the present and the future and reinstates us as individuals immune to the influence of illusions, fully aware of the values of time and space occupied by or inherent in images and things.

Without objectivity ruling over the Senses, the process of thinking, directly influenced by them, produces erroneous activations that act on all vital centers of the organism. They therefore function in an unnatural state, producing a disharmonious functionality and hormonally imbalanced secretions. In this manner, we arrive at a level where unnatural vibrational factors enter the special space that is the seat of Thought. There the first concentrated union of messages occurs. These messages, shaped by their chromosomal expression and the magnetic-attractive preference of the subject, effect a distortion of time. Then, through the center of time a judgment will pass and via the sympathetic system will demand that the control center (near the epiphysis) secrete a hormone. Under special guidance by the control center this hormone will, as a dominating agent, induce a condensing configuration and a vitalizing expression in the spinal cord. Now, with the spinal cord functioning as a regional center and thus more sensitive to external influences, a new secretion from the central kinetic nervous system is ordered for the implementation of the instructions that first appeared as a message in the Essential Visual.[91]

At this point certain other Positions may appear, which often present themselves during the functional impulse of

---

[91] According to physiologists specializing in the nervous system, thought is the most composite and marvelous function of the brain, and is effected with the participation of many centers with varying governing manifestations and multi-connected permeability. Many helixes of the temporal and occipital lobes participate in the formation of thought, with the assistance of mid-cerebral centers. The limbic system and the hypothalamus are believed to participate at a different level, but also as transporters of messages.

The process described here is revealing, in the sense of participation of the spinal marrow of the kinetic and the autonomic nervous system. Once again the fog of analytic medicine is dispersed and the functioning of the organism as a whole is revealed. [A.V.]

the activation for acquisition of the desired object, creating distortions in functionality that our perceptive mechanism interprets as cowardice, which puts an end to our efforts. This is due to genetic causes. Moreover, half of these Positions derive from a very special point, with which I am now quite familiar, having been the healer of so many illnesses, all psychological in origin. If we go far enough back, we will see that all these Positions derive from the parents (especially the mother), eventually influencing the formation of the constitution of the newborn infant which, under the influence of the environment, will manifest a reaction affecting his activities. This is classified on a numerical scale starting from the number 5 and extending in two directions, decreasing, i.e. 4-3-2-1-0 and increasing, 6-7-8-9. Whichever direction the individual follows during his life he will experience the corresponding functionality and, according to his deeds, he will reap his rewards.

In all this there are specific causes, each of which shapes a particular type of manifestation and at the same time an emotion which, because it is experienced disconnected from the Law of Justice, creates within us a sense of protest against whatever may happen to us that we deem unjust. If we consider a certain person to be an enemy, then we cultivate a hatred for him, which generates a desire for revenge. And if we cannot stigmatize anyone as our enemy, then we direct an almost blasphemous protest against God for our "burdens." All this functions in the world of the unconscious, the world that influences 92% of the subjective Element. Thus, without true knowledge of reality, we become trapped in a space where all are attacking each other and all are attacking themselves.

Thus, in spite of our belief that we are striving to create a beautiful life, our erroneous interpretations and illusions actually lead us to greater suffering. And the tragedy occurs when we enter the life hereafter. And I say this because I know very well, and have proven it thousands of times to thousands of people who have visited me asking about people important to them who, as far as you are concerned, are dead, but who have actually been placed in a realm justified by their deeds. In our present course we are involved in nothing but a great struggle to enter that space, and we attach ourselves there with such binding strength that it will be practically impossible to extricate ourselves, since the way out is essentially unknown to us. And of course this space is none other than the space of the "damned," which is very far from where the Offer of justice exists.

There, not all the prayers in the world nor the often self-proclaimed masters of the Earth can save us, except for the one whom the All Holy Spirit has ordained to see everything from the depths of the Earth to the ninth heaven. And by this we mean all those levels with fully-shaped Positions and Anti-positions up to the eighth heaven, created by the Most Merciful Creator of the Universe for their functional progress, from which no created Position, at whatever level, is able to escape, save for he who was chosen by the All Holy Consubstantial Divine Trinity and enlightened by the Holy Spirit. Only he has the ability of Omnivision, that is, the knowledge of the beginning of Creation up to the entire functionality of all creations. He alone has the authority to lessen their punishment and ameliorate their Position, because he is identified with the Justice of the Creator, and his entire emotional field is attuned to an integral vibrational functionality which will lead him to a higher sense of responsibility with regard to his mission, in spite of His vast desire to embrace, to help and to heal. And while on one hand he will feel sorrow, together with unfailing love for men, on the other hand he will exercise absolute self-control, which will fill all of his being with a vibrational lyricism that will shape a message in his chromosomes regarding the imperative of each one's specific course within the space of freedom and justice that the Creator has provided.

Thus, He who Derives from the Great Nucleus feels that absolute justice is awarded to everyone, exactly as each man has chosen. But he also sees the most important thing: that Man, who is shaped in such a fashion as to be able to function on this level of Life and perform his works of his own free will, is, in the main, bound by them to such an extent that, if he does not control his subjectivity, his actions will lead to a fateful outcome, one which, with a little bit of objectivity, we may all understand well enough.

And all these things that exist and function will have to be reflected in us trans-substantiated within our molecular system, from where they will exert their influence on the emotional space leading to action. Now we must pay close attention and see how, through our own particular make-up, we function so subjectively that what we seek becomes so compulsively desirable that its acquisition generates emotions of semi-divinity and absolute grandeur. However, looking at things objectively, we will become aware of the many injustices on which all of our goals and acquisitions were based, and also realize that we give such exaggerated importance to the injustices caused us by others that it is easy to excuse our own injustices.

All this provides proof that Man is composed of two Positions which, though they operate during his course here on Earth, have a special significance with regard to the individual's evolution hereafter, since one influences and is influenced by the other. One of the Positions is the functional Element of Man called the Unconscious. This is greatly influenced by the shape of events and appearances and is subject to the Law of Transmutation and Metacycling. The constitutional Elements belonging to it are the four Senses, with the essential participation of the fifth, sight, that creates a special animation of the image created for us by one of the other Senses and activates it in the nervous system as a representation of the subjective. We then perceive the image as a logical validation of our self, but also as an Offer leading to happiness. The second Position, that of the Consciousness of higher Man, controls certain basic functional Elements which constitute 8% of the scale of the Unconscious, and are subject to the Law of Evolution. Its mission is to project its Position through a persistent effort to stabilize its Elements in the basic Positions of the individual Nuclear Soul and from there to activate, by means of the nourishment offered and through a process of cooperation, the Order of Logic (Rationality) in the domain of Consciousness. This Position is divided into two parts, which are common to both sexes. And each part is composed of four Elements or qualities. In the male these are: Respect, Appreciation, Evaluation, Offer (assistance). In the female they are: Evaluation, Appreciation, Respect, Hospitality.

It is these eight qualities that shape the entire social behavior of the individual so that he can enter the level of human co-existence and co-creation. Depending on the degree of his integration as a person, certain biological and biochemical deficiencies arise with regard to these qualities. The Law of Creation creates a drive toward union with the proper individual to complement these deficiencies, which leads to the ultimate creative task of perpetuation of the human species. When this task is carried out as it should be, we will feel absolute personal fulfillment and a sense of serenity and tranquillity. Then we will experience that characteristic attraction that makes us want to be near one another and we will see and be able to clearly discern that multicolored aura engulfing us in its luminous rays and transporting us into the rhythm of great joy called happiness. This will lead us to an internal state where we hear the voice of the Soul calling us to follow its path through our deeds. And when the time comes for us to leave this Earth, we will find ourselves amidst the great reality, where a hundred suns illuminate the deepest darkness, and all our undertakings here on Earth will be seen so that we are conferred our place in either the realm of Offer or in the world of deprivation, on the basis of the unchangeable Law of Justice of the Creator. These two realms occupy a multitude of levels, ranging from that of the most minute Offer all the way up to that of sainthood for the Soul, and from that of minimal to that of absolute deprivation, which means hundreds of years of bondage to Earth and even servitude to the demons.

Chapter 12

THE DODECAPUS COMPLEX[92]

All of this is the Truth and nothing but the Truth. It has been proven hundreds of times by the people who have visited me, who have asked for and received proof, verified by those who made the effort, at certain special times in their lives, and acquired the ability for research. I have also been endowed with the special ability —how this came about cannot be disclosed here— to see and to reveal all those things that through the years mankind has striven to know: the secret codes of life that pertain to Positions, Anti-positions and the creation of various conditions within people's functionality without the slightest trace of injustice. But I believe that there will be time in the future to analyze all this. In this book my aim is to speak about life here on Earth, which men desire and strive to know and which, unfortunately, continues to be an ungraspable mystery, a fact that entraps them in the seas and tempests of magnetic desires and renders them slaves to their

---

[92] Dodecapus comes from the Greek *dodeka*, meaning twelve, and *pus*, meaning feet or tentacles.

weaknesses. These weaknesses are shaped and develop under the influence of the **Dodecapus Complex**.[93]

The Dodecapus complex is the one that dominates the chromosomal system of Man and permeates his emotional space preventing the individual himself from functioning as a unit and as a social being in order to meet with a matching Element (the perfect partner of the opposite sex). As we have already said, this Element (partner) is the one that the Creator has placed in a symmetric Position to each of us for the purpose of offering his individual sociability to the human Element and successfully

---

[93] Here we find, as will be analyzed below in the text, a multifaceted Position of the Oedipus complex, a complex occurring during the normal psycho-sexual development of the child, in which both parents are involved in a competitive manner. Thus, the little boy feels a sexual attraction toward the mother and, unable to find an outlet, develops a hostile disposition toward the father. The opposite happens with the little girl. This situation is, of course, resolved as the child acquires the mechanism to idealize the parent of the same sex and identify with him or her as a role model. There are, however, many diverse cases of pathological investment of psychic material with roots in the Oedipus complex, which the individual carries into adulthood as character flaws or even as symptoms of mental disturbance.

It is interesting that psychiatry had the need to name the complex after the hero of the classical tragedy, in "recognition" of classical Greek wisdom, which may perhaps be able to show us the way again. According to the teachings of Ioannis, the complex is named for its resemblance to a being with twelve tentacles, something that reminds one of the octopus or the Lernaean Hydra of Hercules. And perhaps mythology, by making Hercules kill that beast, wanted to stress the need for liberation from the complex that fixates within the lower self anyone striving toward evolution. However, whatever the origin of the term, semantics keeps coming back to the figure 12 in endless cycles, conferring upon the Oedipus complex a more universal and complete form. [A.V.]

accomplishing his mission to perpetuate the Life Cycle here on Earth. The recompense for this union is an immense emotional elation in the individual's visceral space, which traces the word Love in bright letters on the luminous horizon and fills his entire Soul with it, reaching a Higher and Supreme divine realm governed by the Higher and Supreme Positions in the Hierarchy of the Creator. Only if we follow these functional principles will our perception with regard to all domains of everyday Positions develop, distinguishing good from evil, beautiful from ugly, beneficial from detrimental, while at the same time we will acquire the ability to see not only the immediate but also the distant future, far beyond what is referred to as "death."

However, people immobilized under the dominance of the Dodecapus Complex are left without any possibility of knowing their own selves. Because of a certain Anti-law of Creation this complex has a legitimate capacity to coexist in the subconscious world and to function in the unconscious with a tendency to dominate. From there it begins its activities, eventually bringing the entire cellular system under its own vibrational influence, with participation of the subjective element to such a degree that 92% of the emotional world will undergo confusion. As a result, we become enslaved by the subjectivity of the unconscious, which leads us, like the most insolent beggars, to seek from other people fulfillment of whatever false needs our complex has projected onto our emotional field. When these people do not respond, we turn against them in the worst possible way. And this happens because we know nothing about ourselves.

One of the many pieces of evidence of this lies in the relationship between man and woman. And I ask you: have we ever been able to identify the main emotional Elements of the particular impulses leading us to a meeting with the opposite sex? If we knew which Positions of our organism receive, and in what order, the stimulating impulse that mobilizes the individual into seeking the imperfect ecstasy of this meeting, then we would be able to acquire infinitely advanced perceptive awareness. We know all too well that the very Body that invests the Soul is shaped by central nerves with many divisions and innumerable subdivisions extending to the entire organic system, and networked by certain special functionalities that have been named Senses. These constitute important Positions for Man, since we could consider them as extensions of the Soul, ordained by a certain Law of Creation to be at the disposal of the Unconscious and the Conscious, which are both located in the Subconscious. From there the emission to visceral space is generated, and from this the formation of the emotive object of desire begins in its turn, activating the nervous system so that the individual will find himself under the influence of either the conscious or the unconscious. When the individual, even at the time of his conception, is influenced by parents who are ignorant of proper conduct, then the balance tips toward the unconscious, with the result that the individual becomes vulnerable with regard to complex-induced states. The most powerful of these is that of the Dodecapus Complex.[94]

---

[94] We should make clear here that, according to the teachings of Ioannis, the subconscious is a much broader domain than that defined by Psychiatry. Here lies the animate expression of being with its conscious functional activity (the conscious) and unconscious instinctive activity (the unconscious) but also the non-animate (unmanifest) existence, that is, the other Element with the divine mandate to desperately seek union with the

The truth is that it is very difficult for anyone to understand the role of the unconscious. I tell you also that millions of people, even as far back as prehistoric times, have tried to understand what is hidden behind the activities that we, with the limited subjectivity of Reflective Visual perception, see taking place. We are able to judge the unreasonable acts of the unconscious in others, but we are unable to perceive and isolate them within ourselves, because under its guidance, we become subjective with regard to the causes of our actions and rationalize them away to places where they cannot cause us pain. This is how the Dodecapus Complex operates, with its many complex-ridden psychological ramifications. Thus, without realizing it, we find ourselves emotionally confused, which leads us to dead-end attempts at solutions, resulting only in increased confusion and eventual regression.

In this way the individual finally loses sight of the essence of the quest for self-knowledge and looks for scapegoats to carry the burden of the impasse imposed by his own problem. Prospective scapegoats are individuals who, in our opinion, have treated us unjustly, and as a consequence we feel "compelled" to turn against them in whatever way our constitutional formation permits. (Based on research I have been conducting on thousands of people for a period of 40 years, beginning at the age of twelve, I have concluded that revenge is entirely a personal matter, dictat-

---

individual existence in order to fully implement man's natural course. In the subconscious also resides the supplementary protection of divine providence, which promotes and heralds, as far as it is permitted, the desired union of the two Elements. [A.V.]

ed by the constitutional formation of the individual and manifested in very specific behavior.) This regression absorbs the time and
strength we need to achieve the beneficial result we seek and,
above all, the tranquillity that could lead us to mobilize ourselves
more efficiently toward a brighter future. But during the process
of regression the nervous system is disturbed; crises erupt with
no outlet, stemming from the need for relief and taking the form
of a wish to annihilate the culprits in any way at all, even through
self-destruction. One form of self-destruction is loading our selves
down with stressful situations, which are primarily responsible
for every type of disease within our Bodily space.

Here we can see clearly that the disturbance caused by
subjective emotional regression, a product of the Dodecapus
Complex, confirms the findings of classical medicine, according to which research on the family history of the patient
establishes that a certain percentage of illnesses are due to
hereditary factors.[95]

---

[95] A lot has been written with regard to inherited disease, since this is a
field of great interest to researchers.

There are diseases where an immediate correlation has been established
with an inherited defect in a specific part of a chromosome (gene). There are
other diseases where a correlation appears with many defects in various
parts of one or many chromosomes. Finally, there are still other diseases for
which the probable cause is some genetic defect, but it has either not been
found or is not able to develop the disease by itself but needs the concur-
rence of other factors (dietary, environmental, psychological, etc.).

It also appears probable that an important role is played by the permeability of the expression of the genetic defect. That is to say, certain
defense mechanisms may develop in the organism that will impede the
manifestation of the disease, something that could be transmitted to subsequent generations. [A.V.]

Now imagine how many occasions I have had to verify the information I am now relating to you with regard to human functionality during the many sessions I have had with individuals. For I see everything exactly as it occurs inside each person's Cycle, as it is delineated and determined from conception all the way up to his departure from Earth to continue his existence elsewhere. We call this departure "death," but this does not reflect the truth, and it therefore does not represent reality. On the contrary, Man strives to believe this solely because he wants to avoid responsibility for the consequences of his deeds, for which he will be called to account. For he has never considered the fact that the Creator has created with great perfection the animate and —according to most people's perception— non-animate Elements to function at their respective levels. Nevertheless, above all else he has created Man as leader of all animate Orders, and it is therefore not possible for him to have neglected to furnish Man with all the characteristics that will enable him to recognize the Elements of his own constitution and follow his natural course of development.

Most people, since they have never really delved deeply into themselves, cannot discern many of their functional characteristics, and this generates an emotional sensation located mainly in the space of the Sensory organs and strongly influenced by the unconscious. This sensation is subject to certain false imagery that initially stimulates a feeling of fulfillment, which soon fades until it is entirely lost. Thus, we begin all over again, and soon find ourselves in new illusory imagery with the same results, so that the only thing achieved is the filling of our memory banks with the activity of illusory representations. These soon begin directing our lives and this almost always prevents us from seeing that we become voluntarily enslaved by the illusory feelings of the subjective Positions of our wishful thinking, otherwise known as "ghosts from the past," whose detrimental influence we have analyzed earlier.

This is the basis of the Dodecapus Complex, and it acquires a hierarchical place well above the Orders of biological cells, with extended diffusion into the nervous system. There it forms a false perception, which fills the emotional void in the visceral space, nourished by the semi-latent Position of the Senses that encompass the emotional centers. Because of this developing void, Man is led into Decline which deprives him of the ability to express his special and characteristic individuality in an integrated way and develop a social personality that would have a positive and beneficial effect on the course of his evolution. On the contrary, he becomes filled with invisible fears that force him to seek protection from the similarly invisible dark projections of the unconscious. Thus he returns to the bosom of his mother and father, not in the way Nature specifies for his age, but by a chronologically inappropriate undermining of his Position so that his falling back on the mother or the father expresses a regression to a stage in childhood he does not have the will power to prevent. The Dodecapus Complex dominates him. We see that the individual, under the influence of this complex and without personal will, is subjugated to the semi-latent thinking patterns of the parents, instead of progressing in a creative, autonomous way.

On one hand, we have an individual seeking the natural outlet of independent, autonomous action, while on the other hand, regression keeps leading him to the supposedly serene harbor of parental embrace. How is it therefore possible for an adult to be creative and cognizant of his self, when he is entrapped in this *complex of childishness?* — a complex that consists of many other complexes rooted primarily in the constitutions of the parents. And we now know that this inner constitution shapes the behavior of the parents toward each other and consequently shapes the family atmosphere they create. Therefore, it is instrumental in both the chromosomal formation of the young individual and in its establishment within all his functional fields (natural, biological, expressive, behavioral, developmental).

And so, with a complex-ridden constitution, the individual is forced to exist in a state of an invisible and unspecified abeyance, until the opportunity arises for him to express his complex-induced desire, believing that in this manner he will be free from the deficiencies he perceives in himself, and hoping to be reinstated into the world and its events. Thus we enter the first great struggle: to become an impressive image, followed by a second struggle to immortalize this image. That is, we strive to immortalize our own image-idol out of a refusal to know ourselves due to an indiscernible fear that we are deficient. However, these struggles demand the means to bring our efforts to fruition. And our illusions lead us to the pursuit of money.

Indeed it is money, we say, that will elevate us to the bright heavens of complete self-actualization and reinstatement. But money can also lead us to the dark heavens of eternal fear and immense pain through the Law of Universal Justice — two opposite paths with the same vehicle. And this is because Man created the concept of money in order that proper cooperation in transactions and appropriate rewards may exist. And all the conditions devised and being devised by human societies allow the individual to handle money in a truly authoritative manner, if he wishes to function with a focus on his evolutionary progress. Unfortunately, however, the deceiving, ever-changing images called illusions exaggerate the importance of money out of all proportion, giving it magical properties that are supposed to heal the deficient nature of the individual. And he of course becomes inexorably subservient to it. Thus the servant becomes the master with his creator as his slave, opening wide the road to the lower levels of Life, because ***money was created in order to serve Man and not for him to serve it...***

In this manner, whoever is destined to ascend to higher levels of consciousness experiences his Decline with an indeterminate feeling of guilt that is transformed within him into rivalry. The accompanying fear demands action from him and finally all of his thinking generates the idea that somebody is after his "acquisitions". In reaction to this, he increases his possessions, acquiring more and more, so as to become invincible and at the same time "crush his enemies." Because I state again categorically: Money, in its true nature, was created with the need for a master who will direct it. If it does not find one, then it will create a slave, leading him to inexorable strife, rendering him subservient to illusions and dominated by uncontainable fears, so that fear and pain will be his rewards during his presence here on Earth.

As for his future course, what can I tell you? I believe words have not been devised as yet that could describe all that I would want to reveal to you. For if you could see all that

I see and could hear all that I hear, then you would prefer to be deprived of many things here on Earth, so that you might be better off in the hereafter. And this is due to the following: In the hereafter there is no opportunity offered for the betterment of the individual's Position, though he may have recourse to prayer and penitence toward the Universal Hierarchies, asking forgiveness for his errors and elevation to a luminous path. Nevertheless, **no hierarchical Order is permitted by the Law of Justice to intervene in order to better his Position**. Because if this were to happen, it would be unfair to others, something that of course has been stated extremely well by Our Lord Jesus Christ in the words: "Not a single hair on your head will be unfairly treated by the Father." He has also proclaimed that a man who has been made into a slave of money has fallen to the lower levels of life and deserves nothing but misery. Because "only Paradise is true happiness for man." Thus "it is easier for a camel to go through the eye of a needle than for a rich man to enter paradise." By the word rich He means a man enslaved by money, one who has transformed it into his idol, thus worshipping it as a God. But the God he has created is not able to restore the two Elements of his self (the Body and the Soul).

The rich man approached Our Lord Jesus Christ and asked him what to do in order to enter the kingdom of Heaven, which means total liberation from the lower levels of life here on Earth and even more so during the hereafter. For only here on Earth does the opportunity present itself for such an immense transformation. And only at the hand of someone who derives from the Holy Consubstantial Divine Trinity and is given the authority to see, analyze and dispense not only the Creator's justice but also His benevolence, showing men the path to higher levels of Life, to the kingdom of Heaven. And the Lord answers him: "Distribute your possessions and follow me..." This means that all his possessions were acquired through erroneous behavior, in excess of permitted levels of exploitation and by means of unfair treatment of many people. In this way Man becomes attached to his possessions, and only when he casts them out from within himself with absolute humility and, invoking the benevolence of the Creator, follows His luminous path, has he any chance of changing his course

All manifest things are set in place by the Laws of the Father Creator of the Holy Spirit and the Son, together with the initial conception of the creation of Universal organization in its Elemental composition and expression, so that everything may exist under total yet minute control. And things are, furthermore, exactly the way Our Lord Jesus Christ presented them to us, teaching us through His Word, His Offer and His actions, what we must truly heed and apply here on Earth so that we may pass onto a different level of perception that will help us understand the meaning of Life, its mission and its values.

When the Lord tells us to go in Peace, how much do we really understand of what this single phrase offers us, if we could comprehend its true meaning? Now we hear many people advocate Peace, and in its name we ourselves even give advice to others, without going any further than the mere utterance of the word. How far we are, really, from the Lord's genuine efforts to assist us in finding our true path — the path marked off solely by our own personal advantage! And do not believe for a minute

that everything happens so that we will worship Him and hasten to avow that we are with Him. For this is a ridiculous
thought, because He is the Creator of the Universe — a universe
that Man strives with great persistence to fathom, while at the
same time he is unable to conceive of the many levels of Life on
this Earth that he rules over. Since, therefore, we are unable to
see our greatness, let us not deceive ourselves by projecting our
uniqueness as the only animate beings in the Universe.

The Creator has given us so much and placed us above all
these levels of Life on Earth to enjoy all the goods offered by
many other Orders of existence. Then why, you will ask, has
He has not freed us from the mysterious molecular system
that carries the dark Elemental energy of the unconscious,
which stimulates shadowy functions, accompanied by the
need to experience biological pleasure and to exhibit it for the
admiration of all of society?

One could give many answers. I will start by giving you the
main point, because an extensive analysis is beyond the scope
of our daily functional needs, as we perceive them, and is rather
difficult to understand. I shall try to give you an example. There
are many researchers and inventors, at various levels, who
manage to understand to a greater or lesser extent, depending
on their efforts, the object of their search. And among them,
there will be one who has understood enough to be led to a discovery so important as to surprise everyone. He consolidates
and integrates the finding, gives it form and presents it to others. They admire his ingenuity and immediately start to analyze
the discovery, disclosing it to various people. Indeed, certain
functional aspects emerge from the analysis that are contrary to

conventional perception up to that time. Then, acting out of their subjectivity, they express severe criticism and a rigorous stance with regard to the initial discovery, as if they were "experts" who knew better. And as if this were not enough they proceed to suggestions for improving the discovery, belittling the initial discoverer. It will not be at all strange that in the end the discoverer himself will not be able to put in order or assemble any part of the resultant artificial contraption, which now bears very little relationship to his initial accomplishment.

And so we see that the Creator has conferred upon this creature called Man such a specially crafted composition that it gives him unlimited potential within the immensity of creative beauty. He can therefore easily perceive all the molecular levels that delineate their course according to the Lawful order within the infinity of Creation and the minuteness of their own existence, in order to complete their rising and setting at the time of their transmutation within the recurring Cycles ordained by the Law, for their integration within the mission of all Creation, but also within their own individual mission. However, we do not recognize that everything we see and admire —all that the Creator has shaped— is merely a continuously transmuting mental image or representation, not in synchronization with the temporal stability of our own course. And this is why we perceive it through the limited Reflective Visual system of subjectivity. Thus, under the influence of the unconscious, these representations generate illusions that lead to thoughtforms that are very far from the Creator's work. It follows, naturally, that we are ignorant of what we do and whether or not it is to our benefit.

Many people have visited me and have asked me to solve what they believed to be problems that others had created for them, or so they said. And I helped them, as much as my time permitted and as much as each was entitled to, meaning that depending on the degree of trust each had developed within himself, he received the appropriate help (Offer). For I am ordained to try and activate the individual toward the enlightenment that will empower him to expand his awareness of the true causes of situations, so he may take the course that is most beneficial to him. And I see that each becomes stuck on the so-called problem, going over it again and again and blowing it up to such an extent that it affects the nervous system. It is this that creates confusion, the master well-versed in wreaking havoc through the weakening of special centers of the organism, with detrimental consequences to the Body.

And how can Man recognize his true natural functions when, entrapped by the Dodecapus Complex, he is no longer self-directing but is bound by the weaknesses that dominate his Senses, which are imprisoned in the illusion-producing unconscious? It is therefore quite clear that the unconscious represents the Law of Anti-position —of the Negative— in the human biochemical and biological Order. And this negative functionality leads the individual to confusion, to Decline and degradation, with corruption as the sole result, not immediately perceived. This Decline does not offer him any space for happiness or respite, but only a relentless and uncontrollable speed filling him with urgent desires that demand fulfillment, only to generate new desires in an endless cycle. And functioning in this manner, Man is obliged to accept things as they appear solely to feel conventionally correct and socially acceptable. When the consequences of his actions become apparent, then he turns against others or against the Creator. In the end we see Man fighting against himself, and the Creator striving to protect him from his own self! How then is it possible for him to penetrate other dimensions of lower levels of life and understand them for his own benefit? How will he be able to perceive the higher levels? This is the place where Saints operate, that is, individuals who, with great effort and armed with prayer, managed, through the grace of God, to transform a dark wall into a luminous path. This path has embraced them with humble grace and has led them to God-given habitation, and they have been united in this way with the boundless emotional luminous functionality of the creative Universe in the eternal luminous path of evolving humanity. Truly, such people have an excellent chance to enter the kingdom of Heaven.

Those who pursue a course of specialized studies, acquiring certain aspects of Knowledge, are led to the writings of people before Our Lord Jesus Christ, without however being able to see things with the eye and the mind of the observer (that is, objectively). For what was written then aspires to represent the complete knowledge through which the Creator has shaped the countless levels of the whole of Creation so infinitely rich in expression. And these levels are impossible to conceive by even the most evolved man on Earth, not even the first among the Saints. Only those who have reached the state of supreme initiation, having passed through the Eighth Heaven, may understand the infinite delineation of created levels of animate

258

expression. It is very difficult for me to express in words what happens in the Eighth Heaven, because our vocabulary has not reached the functional level at which the appropriate words may be formed on the basis of conceptual perception. For the Elements that traverse, in an infinitesimal interval of time, the heavens of contraction and expansion (that is, the Eighth heaven) are absolutely assimilated within each other. Nevertheless, at the same time they remain distinct, functioning in the revolving time that traverses each of these Elements separately, as prescribed by the Law within the scheme that contains both the infinite and the infinitesimal. In this manner they implement the temporal genesis of the Macrocosm within the Metacycling Order of the Microcosm, bringing about the expression of the determined level on the path prescribed for the individual within the whole, with the concomitant Offer of the Universal Authority of Creation. Thus the Elements acquire the creative expression of individuality, and also bear the actual consequences of their own past actions, without any obstacles to the reaping of benefits.

And so it is verified that the Creator has endowed us with free will, along with intermediate messages that call attention to the dangers in the paths opening up before us. Of course many factors are at work impeding easy reception of the messages, so that special effort is needed to avoid being carried away by ephemeral false illusions that fixate us in the avenue of the present. Then, unfortunately, the following thought comes to us: "Here is God the servant, who will offer me material goods for my possession and will lead me to future immortality, making me an indestructible God on Earth." But when the biological Order of Man reaches a point when all his cells are in a state of Cyclic transmutation, the individual will find himself faced with difficulties, his endurance reduced inasmuch as his defense Elements are not at their full strength. So environmental microbes, those special Elements of Natural Law, will invade and consolidate their centers at some point in time, and from there they will attack the organism. Then neither material goods nor God "the servant" will be able to render the individual immune to this attack, and all the self-assurance he has built up with so much effort will crumble.[98]

We see quite clearly that people who have pursued a course of study and research toward true knowledge have not, as I see it, taken a totally correct direction. This is because they start from an inner reaction rooted in the fear of confronting visible and invisible situations that, without

---

[98] Here let us intervene in order to say something that medicine knows well but tries, at the same time, to ignore. Every disease is analyzed with regard to its cause, in an attempt to locate the pathogenic factor, so as to isolate it, to learn its natural provenance, to find the means to eliminate it in the laboratory, to produce a medication tolerated by the human organism, to offer and complete therapy in the most appropriate and expedient way. However, the inverse process is not systematically studied. Starting from good health, how do we arrive at disease? Why did a certain disease appear in this particular person and not in the next? Why at this particular time and location? Why do these murderers of humanity change form at given times, making medicine conduct a life-or-death struggle without truly knowing either life or death? What prevents final victory?

The inadequacy of science, as we see through Ioannis's teachings, has to do with man's inadequate perception... [A.V.]

their realizing it, furnish evidence of their insignificance and inability. They then seek power through social recognition as individuals with special abilities. And they make no attempt to see the dynamics of their own selves —how they are made, how they function, what the time of their residence here on Earth is, what their prescribed course is— nor do they attempt to find the sources of their fears and their many dependencies, and to get inside them, transform and subdue them. Instead, they turn outward in search of more skilled researchers so as to acquire some of their powers. Then they parade around everywhere peddling their "wisdom" like merchants, in accordance with their own subjective perception, making others follow and recognize them as representatives of God. From that moment on, erroneous perception with regard to the true Creator begins to form, as does the gradual distancing of the individual, but also of entire societies, from His Truth. And while they speak of God and believe that He is close to human pain, in essence this is not so. Because they do not know their own selves as they should, and consequently they do not communicate with the higher Element in themselves, which is the only one that may succeed, through the Creative Hierarchy, in knowing the Creator.

Chapter 13

THE SOUL

The Universal Law of Creation has set up Rules for the Orders of the functions of the *Macrocosm and the Microcosm, to ensure that they will always maintain the precise motion and activation required to carry out their mission, followed by the transmutation that brings to completion the time cycle of the organic system formed by these two co-existing entities, in perfect coordination. Then, on the basis of the unchangeable Positions, they will enter the corresponding system-unit in the appropriate proportions to offer the Higher Etheric energy needed as nourishment by the lower Element. If it succeeds in entering the space-time domain of its assimilation within the higher Element of the Soul, this part of the entity will be offered two distinct directions, one leading to higher and the other to lower fields, distinguished by the difference in gravity and in Universal Orders appropriate to each of them. This is therefore the most crucial and important moment for the Element called Man, for it is during this moment that the great meeting of the two Positions of the Soul and the Body occurs.

Here let us refer briefly to the **structure of the Soul**. This is the unchangeable creation of God and is composed of four quadrants divided into three Positions as follows: Half of it (i.e. two quadrants) constitute the **Inner Human Position**; another quarter is the **Intra-stellar** Position and the fourth quarter is the **Messenger** Position of the divine Creation we have named the Soul. The Inner Human Position resides within the Body and is responsible for making contact with the lower human Element. It is there as a Nucleus of the higher Position with respect to the lower functional system of the Senses, in which it is entrapped by the magnetic gravities of the Eighth Heaven amidst the congestion of ever-changing expressions of worldly sensations. The Intra-stellar Position, which is also the Divine, is at the supreme level of the Order of human evolution which is part of a special domain of the absolute UNITY, and always moves within universal luminescence and prescribes the low and lower activations of the individual within the framework of his Psycho-Somatic interaction, as well as his high and higher functions, from the most to the least obvious. The Messenger Position of the Soul, which is the most important, is situated closer to the Inner Human Position and is responsible for transporting the messages from the "stellar" environment here to Earth's level.

Depending on our emotive functionality we pose questions with regard to our actions and those of others, seeking their causes. Perhaps then we will remember the words of Our Lord Jesus Christ who said: "*Go forth from wherever you are not wanted and shake off the dust from your feet,*" which makes it easy for us to understand the characteristic reactions motivating our actions. Because usually, when somebody treats us unfairly according to our perception, instead of "going forth" we end up committing acts that create controversy, and this shuts us off so that we are not open to receive the communications of the Messenger-Soul. And we miss the opportunity to hear and see objective explanations that might benefit the higher, low and lowest parts of our Ego, which is merely an extension of the Soul through the Senses.

If we conduct thorough research with a desire for perfect objectivity and in absolute serenity, we will see that Man is a creation within the totality of created Elements of this functional Order. So, in order to form a valid opinion, we must show infinite respect to the entire created totality and turn our attention to a much higher power, one possessing a creative potential impossible to grasp with our extremely limited perception. For this reason, as I have already mentioned, we have to turn our entire being toward the act of saying, with great piety and in our inner voice: "Benevolent Positions of the Universe, you whose conduct toward the higher Powers is perfect, we ask you to enable us to cooperate with the higher and lower Elements of our selves, shaping our entire individual system so that we may function in a high-level vibrational state toward creative Peace."

Then the higher Positions will accept you into more luminous fields, cleansing you, through the springs of higher energy, of even the smallest amount of bio-genetic residue from the lower levels. Your emotive functionality, in a state of continual transformation, will begin more and more to develop in you the desire to become simpler, and to find the time to express your humility to the higher Positions, seeking their help regarding your entry to the higher levels where those supreme Positions exist in eternal functionality, in close proximity to the Creator. Then, a new and fervent desire will lead you to a state of activation during which your own voice will emerge from within you, saying: "Glory be to the Omnipotent Father and Creator of All. Glory be to the Small, Great, Supreme and Infinite Hierarchical Orders, you who, through your most valuable functional activities and services, find yourselves in these fields of harmony and everlasting joy, with an infinite desire to offer help to those who ask."

You will then feel a strong need to function in the world with great humility and respect for all that the Creator has fashioned within each Orderly Position. At the same time you will beseech the Father, through the Hierarchy, to give you the perceptive awareness to know all evil desires in others, with the sole purpose of benefiting your own Body and Soul. It is only then that you will feel true joy, because you will have understood what the word Creator means. Only then will you come to understand one who has striven hard to be worthy of that which can instate him within the immense spaces of serenity and inner peace. But you will also learn to discern those who have made no effort and remain hopeless and without salvation. Only when their Body is undergoing some sort of crisis do they develop unreasonable demands and ask, with hypocritical tears, for help from higher levels and the Positions of the Saints. But they fail to understand that in this manner they are burdened with greater responsibilities to change their behavior not only toward themselves and others, but also toward the entire Hierarchy. Instead, they forget all about this and indulge in the same behavior, with the result that they find themselves outside of their natural state and their functional social mission. Unable to know their own selves and their own best interest, how then can they come to know even the smallest detail concerning the individuality of the Creator?

There are special moments in the course of an individual's life at which certain presences appear before him, even as the current of illusions carries him along into imagery of his own fancy, but he is unable to discern them because his attention and inquisitiveness fail to focus on the parallel levels of the natural world. It would be a happy occurrence if these presences were always to derive from Divine space. However, this is very rare because the individual must first ascend to the vibrational functionality of higher levels and to a comparable degree of Higher Sensory Attunement, so that his functional perception may develop to the same level of productiveness. This means to have clarity without confusion, along with the ability to make correct evaluations with regard to people, their actions and their ideas, without adversely affecting the course of life, that is to function in the manner in which God's elect have functioned and continue to function. Because you should be well aware that in order for this invaluable Divine gift to be conferred upon us, we need to have made the correct preparations. It is like inviting people we are anxious to please to our home. In such cases we prepare the place, we procure the necessary goods and we foresee every eventuality so as to provide a truly enjoyable time for our guests. Only then can we feel hopeful that they will visit us again and that we are part of the same social milieu. We should note here that within the social environment there are individuals who have the right to evaluate others by virtue of the behavior and the self-respect that their natural constitution or their personal effort affords them. There are also those who are incapable of any evaluation, because they are slaves to their appetites, fawning after physical sensation. You can expect nothing but harm from them and all you can do about this is to keep your distance from them because, unfortunately, their thoughts, and especially their actions, can cause great damage.

You must believe that everything is being written down in the Universal Book of everyone and everything. This is why special care and attention is needed, because this is the only chance we have. Bear this in mind. Only here on Earth may we transform ugliness into beauty, darkness into light, wrath into serenity, fear into power and sorrow into joy, because this is what the Law of the Creator ordains. After that only an Offer by people here on Earth may change the picture. And when I say an Offer, I mean an act of devotion to someone's memory, like the offering of wheat, the lighting of a candle and other such votive acts, depending on the individual's religious background. Here, however, care must be taken. If you perform an act of Offer while dominated by inner feelings of deprivation and of sadness, you will hinder the progress of the recipient. This will considerably limit his freedom, assuming that his deeds have given him the right to move freely toward completion of his Cyclic course, and this will create unhappy circumstances for him. Then again, if his deeds were so good as to elevate him to supreme levels, he will send messages that are hard to decipher, as you can imagine, — messages meant to correct the behavior of people here on Earth toward those departed from temporary existence for their true residence. Such behavior toward the departed also creates confusion within your own emotional field, causing an organic Decline in health.

And while we are on the subject, think a little of the Position of those who enacted evil deeds during their life here on Earth, who became enslaved to money, induced others to unlawful transactions or took advantage of fools. They are condemned by the Law to immobility under intense atmospheric pressure, which makes for a very unpleasant state. This sentence extends from 30 to 999 years. For those who killed for money, the Law reserves an immense sentence, which extends up to 10,000 years. Everything works with such Law-ordained perfection that NO ONE is treated unfairly! Here I would like to inform you about the existence of four overall categories of punishment to which Man may be subjected, each having many sub-categories that apply, depending on the amount of culpability weighing upon the individual.

You may remember that earlier in this book, when I talked about marriage, I analyzed the unique opportunity given people to acquire, through this union, the perceptive awareness that will free them from the lower levels of existence and will bless their children, opening up for them the road to fulfillment. However, conflict and the attribution of blame burdens the Position of the parent who brings a child into the world and leaves indelible signs on the offspring of his parental inadequacy as to his missionary duties. In this manner he becomes bound by the chains he himself created, as stated in the holy book of the New Testament: "That which is bound on Earth, shall be bound in Heaven..."

The Laws of the Creator are so precise as to endow each of the created entities with a programmed course through which it will travel, placed in its respective Order of Creation, each voluntarily subject to and executing the duties prescribed for the completion of its Cyclic course, which is continuously transposed from one Cycle to the next until it is consolidated according to the Law of Cycling and Metacycling. This Law has two Positions: The first gives to the individual freedom of action, on the basis of which he will be transported to the next, or second, Position in which he lacks free will but where he will suffer or be rewarded according to his deeds while in the first Position.

This is the irrevocable prescription of the Law with regard to the two Positions, set apart in every detail of their function by regulatory Laws in the following way: Everyone who takes part in the Cycle of Life here on Earth must seek a genuine Knowledge-holder about Man and God, so that he will be able to learn his true Position within the course of evolution. Then, if the desire of the individual is genuine, this Teacher can help him shed his burdens and protect him from the negative influences of his close relatives, and also of others who may cause him great confusion at certain times. Later, during the Cycle of Life in the hereafter, it is impossible for the Hierarchical

Orders to intervene to change his course, for this, as we have already mentioned, would be against the Law of Justice.

Only during very special Eras does the Law of Order and Harmony authorize the creation of new Cyclic courses within the Universal Orders of the galaxies. To this Law belong Judgment and Offer but also Offer and Judgment. Only then will certain specially-endowed Emissaries be sent belonging to the Hierarchy, who derive from the tri-substantial and tri-dimensional Element of Most Virtuous Divine Thought and appear endowed with such qualities as to possess Perception, Knowledge and Authority, regarding the negative fields men have created during a particular Age in the corresponding Solar System. In this way they carry out their mission as perfectly as is possible.

I say this because the magnetic fields of the negative functions men have created are so dense and mysterious that no matter how hard the Emissary tries to explain them, they remain incomprehensible. For men in a state of Decline are heavily burdened by their background, which has so permeated their entire emotional world that it is extremely difficult for them to understand and to change their behavior during the course of their life. It is possible, when it is asked of them, for the Emissaries to reveal many events pertaining to the life of people here on Earth, and to the lives of those departed, to help untangle some of the states of binding attachment. Only these Emissaries have the authority to do this.

However, those who have enjoyed such help must henceforward be very cautious, because they are obliged to show great respect to the divine Orders and to try to develop within themselves the emotions and sensibility needed to reevaluate the course of their life. Now you should be fully aware that, if we do not first come to know the creations of the Creator, that is, ourselves, and then all other things on Earth and in the Universe, how will it be possible to come to know the hierarchy of the Creator and the Creator himself? Do not therefore deceive yourselves, and harbor no illusions as you pretend to be preachers and spout a lot of theories filled with errors that you have taken from others before you whose desires were the same. Because those who follow you, having received the message and shown a desire to approach the divine Orders, assimilate the few correct Elements, but also the many mistakes that have taken hold, leading them to erroneous ideas. What do you suppose you will gain if, while striving to do good, you act erroneously? So beware, for mistakes are paid for and indeed very dearly.

I, Ioannis Tsatsaris, therefore say to you that false prophets and false teachers have always existed, they exist now and many will appear in the future. Only through great effort, with absolute humility and respect for the divine Orders, believing that our true course is to know the natural conditions of our individuality and function for ourselves without depending on these teachers, is it possible for us to discern the Great Invisible Teacher whom the Creator has sent to each one of us. He is indeed the Great and indefatigable, the endlessly patient and immensely humble teacher sent to serve each of us amid the daily problems we create through our petty desires. He takes note of everything and passes on his observations in the hope that we may control our actions, in order to approach and meet this great servant and teacher, TIME!

Yes, it is Time that will offer, in a way that practically no man on Earth can deliver, the most complete knowledge to whomever truly follows it in search of the revelation of objective causes so as to correct the course of his life for his own benefit. Men of Earth, truly, you strive so hard only to destroy your interests, and you do not recognize even the most minute Offer of our Father the Creator. Instead you commit the grave error, through irresponsible and tragically shallow functionality, of severely criticizing the symmetric, functional, and rightful Perpetuation that the Creator has fashioned and has bestowed on his creations. In truth, here on Earth are the roots and beginnings of everything that has brought us to our present Position. And we try through illusions to fabricate various scenes filled with colorful figures that end up like marionettes manipulated by the invisible strings of lower parental desires. And to think that we base all our activities on this, expecting to be rewarded by joy and happiness, which we continuously approach but never reach, because this is the prison of illusory bondage...

This is the plain truth, made evident not only through the special perception I possess enabling me to see and to scrutinize people's activities, but also through the personal testimonies of the thousands of people who have visited me, the many thousands who would like to meet me, and the millions who will seek me out in the future. I am certain that they will offer the same testimony.

There is something else you should know that is very important: It is very difficult for someone's deeds to be revealed to him so that he can recognize his erroneous actions, because these revelations are made by those who have departed from this life. And they are made to me, because I have that authority as well.

Every time someone makes a mistake, certain instinctual emotional chords transmit messages to him pointing out these errors. However, he hastens to justify his error and to put the blame on others, extending and compounding his error. And I say to you that he who does not become conscious of his mistakes cannot possibly develop his perceptive abilities on special topics of concern to all of us, such as the visceral, the nervous and the entire energy system, whose expressivity is projected as Thought. And Thought is responsible for the creation of harmony within the space of the Body. And the Body is the vehicle of preparation for the Psycho-Spiritual world.[97]

---

[97] According to these teachings, we can fill in one more piece in the puzzle explaining the diseases afflicting our nature. The mind, the "thought-producing field" of the individual, through the misinterpretations it fabricates in seeking to justify the false images it serves, oppresses the body by means of the energy system (hormonal and/or nervous), dragging it into a disharmonious state. This happens, in the visceral system, through the detrimental intake of environmental substances and inefficient elimination of useless matter. The disturbed respiratory system has an immediate effect on the circulatory system, with injurious consequences to the digestive system, which becomes irregular and dysfunctional. Without entering into details —let us leave them for another time— poor intake and defective elimination are responsible for the appearance of pathogenic centers which, under certain conditions, will develop into disease. Almost any pharmaceutical or more radical treatment may improve the external picture but offers little in the way of breaking the vicious circle of the disharmonious state, which will "survive," since the conditions for its existence have not changed... [A.V.]

Chapter 14

THE SO-CALLED "INTELLECTUALLY AND SPIRITUALLY ACCOMPLISHED"

Every organized state considers certain people who hold positions recognized by the State or society as Intellectually and Spiritually accomplished individuals, while at the same time it permits them to function and to influence other individuals who will carry on their particular form of work. In this way a society is formed that claims to give precedence to Intellectual and Spiritual activities. In reality, however, it is devoid of any real Intellectual and Spiritual principles and has led Man to the state he now finds himself in. Because these supposedly accomplished individuals, although they have not been consolidated within their own Psycho-Spiritual selves, as required by this higher Order, take many initiatives and address themselves to particular issues that define and pertain to people who are truly aware. They make suggestions as to how to behave toward others, but also toward God in a way that suggests pathological egotism. And so, without proper respect and humil-

ity, some of them readily conclude that they have been designated by Creation itself to direct people toward progressive goals
for the benefit of the nation and the State in the role of national
"creators," while others believe that they are chosen by the
Creator to represent Him according to His wishes and that they
know His plan with regard to Creation and the future of each
individual.

With such delusional beliefs those of truly special Psychic
origins have been misled by the lower levels of awareness and
have developed states of mind of egocentric pathology which
operate stealthily to break and enslave Man in socio-political,
socio-religious and religious sects that proclaim that they offer
salvation — though the one thing they cannot offer is salvation.
I have clearly seen from my research, conducted over many
years by meeting with people of different political orientation,
social function and religious persuasion in various places on
Earth, that all their efforts resulted only in a state of multiform
complexes and that they were not actually functioning in a
manner which would make any real social or religious contri-
butions, whatever they believed they were representing.

Hardly any of these people had acquired the true sense of
equilibrium that offers serenity, and consequently none of
them was happy with his life, and each was ready to put the
blame on others for injustice. It thus appears that the path
they have followed and continue to follow is not correct nor
can it fill Man with certainty and fulfill him in life. And I tell
you that if every individual were to follow the true path of his
natural Position, he would feel sure of himself as an individual and, as a socially developed person, he would also often

feel the protection of the divine hierarchy surrounding him and would feel that his future course was a bright one. He would therefore not be influenced by the negative currents of his times or Age that force him to struggle with various stress-producing problems.

The results produced by many people on Earth from all different functional strata demonstrate the many falsehoods in the political, social and religious Orders that cause Man to stray from his proper course — the best course for him, the road of genuine creation here on Earth and the religious course that leads him to our Father the Creator.

This is difficult for you to envision and to comprehend, because such perception requires a very special emotional desire for and attempt to communicate with the Higher Divine Position. Of course from time to time many people have stated that they saw various Divine Positions. This is not at all strange. Because the Divine Positions can be found occupying spaces where the atmosphere is filled with purity and desire for what is objectively good and not with ephemeral desires of the Ego. And indeed those who encounter such visions along their path must be very careful during their life and correct their mistakes as soon as possible. But there are also others who become trapped by certain expressions of the negative —which is endowed with the ability to present itself either as a saint or as an angel, or even as a good man now departed and advising us from the hereafter— without realizing that it is a biological state of the unconscious, which is pervaded by the biological Position of the negative. Here close attention and scrutiny will be needed, because such advice, offered during certain emotionally-charged moments, may contain a grain of truth, but then entrapment follows leading to irrevocable mistakes.

For the most part, such negative Positions present themselves to individuals who are greatly affected by the sexual Element. This is why the vibrational fields of each individual are almost always found at the two extreme Positions of our selves. These are, on the one hand, sensually motivated desires that fall into the category of sexuality and, at the other extreme, their transmutation into either intense religious zeal or political, ideological, and social activism. In short, both these extreme states act on the visceral system, which arouses the Senses (primarily that of touch) and, with the stimulation of the Reflective Visual as well as the entire visual system in its Bodily dimension, an image is formed that energizes the individual into a position of action. This action initially leads to an acceptable result, but is then rejected and taken to the other extreme, and everything is repeated in an endless Cycle, without any hope of finding the right road.[96]

---

[96] It is worth noting that an entire school of thought in psychiatry, lead by the great innovator Sigmund Freud, was based on the principle of sexuality. This school maintained that the libido, or sexual drive, is what shapes the individual's character and that, when properly balanced, it provides good health. Freud himself, toward the end of his life, put forward the idea of a different motivating force with regard to personal development: The death instinct, which cultivates creative activity but also preys upon individuals; an instinct that leads the mind to metaphysical quests and which is, according to his teachings, the opposite extreme. It is also quite typical that these two trends in human nature become dominant in states of schizoid delirium, during which the unfortunate patient, if he is not under the illusion of a magical or divine influence (I am Jesus Christ, I communicate with the Virgin Mary, etc.), delves repeatedly into matters of a sexual nature (thoughts, illusions or even acts...). [A.V.]

I am telling you once again now that it is very difficult, I dare say impossible, for the human mind to conceive of the individuality of the Creator. Because, as is also correctly determined by medical science, people use only 5-7% of their potential powers of performance. Let us say that there are even some who function at a level of 30%. These people will have increased perceptive awareness in the domain of subjective desire, with which they will be able to analyze many things that would be unheard of for others. Once they realize that they can make others believe in them, their unconscious leads them to apparent but false truths, nurtured in negative cores, and they begin presenting themselves as experts in their particular field of activity able to resolve issues and obtain very good results.

Take, for example, certain people who know the laws of the State quite well and who, often seized by an egotistical enthusiasm when they find themselves in the company of others who have no such knowledge, will lecture at great length on their ability to come up with desirable solutions for legal problems in general. They thus exert influence on others, persuasively exhibiting their reputedly well-established legal competence. However, we can be sure that they often lead others into making mistakes and cause them to get themselves into trouble. Because it has been established that these reputedly legally competent people are driven by megalomania stemming from fear and feelings of inferiority. In their attempt to become socially prominent, they become entrapped in confusion and are unable to distinguish right from wrong, beneficial from detrimental. This is why their advice is dangerous. And just imagine that we are talking about people who have studied law and have delved into legal matters, although their true meaning escapes them.

If you think about this now you will realize how difficult it is for anyone to know the Universal Laws that have been laid down by the Creator to bring about order in the transformations and creative activities of the Elements, whose number cannot be grasped by human perception. If they could conceive of even the most minute detail, anywhere from the nature of the molecules up to their composition and development culminating in the expression of the Element's Position, then they would be very careful when speaking to men of Creation, and even more so when speaking of the Creator.

It is quite amusing for me to hear talk of God by those who have not been able to talk of Man, and especially by those who go so far as to write books as if they were the unique apostles of God, representing Him here on Earth. In order to expose the gamut of illusions that creates the lethargy they have sown throughout societies, I will mention certain things that everyone should know, especially if he is among those whose Position has called upon them to strive intensely to transform certain conditions ordained by the Law. At first glance, these conditions appear to have come into their lives in order to set up obstacles so that they never achieve their dream — a dream whose initial aim is almost always to gain for the individual the power to exert his influence over all his inferiors, but also over all his superiors. Within the framework of this desire the unconscious takes over and, as I have already mentioned, plays a dominant role in the course of our lives. It establishes itself in the domain of illusions (i.e., the creative extension of the Senses) and, through its central core, interacts with the Senses, passing on to them its negative influence. It is identified with the by-products of magnetic gravities pervading the atmosphere created by thoughts and perceptions that form strong vibrations which are stored in the subconscious of each individual, without his being able to comprehend why all of these thoughts and perceptions are produced or appear at any given moment. Such a thing happens because the traditions of a particular Age, shaped by the actions and desires of previous generations, modify these byproducts and pass them on to the next generation, perpetuating the path of confusion. This results in internal strife and almost always leads us, through the projection of illusions, to the fabrication of an outside culprit deserving punishment. And of course we do not realize that this creates still greater confusion within ourselves, which will later have an adverse affect on our material Body, with the nervous system as the first victim. For this reason I have determined that the emissions of the unconscious dominate 92% of our functional energy, leaving only 8% to the conscious. Medicine has also determined the value of 92, albeit in a different context.[99]

However, I know what the centers of the nervous system

---

[99] Reference is made here to the polarisation potential between two connected neural cells, essential for the transmission of the nervous stimulus, which is around 90 mV. [A.V.]

produce. For with the aid of the thyroid gland, they direct our actions — actions which, impelled by the magnetic fields created by desires resulting from attachments to "idols" (illusions), fill our Bodily molecular system with burdensome extra Elements that also work within our biological Order. These are added on to negative Elements that are the products of both our biological relationship to our parents and of the influence of the more or less immediate human environment in which we are ordained to exist by the Universal Law. This disturbs the Entire Created Element (our biological Body) which in our perception is a "machine" of many parts. Medicine has taken great pains to analyze this "machine", identifying many of its components, confident that it has determined their precise function within the integrated framework of the greater organism.

We have, then, various centers vital to the efficient operation of the organism that represent one Position. However, this visible Position or Bodily entity —the one under control — also harbors an invisible Etheric Position with which it must coexist and cooperate so that both can reach their destination and the complete functional restitution of the Element. Each of these Positions is itself composed of two others, one higher and one lower. Higher Psychic and Bodily structures reside at the higher Position of the visible and the invisible. Correspondingly, the lower Positions contain the lower structures. The lower Psychic structure contains the Senses and their extensions, the illusions. The higher Bodily structure labors to supply the organism with the necessary biochemical energy, while the lower Bodily structure is supplied with unwarranted energy from above, fostering uninhibited actions that encumber our path. Yet we are called upon to transform all of our Elemental endowment into virtue and energetic readiness for exaltation.

If Medicine paid particular attention to all this and applied itself seriously to this task, then it would indeed learn about the origin of the two Positions, which would lead to many discoveries. Only then could it offer what is appropriate to Man, and only then will those who serve it become humankind's true leaders in matters of Body and Soul. The Creator has composed every Element of flora and fauna of billions of individual Elements which trace infinite Cyclic courses at distances infinite for them, in Order of time and space perfectly determined by the particular natural Law pertaining to each. Each of these individual Elements is placed at the service of the Law of Offer, that is, the Law the Creator has ordained for perpetual Creation. This Law has two directions, one leading to decay and one leading to incorruptibility. These delineate the course of every Element, determining and directing the apostolic Position within which it will pass its life.

Naturally the Element called Man is placed in quite a different Position, one that is above all other Elements. Plant and animal Elements have also been placed by the Creator in the order of progressive Positions. Plant Elements fill the environment of our own dimension, but also of all other dimensions, and place their individuality at the service of the Law of Offer so that the animal Elements, depending on their formation and structure, may enjoy what in our language we call nourishment. Through this nourishment, the biological Order is controlled and the expression of Life-sustaining and functional effectiveness of all mobile animal Orders is regulated and realigned, with Man the sole exception. Man possesses the kind of perception that permits him to make choices about his personal situation. These choices, limited by subjective barriers, lead to erroneous evaluations of what Nature has created and offered to him, and to misinterpretations of the Creator's Offer to him, that is of the knowledge whereby he can dominate all vegetable and animal Orders, so that they may surrender to him the Elements indispensable to his biological system for the perpetuation of its animation and Metacycling.

If we were to make a serious effort, with genuine desire, we could arrive at the source of the causes that create internal and external interactions in Man. Then we could obtain a true perception of Man, of his course and of the reason he is in this state today, and although almost all of us are aware of this, we keep it a secret and pretend not to know. Because genuine activation toward the road to ascent would reveal that Creation has innumerable levels of Positional expression, each in its category under the Law and following its course on the basis of the magnetic activity permissible under the Law within the positive and the negative, performing its task as appointed within the Order recognized by the Hierarchy of the Creator. Man then begins to feel the true workings of the Creator and to see his Position in the Universe, recognizing the true course he must follow in order to arrive at his own consummation, which is to assume his

Position in the hierarchy of the consummate Order of Beings evolving toward luminous paths.

But Man is in a state of great confusion, and when he receives messages from the divine Position of his Self, the Higher Ego, whose mission is the restoration of human behavior to its proper course, an invisible emotion entraps him in regressive memories within the phantoms created by illusion. From that moment on we dredge up the inherited memories of the subconscious, and it is very difficult to perceive what this domain is like and how it functions. But Man, having reached this point through his previous erroneous actions, has already created great mental confusion. This causes him to function within complex-induced states, due in part to his own attachment to memories of the past, and to the fact that he has no model to function as an emotional impetus for his liberation from the enslaving atmosphere of the Earth. The organic functionality of that atmosphere is to curtail freedom and subvert it to a state of Decline. This produces subjectivity of judgment in the individual and, as the Rule of survival prescribes, he becomes part of the struggle to produce the "Earthly goods" that supposedly bring happiness as defined by men. And he pays absolutely no heed to the words continuously voiced by Our Lord Jesus Christ to the effect that one must "toil" to enter the Kingdom of Heaven, while nowhere does He refer to the kingdom of Earth, as men struggle to create it. And this is, notably, the enslaving kingdom of that which is by right the great ruler of the Earth and is called *the Negative*, leading Man to his eternal downfall and Decline toward pain and horror.

I believe that whoever can perceive the composition of and connections among the many levels of created Life, and consequently between their biological Orders and their animate expressions, will be able to see the domain of the subconscious. And then he will learn a great deal about Man, about life here on Earth, about life hereafter and about the Laws of Offer and the Laws of Punishment. Then he will be able to see and to speak about the creation and functionality of all systems and also about our Father the Creator. And I use the word Father to include the entire Universe with all the universal functionalities created by this Position, with infinite levels of expression along their course laid out according to their constitutional formation, expressing their individual functionality as dictated by their particular stage in time as prescribed by the universal Law of Positions and Anti-positions. Out of all these, only very few characteristic examples can be mentioned, due to the enormity of their numbers and also to their specificity within each individual. If, however, the individual understands them he can discern and differentiate between Positions and Anti-positions, so as to act upon them as an individuality and direct them when necessary, or ask for help from the Higher and Supreme Orders so that They will provide this guidance.

Because after the long path I have traveled in this life, aided by the presence of the Higher and Supreme Positions, I confess that I have seen many things in men which, when I looked at them subjectively, made me feel sorrow and pain for the drama they keep hidden inside them, as invisible fear immobilizes and imprisons them. I have seen them in the grip of an intimate bipolar desire, on the one hand striving to win over and cling to other people, and on the other hand being led to absolute irresponsibility through continuous rejection. And I have seen, and am still seeing, the great and useless struggle many conducted and continue to conduct, only to end up entangled in their lower selves under the influence of the unconscious, which creates the world of illusions — a world that creates difficulties, unreasonable desires and emotional regressions, leading to loneliness and dependency on others. In this whirlpool, their illusion-fraught Ego leads them through the present with glimpses of a future that promises only disappointment. They then regress to the past to reproduce the few happy moments they have experienced, without realizing that those moments paved the way for the ones they later reject. Thus, while the Law of Life propels them forward, they appear unready to function naturally.

In the midst of this disturbed state of mind and disorientation of Man, there suddenly appear certain individuals pontificating on the Divine Hierarchy, neither knowing what the true Divine Hierarchy is nor how we should assimilate it so as to accept the Laws of the Universe exactly as the Creator has decreed. This is confirmed by the many sects that divide people into various groups, in ideological conflict with one another. Very often, in fact, they even express such conflict openly, each maintaining that their religious persuasion is the correct and only one that will ensure serenity here on Earth and paradise in the hereafter. This argument is, however, immediately refuted by their behavior toward themselves and toward others. For if a man finds serenity and tranquillity, then he has no desire to be in conflict with others, either verbally or physically. But through my many trips to various places in the world at the invitation of individuals belonging to different religions and sects, I must conclude that in these individuals no true serenity exists. On the contrary, every time I offered my opinion as to how we should function within and beyond things, I received the same monotonous answer over and over again: these are stressful times.

And I ask: what exactly is this stress? I am certain that you are not in a position to answer, at least not the way you see and think about those things that shape the conditions of external factors. Your weaknesses attract artificial external conditions that easily superimpose themselves on the emotional centers and occupy a dominant position, driving you like wayward sheep. Have you ever suspected that you might be making some mistakes, you who have been proclaimed teachers of the Earth, those of you who taught then and those who are teaching now? Because my questions are heard *by those departed as well*, wherever they may be. Of course, to those who are here now these words sound strange, unless you have worked with patience and persistence on the messages you have received from the Supreme Hierarchical Order of universal harmony. Because these messages deriving from the Higher Ego, when heard, pacify and assimilate the lower ego into a common search for the third Element, the Divine.

This presence is clearly evident in the reference of the

Holy Book to the celebration of the baptism of our Lord Jesus Christ in the River Jordan, where the third Element is so clearly revealed to us. This Element was, and is, for the Lord, the Holy Spirit, while for us it is the Divine Spirit in each of us. And of course, when the individual enters such levels — levels that almost no one has ever reached— his vibrational field is shaped into a special elevated functionality on a transformed level, which expands his endocrine system and establishes him in that state of readiness in which the radiant fourth Position is assimilated into the Three-fold Element, paving the way for the great Exaltation to occur. There the individual, now fully established in a higher emotional Position, is able to see everything and easily enter into all spaces occupied by Man or other species of Life in their biological Position and functionality. At the same time, he will have before him the slate on which every action and functionality at a given time and place is recorded and interpreted. Then the individual —whose four-fold substantive existence is locked by a code that cannot be revealed here— will belong to the Order of Offer for himself and the Order of usefulness for others toward Psycho-Spiritual evolution within the universal progression of functions.

I am not permitted to go into particular detail about the time-space directives of the Law. As ruling Positions they bring to the surface the Elements of Seeking and Offer, whose dimensionality is delineated and assimilated in the molecular system of every individual, from whence these Elements try, assisted by the higher authority through Metacycling and transformation, to express their presence and help the individual to follow his own best course. But what I observe is that, save for our Lord Jesus Christ and those chosen by Him, that is, those who have come from above and from special Positions, very seldom do we find someone who has, now or earlier, passed through all these levels so that his molecular composition has acquired the biological endowment and functionality that would make him worthy of being a teacher and leading the Orders of Mankind onto the necessary course toward the discovery of the true self.

Among other things I have observed from the myriad of books circulating in the world is also this: Almost all books, in some literary form or other, offer some type of suggestions for self-improvement, and indeed a great many expound theories as to how to accomplish this, saying that through these theories the individual will enter into special domains and will see new Positions that will bring about the fulfillment of many desires and aspirations. This may of course happen, but one cannot really tell if this is a genuine creative accomplishment or an illusion. In the latter case, the illusion will create a frivolous state of mind that, upon passing, will leave a great void in the emotional Position. Because, when such opportunities are given to us, if we do not make use of them through our true selves, we will be subject to errors not easily corrected — errors having to do with sentimental desires stemming from illusions and geared, on one hand, toward the organic field that demands satisfaction through the nervous system and, on the other hand, toward the lower intellectual level, which gives birth to the false perception that we are among the chosen of the Creator and have been given the right to lead others, whom He will acknowledge through us.

It is of course possible for anyone at all to become one of God's elect, if the course of his life is dominated by humility, objective judgment, great desire and diligence. We should never feel wronged, even when we have been treated unfairly. We should take care not to give others the opportunity to treat us unfairly. We should not be carried away by other people's promises, as they might contain hidden traps that could make us indignant and angry, causing us to stray from the right course. We should never attempt to appear to others as all-knowing. We should always have recourse to inner prayer. When someone comes to see us with whom we are obliged to have transactions, we should erect in our minds a luminous cross in front of him, so that we may have the help of the higher Positions. We should always remember not to trust other people too easily because it is easier to win first prize in a lottery than to find people who respect themselves and who will, by extension, respect you.

Because it has taken people on Earth many years of toiling without direction to bring their complex-ridden selves to this point, where the entire higher Element has been subjugated to the lower, which resides in instinctive centers of the Senses, generating emissions to the surrounding Sensory space and forming desires of a lower Order. With his perception Man assumes that each of his desires is natural and tries to fulfill all he can among the many types presented by the lower level, whose primary goal is to make these illusions seem bright and attractive. What is difficult for him to understand is that, behind each desire hides a vague fear, further complicating his existing complex-ridden states and leading him to make hasty decisions aimed at fulfilling this desire before the fear becomes unbearable. At such times men receive messages in order to control their actions, but most of the time their illusion-fraught conscience intervenes and justifies these actions as natural and necessary.

Here we must observe that Man is, at present, at the most critical point with respect to his Psycho-Sensory nervous condition, something that becomes evident from the following. Though he is offered so much in the way of nourishment, transportation, entertainment and information from all over the world, these things are not able to satisfy him or instill in him a sense of happiness, and he resorts instead to various other means to help him get back on his feet, i.e. to medicinal drugs, which are mostly pseudo-supportive. However, these do not often produce the expected result of fully restoring his health. If they did we would not keep hearing every conversation conclude with the phrase "my problems are due to the stressful times we live in." This phrase is very widely in use and makes everyone transfer blame to others and turn against them.

A great many people turn to religion, seeking fulfillment that they cannot find elsewhere. However, when fulfillment is not achieved, due to their ignorance, they have recourse to other areas on the fringes of religion, seeking solutions, but to no avail, from "enlightened" fortune-tellers and various other creators of illusions that Man has named "magicians," who claim that they can help anyone. You would immediately see the truth in what I am saying to you if, even for a minute, you could see what I see and hear what I hear with regard to man's life here on Earth, but also with regard to his life after he has departed (after death). We have all read books showing various paths to "happiness," written by the so-called great who have appeared on this Earth, but we may observe that these experts and those considered emissaries of the Divine Position, who appear more and more frequently in our midst, are, and unfortunately will always be, unable to attain it. And I, Ioannis, say this to you because you should know that I possess tremendous powers enabling me to see all people on Earth from my tiny office, an ability I have had ever since I was a child.

Another extraordinary thing that happened to me is that I was not content with these divine Offers, but my desire led me to investigate whether all the things I perceived in people in a mysterious way were indeed true. Later, I ascertained the truth of these revelations through extended research during my forty-year silent passage as a man of religion and of the world and as a participant in the great struggle for survival. Because although as a child I had no help from anyone, I nevertheless managed, through carefully planned efforts, to achieve a better standard of living. And then I made a great effort, stemming from my own impulse —a strange one for you perhaps, but not for me— to put all I perceived into the proper words. And I say this because I had little schooling and had to read certain books in order to transform the terms in which I received the revelations by the divine powers into the language of men which, you must know, operates on two functional levels: the level of Thought and the level of speech (sometimes we do not say what we think...)

In this way I learned a great amount with respect to the terminology of things in different areas of thought. And I now realize that many people possessing great facility in language have missed and continue to miss the true meaning of some very specific points. And I say this without any reservation, because in order for the exact meaning of something to be expressed, a certain degree of higher perceptive awareness is necessary so that the topic can be structured correctly and its essential meaning rendered in a manner conforming to the social time and place so it can be delivered to the functional members of Society and also appeal to their emotions, which will produce the desired outcome. Only then will things follow and serve their creators and not vice versa. I assure you that the reverse is completely against the Law of Creation. The laws of the State may change according to the desires of the rulers of the State, but the Laws of Creation never change. It is only the levels and dimensions of things created that are in a state of change, with the whole remaining unchanged.

Man on Earth is subject to change, and the messages he receives from his higher self tell him to obtain knowledge of his own Position and of all the Elements of the Earth, which are also subject to the Law of Change. Thence he will begin, with boundless respect and gratitude toward the supreme hierarchical Orders so they will acknowledge and accept him into their space, to develop his perceptive field so that he can penetrate and intuitively comprehend the various created levels of Life, as well as various Positions in their functional state, in their individual expression and in their social surroundings. Only in this way can our intellectual and spiritual perceptions, in conjunction with the corresponding invisible biological centers, develop the levels of our Etheric selves into a harmonious, interactive functional system of the Macrocosm and the Microcosm so that their full dimensions be assimilated in each other. Then our emotional fields will develop the capacity to simultaneously penetrate the lower levels of animate forms, such as those of Life on Earth, as researchers and observers. All this must be done without people at other levels of Life becoming aware of us as Positions (entities) with special abilities, except when permitted by time and place. If something like this happens at an inappropriate time and place, it will be very difficult for them to understand who we are and what they might learn and gain from us.

For this reason, whoever is blessed by the Offer of the great Orders and has cultivated it correctly should feel in his Soul the need to offer to others whatever he is able to absorb within himself. It is certain that everyone has the ability to offer, if only he knows how and when to present his offer, as it is very dangerous to enter into an action of Offer without knowing the origins of this desire. What people call "Offer," in its true Position, has two origins: One is the higher Psychic space and the other the lower Psychic space, which produces illusions and is a center of projections replete with fears. If the Offer derives from our Psychic hypostasis (our

Soul), then the reward will be a feeling of beauty, filling us with elation and optimism about the future, that is, with "happiness." But if it derives from our subjective dimension, where fear, overestimation and hyper-sensitivity reside, then we offer in order to receive in return, and we therefore find ourselves in a state of expectation and demand. However, for our Offer to be returned, others would also have to think and feel as we do, something that again would not lead to the right course. If we evaluated things correctly and objectively, we would see that whenever we give we are almost always driven by a subjective influence, which creates demands. Regarding this, I have observed that people have various notions of demands, due to individual differences in the formation of inner constitution. Let us remind ourselves here that the Position of the negative is placed in the domain of the subjective, which is influenced by the unconscious, which produces illusions, and these in turn produce false images. On the basis of these the individual, according to his constitution, formulates the evaluations that lead him to specific demands.

In all of this there is another important factor that plays a primary role and that factor is the parents. This is an extensive topic with multifaceted aspects that shape the visible and invisible personality of the individual and, according to his constitution, create complex states that intrude into the created individual and establish themselves in the instinctive centers of the nervous system, from where they induce lower-level feelings of fear in him. In his effort to become free from them he does not suspect that he is creating unbearable dependencies, and expects others to liberate him from this psychological pathology. This is, however, very difficult, since others are also in the same complex-ridden space, with similar fears and in the same state of expectancy. How then would they have anything to offer? *"Thou canst receive nothing from one who hath nothing."*

These congenital and acquired characteristics that shape and nurse the individual in the space-time of action and reaction have five main origins: (1) the origins of the Senses and the Soul (individual); (2) the parents; (3) the environment; (4) tradition and (5) the Times (the Age or Era).

(1) The origin of the Senses and the Soul (individual) is a vast and important subject that is difficult to cover completely. Because, although the individual derives from one source, at the same time other sources coexist and complete his individual presence under those Law-perfect Rules that establish the Element, according to his Order, in his bipolar state and his natural space. It is impossible for a man who has not reached the highest levels of knowledge to understand exactly what this means. There are some people, however, whose perception at certain times expands enough for them to intuit many aspects of their natural state, either in their consciousness or —at particular moments in time— in their unconscious. When these individuals perceive consciously and have immediate recourse to prayer, with absolute respect toward all creations of the divine Orders and absolute humility toward the entire hierarchy of the Divine, then they will slowly come into alignment with the perceptive

awareness of consciousness, and when they concentrate they will begin to acutely feel everything they have desired from all Positions and levels of all dimensions, and their minds will receive information. Only then will they be able to know Man and to know which activations shape his functionality and place him on a scale according to his true individual state, that is, in accordance with the expression of his origins. Because you must understand that only when we function objectively will we find ourselves in the place that supplies the special Element with which all-pervasive perception is formed, so that the individual may enter not only all levels of human functions, but also those of divine Positions along the entire scale of all created animate Positions of the Creator. Then the work that the Law has prescribed for us will be completed and our origins will be fully established.

(2) On the basis of the above, the man-father and the woman-mother will endeavor to impart a fully developed constitution to the child, and thus, with their first essential contribution, help the child along his course here on Earth. On the other hand, the Law has granted to external agents such as relatives, teachers, state functionaries and especially priests, who together compose lesser and greater society, the freedom of will to act from any altruistic or latent Position they choose on the basis of their bipolar nature. In this manner they will impose their particular presence and conduct upon the individual, influencing by 50% his individual characteristics. If this influence is positive, then a harmonious functionality will be fostered. If, however, it is negative, due

to disharmonious Positions, then the lower centers, that 92% of the vital space of subjective conscience, will be stimulated and the individual driven to the space of lower illusory functionality, committing many mistakes that will alter his course.

Mistakes are not events that go unnoticed in the history book of an individual's life. On the contrary, even the most minute mistake is recorded, and is thus endowed with the right to project its Position at a given time within the framework of disharmonious Decline. This Decline encompasses not only the nervous system but the entire being, and is not restricted merely to the individual but also extends to those who are emotionally and sentimentally attached to him. These individuals will suffer a part of these disharmonious conditions, since their emotional receptors easily tune into these states of Decline, which invade special individual Positions related to the mind. Very often they deprive the mind of the clarity of events and then the individual is enveloped in an invisible shroud of confusion, desperately seeking a solution. But all this happens under the influence of subjective demands shaped and handed down by those before us. Just think then of the effect of the internalized influence of the parents, especially the mother when the natural inclinations shape and direct the nature of each sex, male and female, to conform to the special reconstructive emotional activity geared toward the meeting and union of the male and the female Positions. The purpose of this emotional activity is the formation of an inner representation of this meeting from two sides: one as the manifestation of the individual nature, and the other as the attainment of the ideal atmosphere we call happiness. And this is done for the creation and mutual Offer, from male to female and from female to male, of their exalted visceral states. During this process, a magnetic attraction accompanied by subsonic waves generates a frame of mind that makes us feel that in this particular place, through this particular functionality, we will attain endless beauty, and we feel an awe that cannot be expressed in words, except when we are inside it and it inside us. Then we are complete within beauty and this beauty is the happiness of our future. With these few words I describe the functionality pertaining to the union of a male and a female that the chromosomal Orders, through inconceivable penetration, infuse into the hierarchy of organic structure in order to shape the emotional fields. These will then produce the sensitivities that create the desire for us to undertake the necessary Offer of childbearing, without which our Position could not be completed in its organic functionality.

This is exactly how the presence of need within man and woman occurs, and it appears that an active part is played only by the lower level of Man, in this way producing a result that is plain to see if you take some care to look inside yourself or around you. Because the easy solution, stemming from subjectivity, is to excuse ourselves and shift responsibility to others. You must learn that to make excuses for one of your mistakes offers you nothing, because this only paves the way inside you for entrapment in an endless chain of mistakes you will certainly commit. And then what sort of legacy will the welcome or unwelcome child that will come into this world inherit from parents who are irresponsible, socially inept and maladjusted? Because no one has considered the responsibilities he takes on or what he must know before embarking on this act of creation.

The truth is that until now no one has understood Man in his bipolar Position, so as to be able to speak about and analyze the two Positions that are manifested and coexist with the other two of the higher self. Basically, however, no one has as yet analyzed that special Position of human existence of such great importance to the perpetuation of the life of humankind, the woman. No one has approached her Psycho-Somatic Position so as to form an opinion of any relevance with regard to her biological functionality and the blueprints of her emotional functions and manifestations, which are devised on the basis of the Position she occupies. Not even she herself has the ability to reorder her biological reshuffling at certain particular times during the course of her life. Only Our Lord Jesus Christ, at certain points during His presence, refers most specifically to the female Position, although it has been impossible for the readers of the Bible to recognize this. Perhaps at some other time I will analyze certain viewpoints the Lord has expressed on this subject.

Nevertheless, at the point mankind's Psycho-Sensory states here on Earth have now reached, it is almost impossible for Man to know even one half of his inner world. And here we have a matter of extreme importance. When he who gives and she who creates do not know their own selves, what can they possibly offer to their joint creation? When they do not know why they are here and what they must do in order to properly instate themselves in the natural space of Positions and Anti-positions? When they do not know what it means to be a joint creator and how one should feel in order to offer appropriately? When they do not know what it is they should be offering and when to offer it, or on what set of values to base the Offer? All of this is a set of Rules of faith laid down by the Creator when he created all things, and above all Man, who must possess awareness and be able to function under these Rules as a joint creator. Whoever adheres to these Rules will know Man in his entirety and in his individuality, but he will also know the meaning of male and female, man and woman, what their Position is and what their responsibilities are toward the Law of Creation.

(3) An individual's environment has two Orders: One Order pertains to the relatives, who constitute the space already created around the individual. Godparents occupy a special Position in this Order, since the influence they exert on the individual is very important, especially during baptism regardless of the way it is performed or under what religion or sect. The second Order contains the so-called "representatives" of God and the teachers who, according to the role they have to play during the development of the individual, are responsible for the usual complex-ridden states we fall into, since they are ignorant of their true mission. This confusion leads to mistakes and in turn to a state of expectancy where, as we have said elsewhere, the feeling of injustice dominates, with all the well-known consequences according to objective perception

(4) Tradition is the creation of manifest behavior over time involving communal participation, beginning with one individual whose functionality influences a second individual until a tradition within a small social unit is created. This is extended to other nearby individuals and thence it forms a large ensemble or group, influencing its emotional field, shaping sentiments with regard to the times, events, and habits, finally absorbing them. From that moment on the group enters a state of expectancy, awaiting the time when its emotions will direct it to unite with another group and be absorbed with it as part of creation and establish what eventually becomes a Rule of faith and oftentimes law. Whoever defies law is condemned by the group and is rejected. And at the moment of pronouncing sentence the group enjoys a feeling of redemption, as if it had performed a holy duty toward the Creator and the Law. This most special creation of mankind offers total group communication, with the purpose of somehow promoting good behavior among people. And in this atmosphere a part of Man's natural sociability is developed, contributing to his refinement and shaping cultural leanings. Then the individual appears cultivated within traditional society, and develops the feeling of being a person of value, something that fills him with "happiness," according to the evaluation of his newly-created emotional personality.

(5) An Age or an Era is defined by various factors which are formed and dynamically manifested during the moments of previous lesser or greater Decline, which in turn are the result of mistakes made by individuals involved who were

actively performing their missionary and social functions at the time.

One factor is the behavior of those ordained by Nature and the Universal Law to offer their services to people who, voluntarily or involuntarily, are the reason or the occasion for their coming to this life on Earth. As I have already said, these specially-ordained individuals should be well aware of the responsibilities they are assuming. This has an extremely important effect on other individuals, since Nature and tradition have created atmospheres whose emissions produce in us strong Sensory emotions that belong to lower levels of perception and have almost nothing else to offer except fear and doubt. This produces a reaction of invisible or even visible aggressiveness toward others. Such aggressiveness, which can even lead to murder, is always followed by a sense of impotence and by fear of the laws of the State, of other people, and of the victim himself. At first glance such a thing seems incomprehensible, but do not forget that I am revealing to you the hidden side of people.

The difference that exists between individuals is merely the reaction expressed by each because of his own constitution, from which the action derives. I tell you now that, from the moment that external factors direct an emission toward us or, more generally, toward the entire social group to which we belong, manifest action gradually commences. This entire process is carried out as follows: the impression is first produced in the Essential Visual system, and through the emotional centers of the nervous system, stimulates the Sensory nerve center where the sympathetic nervous system resides.

There the corresponding impressions are activated, producing acceptance or rejection, or some other reaction. All these are recorded in their individual frequency as if, let us say, on a tape of minute width and length with immense capacity. In almost everyone this memory is stored within the total space of the individual, and the Law of organic form places it in a state of abeyance. Thus when the perpetrator executes his wrongdoing, his memory will usually portray to him things and events in a disjunctive and deceptive way, so that his thinking with regard to these things will be incomplete, thus propelling him into chaotic states of mind. This creates certain fears and a rationalization for his act is produced in order to alleviate these fears. However, this memory does not disappear but remains in readiness to reproduce itself. This has special significance and is indicative of the continuity of the individual's course, because what we are and appear to be here on Earth becomes a program for our future course in the hereafter without the possibility of intervention by anyone to better an individual's Position.

The only opportunity for Psycho-Spiritual Elevation **is here**. For this reason the individual is pursued and disturbed by fears and states of confusion, because deep down he knows very well how things are, even though he may say that after life here on Earth there is nothing. But there is. His punishment will be irrevocable, and no one can change this save He who is sent from the hereafter. And you will be able to discern him among the multitude of Spiritual teachers who —whether proclaimed so by themselves or by others— profess to save the world without having the faintest idea about salvation. And you will distinguish him through his revelatory interpretations with regard to the Inner Man and the invisible functional influences he receives from sources he does not know. More specifically, he will know the male and the female in their individual dimension and their special manifestation. Only he can speak about Man, about the Senses, and about the Soul and its lower and higher levels. He knows and can tell you about Religion, how we seek it and why, which religion is sought by the lower levels of Life and which by the higher. He will be able to analyze for you the three levels of religious Positions and functions, i.e., the zealous, the pious, and the faithful.

Today people on Earth find themselves emotionally fixated within a subjectivity that belongs to the unconscious, because of a lack of control over their actions and a passive life stance. They are trapped within an erroneous perceptivity, unable to understand the divine gift offered in response to their individual needs through the Position of the faithful. Only through intense effort, humility and striving toward completion will one's individual heaven called *Essential Visual* open up and activate the special eyes through which he will see into places beyond this life, into everyone's lives here and hereafter, the deeds here and the reward hereafter. Then he will be able to understand what justice is, how it is dispensed and how it is received by each of us.

And only he who sees and comprehends all this and feels a boundless urge to explain it in detail to those who ask with respect and with a great desire to better themselves, only he can free us from the bonds of punishment. Because the authority is given to him and to no one else. This is, more-over, also evident in the teachings of Our Lord Jesus Christ, if we are able to understand these teachings. He always tried to make it very clear, through the Apostles, that everyone has a place within the higher and supreme Orders of the divine Hierarchy, provided that, under the influence of the five par-ticular factors we analyzed earlier, when he receives the mes-sages at the appointed time, he will follow the path of his true future.

However, we follow the path of illusions, and pathological states dominate our chromosomal Order, developing fears that lead us to get caught up in our times. The Age we live in sweeps us up like puppets and carries us along for its own ends. Inside us, on the other hand, tradition will project its own tenets, delineating a confrontation that splits us in two. This division creates in us emotions that are difficult to understand, entangled with feelings of insecurity, leading to violent outbursts of aggressiveness, which also happens to be the dominant characteristic of our times. For this reason the individual must do a lot of thinking when he finds him-self at these crossroads, because, when he chooses a certain path in his life unaware of the responsibilities he is assum-ing with regard to all his creative actions, then there is only one factor that can intervene. And that is Divine Grace, which can indeed save him from making disastrous mis-takes. Because when mistakes pile up disaster is nearby, carrying for the individual a very heavy sentence.

Chapter 15

NATURE AND GENESIS

It is well known that human society began and was created by man and woman. This is almost like the Genesis of Hebrew tradition as told in the Biblical story of Adam and Eve, the only difference being that the story individualizes the situation down to the forms of one man and one woman, which is not correct. This occurred either because, for some special reason of their own, the writers presented the event in this fashion or because this met with the needs of the people of that Age in order to begin their quest for God. And of course the Bible does not refer to the biological order of things and their creation by God as the beginning of the creation of Life throughout the Higher and Lower Universe. This is something that no one who has passed through life on this Earth knows about, except for Our Lord Jesus Christ, and I have only described a peripheral situation with regard to the Lower Universe.

I believe that the Cycle of the Universal cosmic entities has been traced with distorting systolic delineations within their overall individuality. When these Cycles are in this condition, the overall individual is in a state of contraction and the hydrogenic individual has a slow circulatory state. Under these conditions it is very hard for the perceptive capacity of the individual to function in a natural biological Position, so that he will be able to see the course he must follow in order to offer himself what he really deserves. This, however, does not free him from all responsibilities, because the individual, despite the systolic pressure of the hydrogenic system, must be effective in his search for his Etheric Self in its cosmic luminescence so that his condensed Self may become free and function at the level of his Position here on Earth.[100]

As I have already mentioned, there are many individuals who come to Earth from first-rate Positions of the Hierarchy of Light (as there are also others who come from dark Positions). Such individuals should be at least partially able

---

[100] It is well known that the simplest element on Earth, from the point of view of physics, is hydrogen, whose name reminds one of genesis (from the Greek word hydor = water, the fluid of life + genesis = birth). Of course I am referring to the "hydrogenic nucleus" of these teachings in an attempt to place it on well-known foundations. It is certain that the human organism, an Element of the universe, will constitute a miniature —a scaling down— of universal genesis. "Systole" (or contraction) and "cosmic luminescence" are also encountered in the chromosomal cycle. When this cluster of molecules of the nucleus containing the knowledge and the memory of life is contracted, it is considered quiescent. That is, it does not provide the cell with any creative activity; it is, in other words, in a systolic state. However, when it is extended, then it acquires clarity and the cell produces work. To avoid going into more detail, let us return once more to the correlation of biological order with true knowledge of human existence. "Sometimes the truth is so near that we have to go around the entire world to find it. Because it simply is not to be found anywhere else but within us." [A.V.]

to observe and investigate things from their creation to their results, on the basis of messages they receive from the Super-Position, so they may be correctly activated. However, they give priority mainly to their lower selves, shaping their emotional fields so they are dominated by a feeling of apprehensive watchfulness, geared at promoting themselves to others and they base their actions on advice to "be good and not bad," to "act morally and not immorally," to "believe in God and not succumb to atheism." In this way, they are deprived of the strength needed to surpass their congested Bodily Order and perceive their individual dimension so as to know the proper course here on Earth, in the hereafter and beyond, and to be able to give others clear directions. How is it possible for these individuals to teach about good and evil, morality and immorality, religion and atheism? And what then is the difference between them and other people? And what will be their recompense for their functional Position here on Earth? And most important, under what kind of inner integration will they function when that special time comes to enter into marriage? Because marriage, for anyone who enters into this extremely important function, is one of the most serious acts and indeed, for me, occupies the second place in the sacred mission of Man.

The first priority in our mission is to reach integration and evolve as individuals, so as to become cognizant of the Position of our Father the Creator substantiated within us and to show humble respect for the Hierarchy of the divine Orders and become worthy of expressing, with all of our Being and with absolute humility, our boundless respect for

His compassionate Offer to us. Naturally, this was not understood by most of the Great Men who passed through life on Earth, except for Our Lord Jesus Christ, who was indeed the Compassionate Expression of our Father the Creator, along with a very few others who came close to His deeds. For my investigation of human thought on Earth has shown that, indeed, almost 2,000 years later, the greater part of Earth's population has retained their "stone-age" emotional state with regard to religion as a function, and have placed as its figurehead Our Lord Jesus Christ, whose assistance they invoke at their most difficult moments. And by difficult moments I mean the times when they are unable to react differently to what is happening to them, to which they too have contributed, albeit unknowingly. It has been proven that this Universal Glorious Position of Our Lord Jesus Christ —who derived directly from our Father the Creator, and whose protein Elements our planet had the infinite honor of embodying as material form in Earthly density in order to align and substantiate His Position also as Man, something that had never happened since the beginning of life on Earth— came and brought to Earth, once and only once, the grand atmosphere that materialized Etheric molecular entities which in turn entered many human organic Positions as "invaders" of our Universe, as part of the infinite compassionate Offer of our Father the Creator to Man, to provide him with the utmost assistance in understanding the natural and para-natural states under which he functions on Earth. Based on this, Man can decide what is in his best interest and then use this to shape the optimum physical conditions in his organic Position, so he may follow the natural course of Life. This divine grace, the primary gift to perception, offers Man the ability to understand the conditions that prevail in the Lower Universe, and to accept and adhere to the course of his personal mission, whatever the obstacles.

After this comes the second Offer which, in the form of a sound atmosphere and wholesome nourishment, is given to the organism of the individual under the name of *serenity*. Here, within this organic Position, certain entities partaking of these extremely worthy emotions will materialize and take shape and will, like invincible warriors, usher Man after this life here on Earth into the Kingdom of Heaven.

The first of the few Great Men of Knowledge after Our Lord Jesus Christ was Socrates, something that can also be verified by the fact that he had no Earthly teachers but was taught directly by the Divine Wisdom of the created Universe. This is why his social function was to give priority to those aspects of education which form the basis for protection against attacks from the lower levels of the Soul, that is, the Senses. I repeat, the Senses are constructed in such a way as to be influenced by the unconscious to function subjectively, which causes the individual to deviate from true perception. For this reason, Socrates always tried, in his own way, to help men develop their perceptive abilities within the daily course of things, and to know what they were doing and how to proceed in the direction of the Divine Orders of the Universe, as well as toward the Creator of All Things. For this reason, when they asked him "What do you see here on

Earth?" he answered very serenely and correctly: "I know one thing: that I know nothing." If someone uninfluenced by the emotionalism and sentimentality characteristic of human existence and dimension could be found to interpret this, such a person would understand what Socrates attempted to offer to men, especially during that particular Age, when the world was making a profound effort to evolve through active involvement and emotional attachment to philosophical dialectics.

Naturally, in the course of these efforts, many factors intervene that lead the individual into a state of apprehension, to fears and eventually to mistakes. Among such factors are four conditions, out of the five already discussed (in chapter 14), that the individual must deal with in order to function. And since they operate at the lower levels of Man, it is obviously hard for the individual to interpret the coded messages sent for his Psycho-Spiritual Elevation. But, dominated by the lower levels, the individual becomes trapped at the level of the Sensory organs, and then he begins struggling for no other reason than to be recognized by others as being strong, Spiritually accomplished, an elect of God. Unfortunately the Earth is filled with such people. This is why Socrates was trying to make them understand that, functioning in this way, they made tremendous mistakes — mistakes that they have passed on to ensuing generations, reaching all the way up to the present. This type of thinking was dominant during the Age of the coming of Our Lord Jesus Christ to Earth, as the Bible bears testimony. According to its teachings, people, on the one hand, sought help from Him and, on the other hand, were indifferent or even condemned Him. This shows how erroneous functionality leads not only to irresponsible frivolity, but also to considerable ingratitude, another sign of our times and the Age we live in.

As I write these lines, the image of Moses appears before me and asks me to speak of him. Indeed Moses was a good being who tried to follow his appointed path to the work that was to distinguish him within the destiny of his particular ethnic community and of history at large. He tried, through his hieratic circle, to organize his people into a functional society and nation and, through the divine Word, to shape education, that is, the beginning and the end of every Nation-State. Without education one cannot conceive of an evolved society that could be called a Spiritual society, although the term Spiritual describes only a part of the whole, which is Psycho-Spiritual. And Moses tried to lead them to Psycho-Spiritual perceptive awareness, where the religious side of individuals and societies can promote respect, appreciation and, when possible, Love. And he proved this through his own efforts and piety, by climbing Mount Sinai.

But there was one other contributing factor in his case. His entire being was infused with one great desire, that of completing his mission, which was the organization of the Hebrew State. It was indeed a mission of divine inspiration. And when I speak of divine inspiration, I refer to deeds on Earth that have been ordained in Heaven as our purpose. Now these deeds do not fit into one category, nor do they always take the same form. They are not just the deeds of some ascetic, recording for us in a few pages his visions or prophesies concerning Man, or of certain priests, or even others in various walks of life. Each of us comes into this world in order to first perform the work prescribed for him and then move on to other work, the importance of which will determine the hierarchical Position he will be awarded. A corresponding Position will also be assigned to those who do evil, except that those who have sunk to this state will always remain slaves of and tormented by the lower Order. It is of course very difficult for you to see them where they are now, but try to imagine their Position by looking objectively at their social relationships with other people.

If we look carefully, we will see that Moses came here to Earth in order to perform a great national service. He first moved through the hierarchy of Egypt in order to learn how the emotional states of people of that particular Age functioned biologically and manifested themselves according to the traditions of that time. In this way he managed to assimilate within his own emotional field the corresponding fields of other people and to differentiate classes of people with respect to authority. He thus devoted himself to his mission, that of assuming responsibility for the organization of the Hebrew people and for leading them to a place they could occupy as an organized State — a place where they could function under the social Rules governing the activities of a nation and a State, always with an emphasis on religious sentiment. On this foundation social and ethical values would be developed.

In my opinion, this was an extremely unusual effort and

at the same time a very great one, which showed that Moses was a most able national leader, but also that he was especially gifted with regard to his inner Position, which enabled him to bring to light his religious aspirations. This is why we observe him in his every action trying to create and bring out the religious atmosphere, so as to unite his people emotionally and to forge a nation. The effort to consolidate these feelings is clearly evident at the time of his ascent of Mount Sinai, when he prayed deeply and asked the Hierarchy of our Father the Creator for help and inspiration to create a Rule, the contents of which would express the way a community should function and lead the people to an advanced state of religious sentiment.

Moses' life could set a very useful example for every leader who truly desires to serve his people. As they could also draw many lessons from those other two great beings, Socrates, and then Our Lord Jesus Christ. And I mention Socrates first because he came to a people who were very advanced as a State and as a nation, having consolidated the democratic system of government — a system, that is, allowing every citizen to scrutinize the way his rulers govern, without blind obedience to and undue praise for religious leaders, and allowing him to freely offer his opinion, irrespective of his place in society. (He was only forbidden to criticize the works of certain disciplines.) But Socrates, being of such greatness and such singularity, did not hesitate to break down the barriers and, with boundless courage, he decoded and exposed the errors of the experts of his Age and spoke about education, ignoring all those people considered by the State as the "Powerful."

But, as I said earlier, Man on Earth is dominated by two kinds of emotive feelings: the subjective and the objective. The subjective derives mainly from the sense of touch and influences the nervous system, leading the individual to a multitude of lower level desires. This results in the individual creating a central axis at the lower quarter of the Soul, where the Senses reside, and from where he observes and follows things, differentiating among them and making choices. Of course he does not even suspect that by functioning in this way the only thing he succeeds in doing is in creating false idols that cut him off from his higher inner self. However, since he rejects three quarters of his essential (true) self, how is it possible for him to function normally? In spite of all the messages sent by the Law of our Father the Creator, he pays no heed and continues on his way with increased passion for the creation of false idols. And when these are brought down, he feels wronged. And when he develops wounds that cause him pain, he hastens to the Saints, to Our Lord Jesus Christ and to God and asks for their help. When he does not get the help that he thinks he deserves, he denies their existence.

At any rate, we see that the individual is in an extreme state of confusion, and it is very hard for him to understand his existential condition. Yet deep down he experiences a secret fear that something is wrong. Some people are led by this to blame others for what is happening to them and turn against them with whatever means they can, while others, on the basis of messages they receive at certain special moments, seek help from the divine Hierarchies, even from

Our Lord Jesus Christ. Many people who feel they have some special value as men ask for help directly from our Father the Creator... This sort of thing means that they will never receive help, in view of their inappropriate behavior! But this behavior comes from fear and not from genuine desire.

Moses was doing what his perceptive abilities allowed and what he deemed to be beneficial, without of course being able to pronounce judgment on whether this was the naturally permissible thing for his Position. If an individual does not reach the perceptive awareness where he can know exactly his Position and the rights naturally accruing from it, so that his desires will steer him toward self-realization and the enjoyment of happiness, he will not be able to function within the natural creative state of his Order so that his biological Position is in harmony — because the natural state of an individual is based on harmony. And from the moment the individual is not in a state of harmony, the Law of Creation places him in a peripheral, semi-integrated Position.

Be aware that in our present Age various impressions are constantly transferred to our emotional fields, creating certain demands and placing us in the domain of anxiety. We then begin looking for ways to satisfy these demands, making all sorts of concessions, no matter how unreasonable they appear. Thus trapped, we receive a message with regard to our erroneous ways, and then, in a panic, we hasten to justify our choice of path with flimsy rationalizations, saying, for example, that society is at fault, or that blame rests with the politicians, the priests, the judges, the doctors, the teachers and everyone else except us. I cannot say that these people are not also to blame because of the way they carry out their mission, but there is such a thing as personal responsibility. Moreover, the responsibility each of us bears is manifested as various psychological problems he carries with him and takes great care to hide. Through the pressure exerted by personal responsibility, which develops into group or even national responsibility, many people have attempted to discover the cause of this inner disturbance, which is nothing more than the irrational acts of previous generations transmitted to their descendants and constituting a defect.

This entire situation has entangled Man in a state of suffering, leading him to the consumption of pain suppressant drugs created and produced by pharmaceutical companies. He lives under the illusion and expectation of better days to come. But this is hard for him to believe when, from one moment to the next, because of his permanent inner state of uneasiness, he encounters some difficulty that he experiences as a "problem." This difficulty, stemming from internal disharmony, leads to confusion and this in turn to states of inner conflict, revealed through the erratic behavior of the driven individual toward others, thus compounding the "problem." And it is only natural for us to displace many of our problems onto others, while at the same time seeking relief from our tension by placing upon them whatever blame we choose.

When someone's inner state of mind is irrational and he is busy trying to hide this, how can he possibly function as a member of society, morally and socially able to meet existing responsibilities, not to mention those he himself has personally assumed? How, for instance, can he meet a responsibility such as that of the union of a man and a woman in the bonds of matrimony? On the basis of tradition, or the necessity for Life as dictated by the Law of Creation, our biological Position is formed in its natural state so that we may function as individuals in our apostolic Position, and thus make our appearance with our mental and Bodily functions fully activated within the domain of Creation, in order to perform our duty according to our organic substantive existence, which has been shaped by the Creator into a binary state (Position-Antiposition). It is here that the functional emotion of biological need is produced, in such a way that the two individuals, man and woman, are placed facing one another with each of their natures projected in a clearly pronounced form, so that each will attract the other into the inner recesses of desire and both may feel complete and fulfilled. Within this organic process, there are many factors participating and vying to impose themselves and at the same time to lead the individual into their own domain. It is at this point that, because of these factors, the natural course of the individual's functionality is altered and disharmony is firmly established.

I can assure you that in saying all this I am not trying to promote my Position, because I was taught not by teachers of the Earth but by the Laws that the Creator has set down for Nature. And it is Nature that created men, under the supreme direction of the Great Hierarchies, with their mysterious functionality within Creation, which cannot be seen by Beings of middle or lower Creation. It is these Hierarchies that have placed me in this Position of infinite honor and have infused biological Rules into the higher glands of my Body, and other glands as well, so that I could reach this supreme state where I can receive, with infinite awe, the revelations offered to me concerning everything from the infinite Principle of the Creator down to even the lowest Position of created Nature. This enables me to provide answers regarding anything pertaining to Man.

Now, I will simply try in a few words to give you a picture of human nature at this level of life. Our Father the Creator presents to us the hierarchy of Creation as it functions under His Law. Every level of life performs the duties of its level and thus fulfills its mission within its own Order, without deviating from its natural Position. The same is true for all other levels belonging to the Law of functional regetation. And above all of these, He created the Position called Man.

I will now present the created hierarchical Position of Man, based on the revelation made to me in 1965 so that my perception on this subject could be completed. For many of you this is a theory deriving from my own illusions. This is not so, however, because long before I became thoroughly familiar with the functional states of the individual, I was in a position to perceive *his core image*, that is, the exact point of origin of these functional states within anyone's individual universe. I speak of course of the subconscious, the space where the two Positions, named *conscious* and *unconscious* by early researchers, have been placed so as to function and develop their individual dimension. These Positions belong to the organic state of the individual and are exclusively responsible for establishing him in his particular functionality. The primary Position is held by the unconscious, which also contains the subjective Element with its associated illusions. We already know from the above that when the individual is trapped by illusions, he is surrounded by such difficulty and disharmony that he can only be brought back into a natural state through great effort, calling for fasting and prayer.

But, you will say to me, Man has always prayed and especially, after the coming of Our Lord Jesus Christ, those who have tried to seek Him out Spiritually. Moreover a ritual has been established in the religious Order where fasting has a special place. Nevertheless, individuals have not succeeded in interacting harmoniously and in developing a sense of respect. Because, until now, the inner state of the individual has not been analyzed, so as to enable him to establish inner harmony. Great efforts toward this have been made by many people from all walks of human knowledge, but it has not been possible to penetrate the special Position called **mutual assimilation of coupled organic functionalities**. By this term we mean the Position that we have recorded and described as subjective (or as a materialized image) and the Position we have called objective (one of Psycho-Somatic harmony, functionally powered by the Etheric Position of the Soul and the condensed matter of the Body). The subjective Position greatly influences the Senses through the sympathetic nervous system and entraps the individual within an unnatural perspective, from which he observes things under such unnatural conditions that fasting and prayer can offer only minimal help in his quest for a better life. As soon as we stop practicing these, we return to the darkness of self-ignorance and to illusory perception.

As long as we are unaware of the true nature of things, we remain outside the Laws of natural evolution, and this is why we are in this state today. We see wrong as right and right as wrong. How then can human nature function harmoniously? Unfortunately, we are living in an para-natural state, and I am not the only one to say this, for this is obvious from events and conditions both around us and within us. Take, for example, a person's attempts to impress others and make an impact on his environment or exert influence. Such tendencies stem from insecurity due to lack of self-knowledge, and this pathological complex-ridden type of behavior was evident in the past and is still prevalent today among a great many people on Earth. But this behavior does not contribute in the end to their ultimate goal of being fulfilled and finding inner peace. It is certain that, under the influence of this perception, it is impossible for Man to know Creation and to carry out even a small part of his mission as a natural individual.

Chapter 16

MALE — FEMALE

Two factors, first the organization of a nation into a functioning State, and then tradition, contribute toward the consolidation of the religious Position of the nation-State, which confers official investiture to the individual's existential functioning in his presence on Earth. He is thus led to committed coexistence as male-nature and female-nature, which will bring about the natural Cycle of their mission, whereby the physical organism is consummated by means of creative union according to Universal Law. We must realize that two Positions coexist inside us, male and female, with each evincing its presence at particular times when conditions will cause it to manifest its characteristics in the way necessary for the formation of the organic functionality of a woman or a man.

The Creator fashioned Man so as to be above all other creations, and gave us the great gift of being able to evolve into higher Positions (such as those of Saints, Angels, and others), and thus to free ourselves from this level of Life, which is simply an opportunity for us to understand that we assume responsibility for each of our actions on the basis of the Universal Law of Justice. And when the Law determines that the time has come to present ourselves before it, we will receive our just reward. Because this Law will neither add nor take away anything at all. This is stated clearly by Our Lord Jesus Christ in words to the following effect: "Not a single hair on your head will be unfairly treated by the Father." Each individual must recognize the great opportunity offered to him during life here on Earth to ascend higher into the Eternal Community, and to do this he must function both individually and socially under the guidance of his conscience and he must be open to objectivity. Otherwise he will become a slave of the subjective conscience, which will make it very easy for him to become entangled and assimilated by the lower levels of Life where illusions prevail. These create false ideas and idols that stimulate us at the Sensory-organic level of our functionality, causing us to deviate from the true apostolic course that is in our best interest. For this reason, we should learn first to direct the functioning of the Sensory organic level as an apostolic Element of the Higher Nucleus-Soul, and not as that of the lower Orders where the Negative (the Devil) dominates.

And when man and woman decide to coexist and enter the Cycle of creation, having exchanged mutual promises to carry out their natural mission of caring for each other, they should first get to know their existential condition and the causes that motivate them emotionally so that their biological Positions become bound to this very powerful desire for Bodily union. Of course we all know what a high rate of failure such efforts have. We have spoken above, and we may speak again, about individual and collective responsibility for this. But it is individual responsibility that counts most, for it is difficult for us to understand that when we arrive at this position where promises are exchanged before God and men in the new mission we undertake for the continuation of our lives, there is a lot more to it than is normally believed. That is, there is more to marriage than experiencing the joy of love and sharing our lives with someone, which goes on at the mental level of uncontrolled desires that appear in our perception as great needs. These things also have their place, but the natural Order impels us to become familiar with the Position of missionary service (caring), whose function we will undertake to carry out properly. For if we do not learn what is right we will not be able to serve what is right, and as a consequence we will not develop our higher Psycho-Spiritual selves. And when a man and a woman do not evolve Psycho-Spiritually, how will they be able to function as father and mother in their natural Position, with all that this consciously entails? And how will it be possible to foster their inner desire for complete devotion to their sacred task so that the creation of the family will evolve within the sense of Offer, which will also include the beauty of the Soul in its supreme dimension (religion)? Only then will inner harmony be offered to the individual, as the Lord has decreed that Man should live on Earth, saying to him: "*Go in peace.*"

And now let me pose the great question. Have there been men from any missionary level and space who have understood the absolute meaning of "*Peace be with us*"? As far as

I am concerned, there is practically no one. Because the individual who attains this level of perception will be led by the Universal Order of Individualities to the very high Positions possessing the keys to the domes of the Heavenly Universe where our own planet also belongs, and they are many in number. Then he will perceive everything there is to know about Divine Creation and its wisdom, and then he will know the Peace of the Lord.

Let us not deceive ourselves. Man and woman are not yet known, neither with regard to their visceral dimension nor with regard to their Psychic hypostasis. This is why it became imperative, by means of the Rule of Sensory Orders, for human urges to act as a motivation to support tradition and guide individuals toward the sacred ceremony of matrimony. During the wedding ceremony, apart from the ceremonial words pronounced, certain words of advice are offered to the individuals concerning what the principles and foundations of their thoughts and actions should be in order to properly accomplish their mission. If these words register in their consciousness, they will develop two Positions, one of which will be able to predict the benefit or the detriment associated with each of their actions, while the other will develop a sense of objective conscience, the only guiding force able to channel desire into an integrated missionary function.

But as I have already mentioned, people enter wedlock out of a purely subjective desire, influenced by the lower Element, where Sensory-based illusory images dominate. And this is contrary to the Law of Natural Existence, which prescribes that the surrender of individuality to its own existential presence is indispensable for its complete physical consummation, enabling, through acceptance and interaction, the creation of the unity of the whole (Body and Soul), toward the completion of its future course. Only in this manner will the woman's natural physiology expand and the positive endowments of her genes be heightened, taking the Position of childbearing to its harmonious dimension. Then the creation of the smallest social unit, the family, will take place and develop within the natural levels allowing the just allocation of nourishment to the Body and the Soul. This will lead individuals to genuine acceptance and communication between their Bodies and Souls as well as with other people, and by extension to their individual sense of religion (faith), which is also to everyone's true benefit. That is, they will work at this functional creation, because this means the future establishment of their individual Position in the domain of Divine Creation.

Tradition, as shaped by various societies up to the present, has become an end in itself, a kind of duty for all to acquire riches and goods, so as to be considered successful and well established. This is certainly not the best sort of motivation for this level of life. We should not, of course, deny the power of the traditions that have been incorporated into the plans individuals make, but these plans are filled with errors, creating unnatural pressure on the emotional fields of people, who try to escape from this pressure by resorting to ineffective solutions in an attempt to reestablish inner harmony. The adoption of such solutions by large masses of people creates an emotional movement, which is raised to the status of an emotional creed, creating a time of presumed victory against disharmony. And it is natural for this victory to prove a fallacy, yet no one will wonder why. On the contrary, they will seek similar but equally ineffective solutions elsewhere.

Nevertheless, the Creator has given us all the Elements we need in order to pose questions within ourselves and analyze the manifestation of any given situation, and through this we will receive help in arriving at the proper answer. Certain people who lived on this Earth did manage, through inner reflection, to develop their perceptive abilities to the point of finding answers. Indeed, all the answers eventually pointed toward divine Creation and Benevolence. And through them these people bettered their Position and prompted others, through their example and teachings, to embark on a similar course. For were you to become just a little more aware of the unknown Position in which you will be placed in the hereafter, with absolute justice, it is certain that you would then consider carefully each of your acts, laying down the foundations for a proper course.

However, tradition, as we have already said, has a strong presence among us and binds us to situations created by others before us. A large number of these situations are useful to society, but the individual must distance himself from everything that prevents him from following his natural course. For often what is beneficial for one person has no relation whatsoever to the things tradition has made us consider beneficial.

As is shown over time, none of us stays here forever, and if we have perceived even a little of the meaning of the Creator, it is certain that we will realize that life here on Earth is only a part of a larger course whose past and future we do not know but have a duty to learn. This begins with our effort to return to our natural state, that is, to the state of Peace of Our Lord Jesus Christ. Then, with correct judgment at every instance in time with regard to the order of things and the Divine Hierarchy, we will develop, along with the awareness of what Life truly is, a sense of respect for our fellow human beings, and a mutual respect between man and woman. Thus we will lead a very correct existence together, our marriage will succeed and will work in a way that will bring us good results, both during and after life here on Earth.

As I have already mentioned, there are individuals who have such strong characters that they are able to repel the attacks by traditional and more modern-Age states of anarchy and carry out a large part of their missionary work, especially if they manage to marry individuals with similar characteristics. However, the social environment, already entrapped by the irrationality of individuals leading a trivial existence, tries to assimilate such individuals in order to conserve a bankrupt system! And this is easily accomplished, since there are no arguments, knowledge or awareness that can demonstrate this irrationality. Only very few people escape the dynamics of this assimilation and these are the people who eventually maintain some sort of equilibrium in the world. If you were to bring to your mind all the suffering that beleaguers people in our present Age, you would not let even a moment go by without thinking of the advice of John the Baptist: "*Make haste*," but also of the words of Our Lord Jesus Christ, assuring us that "*the Kingdom of Heaven is at hand.*" Note carefully, "*of Heaven*" and not "*of the Heavens*"! *Of the Heavenly Positions.* Whoever does not understand this will not be able to properly carry out his missionary function.

Many will read this but, as usual, they will do nothing more than read, something that Our Lord Jesus Christ, but also the Apostles, have noted: that men living during various Ages have heard and read many things, but very seldom have these things entered into their perceptive awareness. And because this process does not take place in them, they turn to another solution, that of transferring responsibility to others in order to "exonerate" themselves from their own share of blame. But in vain. The individual who comes here to Earth assumes the burden of responsibility for his deeds. The Lord said that even in our thoughts we sin, and this is because whatever is born in our minds, given the opportunity, will exert pressure to be turned into action. Throughout almost our entire lives we function under the direction of the mind, which is, for the most part, subjective.

Thus the individual cannot be social in the true sense of the word and cannot function properly in his mission. How is it possible for him to succeed as head of a family if his subjective space initiates the production of lies? When a baby is born to such parents, do you not think it instinctively senses the situation? Of course it cannot react, since it is fully dependent upon them biologically and materially, but there is also a special reason for this that you may find incomprehensible and that I will try to explain in so far as this is permitted. Those special individuals who came to Earth did not work hard enough on the natural messages sent them by the divine Hierarchies, and on expounding them in writing in their natural structures and thus developing a tradition of functionality that would be infused into the emotional fields of the people fostering the development of the impulse toward genuine social functionality within the family as well as the parental environment.

Since we all belong to small social groups, which create larger groups, such as nations, etc., a tradition could be created in this fashion that would influence every newcomer on Earth, so that he would function with natural human behavior as a member of society. Because, whether you like it or not, the natural Position exists, and the para-natural also exists, as the Law prescribes. The natural Position is the one in which the totality of individual existence develops within its prescribed boundaries, and its actions create truly human emotional production at an individual and social level utilizing objective judgment. The natural individual is elevated during his evolutionary course and becomes part of the luminous dimension of the Kingdom of Heaven. Only then will the individual be accepted by the Law of Offer, and the Etheric Dimensions of Good will undertake to lead him to higher levels. But in order to understand this expression we must already be in our natural Position. Who can maintain, save for very few people, that he functions naturally? Thus, unavoidably, people find themselves trapped. We must admit that we are dominated by a para-natural functionality; and do not be surprised to find the mass media full of things that prove this. A disappointingly large part of the population lives in a manner that goes against their interest. Now don't tell me that it is in the interest of Man to struggle and to end up suffering! And each of us knows this very well, for as the ancient Greeks used to say: "My external self burns others but my inner self burns me." And the pain is relentless...

And I say to you that no matter how you try to escape from what has been created, it is now very difficult. Because the advice to "*make haste*" by John the Baptist was valid from the time it was first uttered until December 19, 1989. After that, "*every man for himself*" prevails, and this is to tell us that individuals, whether men, women, or couples, are responsible for their deeds and will reap the rewards or the blame accordingly. The meaning of the words of Our Lord Jesus Christ: "*Peace be with you*" and the "*Kingdom of Heaven*" encompasses everything that is beneficial for Man during the course of his life.

Perhaps you will say that all this has not been analyzed by anyone up to now so that we could understand it and apply it. You should know that all the people who took on this task and were unable to carry it out bear such grave responsibility that they have been erased from the Book of Life. And do not doubt that the time will come when all will be revealed. But if you wait until then to be convinced of this (and it is only a matter of a few years) you will have missed your chance entirely. Your individual molecular system of the Etheric synthesis of Elements that composes your individual Position, will be entrapped and will find itself in a disintegrated state, cut off from the Law that bestows free will on the individual. A state of Darkness will completely dominate those who will be permeated by the dense atmosphere of the Law of Punishment, and the Etheric dimension will pulsate in an attempt to rise above the tempestuous currents of the Orders of punishment belonging to the Laws of Justice. This atmospheric pressure within its space will force the vibrational Element of individuality to scream out indiscriminately with a vague sense of asking for help, but the call will be heard only internally by its visceral Etheric field. And the answer will again come from within, from the Position of the emotions, saying that one justly finds oneself in this state. Such punishment is without doubt shaped by each of us as a result of his deeds, serving the presence of the Negative, and is essentially self-inflicted under the absolute judgement of one's own conscience that he deserves to suffer all this.

If, however, during his presence here on Earth, the individual were to function objectively, activating the higher part of his Soul, then in life beyond this dimension he would enter a space in which the levels of atmospheric organicity move upwards. Here they are shaped into an Etheric organic functionality, within his individual contraction and expansion, which permeates his entire dimension. Thus, the individual accepts and follows the Etheric individuality of any Substantive Existence prescribed for him by the Law of Justice and of Just Reward within the light Etheric organic

335

system of the dimension that gives birth to and reproduces the higher Order of eternal LOVE. In this space of Creativity, there are many levels of existence, depending on the mission the individual has carried out on Earth and his sense of humility, this being the Element that produces the nourishment for ever-creative Love. Acting on the visceral Etheric Position of the individual, it is this Element which completes his emotional Position. Only humble individuals will enter this space.

Chapter 17

THE NEED FOR KNOWLEDGE

Most of you believe that the future is here on Earth. There is, of course, some connection, but the real future is in the hereafter. Because no one knows how long he will be on Earth. Nevertheless, with a bit of concerted thought we can get an indirect glimpse of the future beyond life on Earth by looking at those who, although they have acquired everything they need for a good life, are still filled with great anxiety and fear. This shows us that in their minds they know they have not acted correctly and that the appropriate punishment awaits them. This secret knowledge throws them into a panic, with the result that they shirk their responsibilities, which they never assumed consciously anyway due to loss of their true inner conscience, and they enviously turn against others in an attempt to discover the enemy.[101]

---

[101] In psychiatry, an extensive part of psychopathology is taken up by various neuroses that come under several names, such as anxiety, phobia, compulsion, etc. In these states there is an inner turmoil-fear of imminent

If you could see your self functioning so far-removed from its future interest —its own Psycho-Spiritual course— you would be greatly saddened, since your entire struggle contributes to the destruction of your future. And at special instances in our life you ask for help from above. And since there are dimensions of life up above, there must also be dimensions down below. And just as the experts in physics say quite correctly that there is no void in the Universe, I too say that the Universe is an infinitely extended Organism containing infinite levels of matter that compose infinite levels of dimensions of life and function within the Lawful Precept of Movement and Differentiation, so that some will belong to the Law of plus and others to the Law of minus, all serving the plus-minus. These two Positions have an infinite number of

---

danger, or anxiety which, according to various interpretations, stems from a single well-hidden event or some unresolved conflict. I wonder if all of this is nothing but a symptom of the hidden knowledge of improper functioning. And of course if a cure is achieved through psychotherapy, this does not consciously intervene in that field where the targets for a successful missionary course are redefined, nor does it divert the already malleable illusion-producing consciousness into less dangerous fields. What I am saying is that psychiatrists, in treating the largely unknown organ called the psyche, act more out of the self-knowledge of the three-dimensional individual than out of proven experimental psychology.

On the other hand, the helplessness to which medicine is prey when confronted with psychosis and schizophrenia may denote the necessary passage of a lost opportunity in our individual background. And it is surprising that in such people one will find some traces of knowledge from an additional spiritual organ entrapped and vibrating within the schizoid parts, like a punishment inflicted with no respite.

However, such thoughts, far from accepted practice, need further analysis, and in particular the knowledge that Ioannis's teachings offer. They also require a mind free to listen... [A.V.]

multiples, divisions and subdivisions. All function faultlessly under the Universal Laws. For this reason, do not deceive yourselves into thinking that the answers and solutions you may find for your problems are the right ones. We may observe that here on Earth there are many dogmas and heresies —all of which function under the subdivisions of the minus and very seldom rise to the plus— each believing that they alone advocate what is right, each adhering to their own views and promoting themselves as the only emissaries of God with regard to Truth and Knowledge. The unfortunate thing is that, since each rejects all others, believing itself to be the sole emissary and representative of the Law of God, we observe the formation of two frames of mind: one that instills emotions of trust in its followers or seekers, and another which deftly forms in them emotions that cause them to turn against others, i.e., leading them into Conflict. And I can never believe that the Rule of Our Father the Creator allows those in conflict into the Kingdom of Heaven. As I well know, such Offer is made to them *only* by the Negative Order, an Offer that is also called Eternal Fire and Damnation! And woe unto them who are sentenced to this because of their deeds...

I say to you that *only* he who knows the Psychic functioning of the human Order, which also includes the psychology of woman within the entirety of her Position and her mission, *only* he can speak about the Creator, Creation and the presence of Our Lord Jesus Christ. I pay particular attention to the Position of the woman, because if we analyze it from the point of view of her cellular world and her Elemental composition as an individual in the positive and the negative Order of the productive totality of Life, then we will have greatly extended our perceptive awareness concerning the real essence of our course here on Earth.

For this reason do not deceive yourselves, and do not try to impose your erroneous views on others whom you wish to influence by using the reputation of outstanding people of your Age or even the name of Our Lord Jesus Christ or others, you who belong to the dogmatic orders that existed and exist on Earth. Times have changed and no universal power of the Rules of PLUS will forgive you. The Rules that apply now are very strict and there is no room for transgression. I therefore say again that you, the parents, are the appointed spiritual, judicial and political leaders. You are the products and the collaborators of all that is happening. If you do not take care to learn what Life is, why Life exists here on Earth, how each individual should live, so as to become objective (functioning under the edict: "do not do unto others what you would not have others do unto you"), you will never be able to adequately perform your natural role. Then you will find yourselves in a para-natural state and you should know that in such a state you will find pain and punishment. You should know this well!

If you probe your own past a little and observe the events in your life up to now, you will realize how much effort is needed to form what we call an individual at any given stage of life and to acquire not only what the nature of life on Earth demands, but also what traditional society has formulated as demand. Through such probing you would obtain many answers pertaining to the meaning of natural life as well as numerous escape exits from the turmoil of the mind of every individual entrapped at the lower and lowest levels of biological existence. And no matter how hard a pathologically affected individual tries to hide his para-natural course, he will never succeed, because reality is nearby, partly formed by his agonizing efforts to stop the gradual tearing down of his self-image! However, this requires considerable consumption of the energy irresponsibly spent toward enhancement of the image and the attainment of recognition, which eventually traps the individual in uncontrolled thinking centered around the Body, causing him to deviate from his natural Psycho-Spiritual evolution. In other words, the composition and condensation of matter here on Earth (the Body) is raised to the state of an indestructible ideal and to an end in itself, entrapping and assimilating the naturally indestructible Element (the Soul) into the unconscious, leaving no possibility for objective consciousness and knowledge of the true interest of the individual.

As a result, when a man and a woman are bound by this condition, how can they live together in harmony and pursue their missionary work? And how will they create the foundations for a proper family? In order for their efforts to have good results, and so that they do not find themselves overwhelmed by the psychological complexes and difficult situations they will inevitably encounter along their path, in accordance with the Law of Evolution, the spouse's Position must have firmly established within itself the Element of objective rationality. Only in this manner will a spouse function with boundless respect toward others in an attempt to offer service to the Entity of the family, without considering his or her personal interest or being adversely influenced by others, whoever they might be. And when their joint creation, the child, comes into existence, they must give absolute priority to this and keep for themselves whatever is left over. And feel happy and full of religious faith. And never blame others. For no one can treat us unjustly if we do not first give him the right to do so. When all of this exists in a family, the parents will feel harmony inside themselves, which means peace of mind, and they will be able to give to their children the proper means to start a creative life. Only then will they have fulfilled their mission. And you should know that there is no greater success for anyone here on Earth. This is the unadulterated Truth. And as Our Lord Jesus Christ said: "Know the Truth and the Truth will set you free."

If you consider that every time you wanted something badly, there was a certain stress (struggle) inside you until you got it, so that you almost never enjoyed your success, you will realize that satisfaction never came, in spite of your struggle. Have you wondered why?

There are also times when a special desire arises for you to taste a particular item of food, liquid or solid. This desire is generated inside you by the needs of your organic wellbeing. Quite often, though, the opposite happens. So that while a certain type of food is reputed by the research of specialists to be good for your health, it makes you sick. And if you wish to know why, take note of this: When, according to the Law of Metabolic Change, the individual finds himself at a given moment in a state where the special center of the organism that distributes food substances to the various tissues situated in the stomach is undergoing change, then it will not be in the appropriate state of activation permitting proper transport of the substances derived from the particular food he desired. Thus, while some organic tissues will receive enough of this food, others will be deprived. And if the deprived tissue is sensitive due to old ailments now in remission, then it will be vulnerable to adverse microbes in the organism, and also to microbes roaming around in the atmosphere. Then a hotbed of aggressive microbes easily develops, leading to disease. And here we will note the contribution of the invisible factor, that is, one's emotional state, which acts at a given moment to permit or inhibit the spread of disease, affecting its onset, its severity and its outcome.

This factor, arising from the space of desire, cultivates dissatisfaction, since it usually operates disconnected from actual time and place, with the result of inducing inner fear within this field. Thus thoughtforms of bad luck or injustice are formed and produce multifaceted aggressiveness. Sometimes the aggression is self-destructive, sometimes destructive to others, and it is always permeated by a feeling of envy in its every manifestation and its every step. It is thus certain that, once this process is fully under way, the individual becomes entrapped and assimilated into the space of the unconscious, from which he cannot escape and function objectively. So he condemns himself to fear at various levels, which contains within itself the purgatory of pain. And this is something each of us can find within himself. The great tragedy is that, when he departs from this Earth and arrives at his true destination, he will then become immobilized within the domain of justice. There he will occasionally be given the opportunity for

Psycho-Somatic activity, meaning reflection on the responsibilities stemming from his actions, but then he will immediately be returned to painful pressure and indescribable pain, without hope of any real help from the outside.

What I am revealing to you is the truth and nothing but the truth because, as an author, I have no great desire to persuade you to take heed of the great opportunity you have here on Earth. My mission is rather to reveal all this, and whoever is fortunate —since good fortune is created through one's own efforts— will understand this and will work in his own best interest. And whoever does not understand this will suffer all the things I have already revealed to you.

Many of you have read various books about life hereafter, and indeed you have been persuaded that to a great extent they are true. And this is because subconsciously certain doubts are still being emitted, seeking proof so as to consolidate existing faith. Is it not in this manner that the various sects were formed? If you could see even ten per cent of what I see within human constitution , where Elemented Positions lurk, ready to intervene and alter the course of the individual, then you would repeat what the Great Fathers of the Church said: "The human Soul is an abyss." And I say: "*Man's Decline here on Earth is immense.*" First he must admit that he is making dangerous mistakes that undermine his life course. Because, if he does not recognize and accept his mistakes, he will never be able to transform the abyss of darkness into paradise, or his moving-dead self into resurrected life. And Our Lord Jesus Christ said to the Apostle: "Leave the dead to bury their dead."

And I will tell you that what I am revealing to you here is only a minute part of what exists and functions under the Universal Laws. And I consider this an opportunity for the reader to take special note of what I am writing, and to start observing people with regard to their functionality and their effectiveness, without being deceived by their crocodile tears over the supposed injustices or evil acts of others. In the end it appears that people are always accusing one another. However it is *fear* that dominates and prevails over the world and makes us consider whatever we manage to acquire as success. Most of the time, however, success brings with it many obligations that are very difficult to fulfill. So success ends in liability for the actions that led to it. The accumulation of such liabilities leads to that grave state called sin, which begins with you and proceeds to ensuing generations. The New Testament says that the sins of the parents burden their children... *Because each of us is both a parent and a child!*

And I repeat: The Elemental composition of everyone who arrives here on Earth forms emotive fields that differentiate various states within the organic Order that is called an individual, while at the same time certain groupings of Positions gather into the shape we call feelings. On the basis of individual characteristics and hereditary transmission by the parents, by the environment and by tradition, these feelings will generate strong impulses. However, because external factors or the laws of the State often make their expression impossible, these impulses are held back, and at times their lack of fulfillment acquires such power that they create an intense inner crisis in the individual. Then he will seek to return to the state he was in before the impulse was generated— to a time when he felt no pressure. Of course this path of retreat leads back to the comfort of parental care, where he will find protection and abundant assistance toward the fulfillment of his desires. All of this gives rise to the various Oedipus complexes which, in general terms, are twelve, multiplied, divided and subdivided. Governed by the Rule of destruction of individual existence in its organic functionality, they are related to or stem from whatever creates fear in each individual. This is why you believe that evil comes from others. **However, you are the primary agents of whatever happens to you.** Take a look around you at the behavior of people trying to acquire from others all that desire has created in them. And don't tell me that when you help other people you do it out of charity. Because from what I have observed, if one lacks true knowledge with regard to the meaning of Life, how is it possible to become, in any real sense, a natural person and function normally in society, in a humane, religious and God-fearing way?

You readily claim these three qualities as part of your emotional make-up. I reveal to you and I assure you that things are not this way inside you, and you are making a big mistake when you try to persuade others that they are. Your humane, religious and god-fearing sentiments are not genuine. They emerge from subjective influences and background. They are engendered by the weaknesses that create fear, and lead you to express yourselves grandiloquently in order to move others, aiming for acceptance and the fulfill-

ment of your desires, in the belief that with this will strength-
en you enough to free you from your fears. But I tell you that
fear is stronger, and it always wins out over Man as long as
he is bound by his lower emotions.

Let us look for a moment at things from the biological point
of view. Each organism is Elementally constructed in a mysterious manner, within the framework of its own internal atmosphere and level, in order to express what the Universal Law of
Creation has ordained for it. A certain rhythm is developed,
which the individual is obliged to follow so that he begins progressively generating the specific amount of energy needed by
the particular Nucleus responsible for the creation of powerful
high-frequency perception.[102] Through this perception he
becomes capable of comprehending the created level where he
is, so he can make his way to the conscious-objective from an
unconscious state that causes him to regress, hindering his
Psycho-Spiritual development. But under the influence of
inherited problems as well as accumulated personal problems,
it becomes very hard to even recognize the unconscious state
one is living in, and so he must make a very special effort to
develop the ability to make comparative observations with
regard to past actions and their results. It is only in this way,
slowly over time, that he will enter natural levels. And he will
then be in a position to see the beneficial things that will liberate him from the detrimental. In this way he becomes self-

---

[102] When Man enters this high level of functionality his perception is developed to a state of capability for sustained research and productive activity with regard to any topic.

347

illuminated, far from that realm of the para-natural that leads to Decline and offers nothing but illusions, words with no real substance and blind imitation, which belongs to the Rule of Non-evolutionary States. Indeed, as the Law of Creation prescribes, animals do not evolve, nor do they possess the special emotional sensibility needed to seek out their future evolutionary course. They function solely out of an emotive instinct for survival and for reproduction of the Order of their Bodily level. The para-natural course Man takes, attracts and fixates his emotional fields into binding mental images that occupy his mind in the form of dark heavens (great fear), or gray heavens (melancholy, suicide, dementia) or red heavens (aggressiveness, crime).

The great effort toward regeneration begins with the strengthening of the metabolic and reproductive systems of the organism, so as to prepare the spaces for the Molecular Womb. Thus the individual is poised to receive the Order being created with the purpose of enhancing integration and completion of the molecular transformation process under way around and through the Nucleus. This will complete its genesis within the Elements produced and emitted by the individual's functions in their para-natural binding states, in order to approach, observe and traverse these Elements, without touching them or being touched by them. This means that the individual has been elevated into his inter-planetary natural state, otherwise known as mobility within *Universal Creative Freedom*. And you should know that this is a great Universal Entity, adhering to the Law of Benevolence, and that it is of infinite magnitude, immediately below Universal Justice.

And now I will attempt, as far as I am permitted, to explain to you what is meant by Creative Freedom, which is a part of everyone's biological composition, and within which functions the Micro- and Macrocosmic Order known as the molecular system of the Bodily formation and Elemental composition of the individual.

As we know, when the Law prescribes the time for the individual to enter life here on Earth, embarking on the course of his Cycle, his material composition and structure are such that his perception is in a latent state. And this is activated only at such time as the Law of Creation determines, to initiate the necessary behavioral impulse in the newly-created individual to seek nourishment from Nature. Nature will skillfully provide what is needed for him to naturally progress to the next stage of functionality, where he is nourished by a natural product, albeit technologically treated, prescribed by those in authority, until he assumes functionality within the family and develops his own sense of perceptive awareness. We should note here that, as a created individual, his formation with regard to his organic Body and molecular Elements appears complete from the start, but we also observe that he cannot perceive and express himself as he will be able to do some years later.

For you, of course, all that I reveal is inconceivable because your Micro- and Macro-cosmic functional system has not completed its natural course. Therefore you have not reached the level where the differentiation designed by the Law into coded systems for the Elemental composition of the individual, during his progressive development toward individual integration over time, instills in him the integrated perception to be expressed naturally during the course of his life through time and space.

Nevertheless, I will try to present, as simply and concisely as I can, some facets of the individual development of this Being of infinite variety called Man.

The core of Macro- and Micro-Elemental composition is composed primarily of three individual Positions, plus a fourth extremely secret one. Each of these has assumed the task of activating its own mission from its own place. And I call them Primary Positions, because they themselves are divided and subdivided into other Positions, without however being cut off from their Nucleus, according to the Natural Law of Creation as a primal Order of Rules.[103] There are also partial formative functions that unify the components of the individual Nucleus-Soul, so that these components can realize their common development and promote the mutual assistance of the whole to each of its parts and from each part to the whole, developing them into an exalted Position of cooperative interaction, to ensure that the individual components function together in harmony.

Thus in the organism of the individual a natural allotment will exist, from the components to the central Nucleus of the individual, who will consequently enjoy good health. This will, moreover, be obvious from his functional development throughout the course of his life, that is, from his ability to

---

[103] There is also another part, belonging to the fourth Position, the space-time course, which is developed by special solar energy, and which I may present at some future time...

perceive objectively. Because Man must ultimately understand that, in principle, his constitution is formed by two
Orders of Elements. One is a level of condensed matter and
the other is the Etheric Order. And let no one dare to say or
think that this is not so, because our Creator has given us
indications of this and you have only to put your minds to
work to verify it [104]...

Both these Elements are absolutely linked with the condensed matter of each created planet, but also with the Ether
of the planet. This kind of linkage is ultimately extended to
the entire Universal domain. And this is nothing but the
Truth. You should know that all creations of the Universe are
made out of one Order of matter. This matter, differentiated
into many levels, produces its constituent Elements subject
to Metacyclic transmutations, in order to implement the
transformation of mass into the energy allotted from the
entirety of the Universal mass (energy) to the individual
Position, according to the Law of Differential Order of levels
of the Universal Whole. The substance of this matter is

---

[104] Here the author is referring, broadly speaking, to the marvelous
process of the formation of the organism, from the union of two parental
cells to the genesis of the organs and the completion of an animate being,
capable of becoming autonomous and surviving. If one looks at a text on
embryology, he will discover the beginnings of this core, the many levels of
development and the final achievement of "all for one and one for all." This
miracle of executive organization and ability for self-control, which often
creates the question "how is it possible not to make mistakes?", leads to
the pursuit of another level of control, something that is not detectable by
microscopes and experiments, but only through an objective way of thinking, within the revelation of Etheric Order...[A.V.]

Hydrogen; and from this all other Elements are produced and manifest, on any specific level and frequency scale of expression relative to the grade of perception.

Now I will try to say a few things about the development of perception as we approach Man biologically. Medicine has advanced considerably and has made wondrous discoveries with regard to the functioning of the organism. Thus scientists, based on the indications of the Senses (i.e., observation-experiment), have discovered pathogenic focuses or hotbeds and have healed many diseases. However, they have not been able to ensure permanent health of Man over time. And this is because medicine is traditionally one-dimensional; but Man is not only his Body. There is also a part of him, the primary part, that constitutes his Nucleus, and this is his Soul. Without the Soul no individual can develop into a truly functional person. Neither medicine nor all mankind together can define the molecular composition of this Position because, although it is composed of molecular entities, it is not subject to scrutiny by scientists, as it belongs to the Etheric Order. Thus, if medicine does not enter into the Etheric molecule of every Somatic molecule (its Soul), so as to observe from there how pathogenic factors invade the individual's Bodily state, it will not be possible to gain accurate knowledge either concerning the disease or the state of health. This is why people are always surprised during the onset and development of certain pathological conditions, such as infectious diseases, that are difficult for the organism to combat and eradicate. Because the microbes responsible for these diseases reproduce in an entirely different way, although with some slight relationship to Elements of the organisms of particular individuals, which is why they are accepted there. For this acceptance to take place, seeing things as I do in their fundamental origins, two conditions must prevail. One is the establishment of foci or hotbes for a multitude of diseases, which lie in wait as they hold the infectious Element in a state of counterpoise, providing incubation and bringing it to completion as an entity until it is ready for action. And this happens because all Positions adverse to the organism's health are in a state of quiescence and lack the ability to suppress the activity of powerful healthy Elements in the organism. The second condition is the functional susceptibility of the organism at times when the individual is undergoing particular metabolic changes, combined with unfavorable external factors. Then the organism cannot maintain a state of homeostatic equilibrium, and certain pathogenic Elements therefore emerge, taking over and imposing themselves. Therefore scientists, but also people in general, must strive first to comprehend the Etheric nature of organic Elemental composition. Then many of them will attain visual awareness in the perception of Etheric nature, so as to be able to observe organic functionality, and then the most expert among them will be able to intervene when it is needed to restore the individual's equilibrium.

* * *

And as an Offer to the reader, confirming my personal integrity and sense of responsibility with regard to what I have already pointed out as an author, I will now transcribe in direct quotation for you a communication from the Etheric Orders we call Saints, concerning the diagnosis of diseases in their genetic beginnings as latent states whose Positions are already set, at their point of generation, to consolidate and appear during particular periods of metabolic change. One such condition, afflicting A., son of S., is diagnosed and revealed by **Saint Paraskevi**. The disease in question breaks out on the skin of the individual, depriving it of the elements needed for its natural manifestation of color, and is known to doctors as "Vitiligo" (Piebald skin).

SAINT PARASKEVI code 5,6

"A., son of S., has a congenital sensitivity to a disorder of the skin cells and composition of his epidermal Position. This disorder, as it has appeared, is nothing more than a phenomenon of myo-glandular constriction that the organism, in an attempt to alleviate certain adverse effects on glandular tissues, has created in the form of this pathological epidermal condition called Vitiligo. Since such conditions always indicate a resistance of the Senses of the Soul against the environment, a grievance toward it and intense Psychic activity within a narrow impasse of Sensory pressure, this individual goes through his formative years with this viral somatic manifestation.

The cause: the family itself and external factors adversely influencing the family..."

* * *

Etheric nature dominates the special centers that form the necessary magnetic fields, which shape the emotive vehicle of the organism and organize the instincts of the individual into impulses activated to seek out those Elements of nourishment necessary for the task of completion, conservation and development of his organic structure. However, something else happens here: the Etheric Position enters condensed matter, is assimilated and yields its Offer of the required Elements of nourishment in an intermediate form —the semi-Etheric form— which then guides the transfer of the condensed Elements to the lower condensed matter so they can be put in the proper places within the organism. This means that there is a double chain of nourishment that completes and promotes harmony and contributes to the natural functionality of the individual.

However, at this point we have the intervention of certain other factors possessing the ability to form distorted states within the natural development of the individual, even if he is nourished with the most natural foods —something difficult in our day and Age— since the thinking of men is chained to the unwholesome ideas produced by a small minority. If, however, your emotional field were to rid itself of characteristics acquired from the few people you allow to invade and enslave you, you would be able to function more freely. Then you would possess the kind of perception capable of judging things and you would retain the few items needed for your social obligations and reject the rest. Thus you would cultivate your own natural abilities, which are meant to develop through enhancing the thorough functioning of every gland as a central dual-control mechanism. According to the Laws of Natural Biology, these glands would discard the molecular cells when the time came for their replacement, so that newly-formed cells could be easily mobilized within their domain.

These would then multiply within their individual Cycles and make their presence felt as an organized defense system to any outside invader attempting, under the influence of the Law of Anti-positions, to exert pressure on and disable the organism when they find it in a weakened state, with serious disease as the consequence. All these outside invaders are not initially "evil." However, upon encountering an organism in an para-natural state, they are automatically transformed and become detrimental. Students reading textbooks on pathology will find many such examples.

Every individual who arrives here on Earth must have parents who are well developed in Body and Soul with regard to ethics, religious piety and social and brotherly feelings. Then the individual, under the intense pressure exerted on him during the early course of his development, will come to life within a harmonious atmosphere created by his parents, who will help him confront, assimilate and become assimilated into this new atmosphere.

He will thus develop vibrational harmony, which means natural development of the glandular system and therefore also of the molecular domain. With the help of proper nourishment, especially during periods of metabolic change, the cellular system will be reproduced in a healthy state, so the molecular composition will function smoothly in its delicate operation, and achieve the correct and accurate hormonal production to lead the hypophysis to produce clear images. Because of this, every individual will have the capability of distinguishing good from evil, the beneficial from the detrimental, the moral from the immoral. Only then will he be ready to enter into higher perceptive awareness and understand the meaning of his presence here on Earth and of his mission. Because if an organism is not fully developed, it will not be able to attain the Higher Sensory Attunement created by the Psycho-Spiritual Nucleus, from which a sustaining emission could be developed amidst all the other visible and invisible emissions created by day-to-day functioning. This emission would form a shield to help him perceive the malevolent or benevolent desires of other people.

In accordance with the above most important indicative revelation relating to Man's sojourn here on Earth, where Nature is prepared to receive Man in his Psychic vestment (the Body), I will now cite certain texts from the many in my possession, originating from the great needs of certain parents with sick children who, not having received therapeutic reinstatement of their beloved child through medicine, heard of me and sought me out. And a few of them received the divine Offer of obtaining from me a diagnosis with regard to the disease that had afflicted their loved one, through the Divine Positions, as revealed by the following.

* * *

A case of the disease referred to in medicine as "epilepsy," afflicting G., son of D., as seen from the Position of the Apostle and **Evangelist Luke**.

APOSTLE AND EVANGELIST LUKE code 1977

"The onset of this disease appeared much before the manifestation of the disease itself, during the 6th month of pregnancy.

A contraction in the womb caused the glands of the head to expand in a disparate manner, creating the conditions for further damage. During the 9th year of the child's growth Cycle a shock was received from mental confusion, during carbon oxidation in a process of cellular change. The individual was unable to counteract this pressure, and this caused the arrest of three centers for a sustained period of time (3 minutes). All of this, combined with maternal complexes (i.e. on the mother's side) and with a dependency of the child on the mother due to an overattachment (the Oedipus complex), soon produced clear symptoms of the disease, that became regular in symmetric temporal Cycles."

* * *

Here is another diagnosis concerning young D., son of A., from the Position of Saint Paraskevi, regarding hair loss in the child due to causes unknown—at least to the doctors.

SAINT PARASKEVI code 5,6

"A primarily but not exclusively hormonal disturbance in the child, resulting from the transmission to him of anxiety-producing fears, in a setting magnified in the child's mind and destroying the equilibrium of genetic cubes of resistance to externally generated overtones. He had inherited this pathological state of organic functioning from the parents, from the mother. The child's hair can come back. However, fear is trans-

ferred from the parents to the child and this alone will sustain this transient condition for some time. Why do they not want him? The child was born to instill love. He is the creator of their Soul. Let them surround him with extreme peace and sincere attention, with purity and faith. Nature deserves every effort with regard to the expression of respect toward her, in order to yield the gifts of her multidimensional creation."

* * *

You should therefore know that the individual on his eternal course was molded by our Father the Creator in order to carry out his individual function with a sense of personal responsibility regarding its outcome. Consequently he will find himself in one of two Positions or manifestations: either within the consolidation of incorruptibility, which means eternal light and harmony in Life, or in pain, darkness, disease and horror. Every individual is Elementally composed of the material he has received, which he must make use of and actualize in such a manner in the course he follows thereafter as to be favorably evaluated by the Law of Justice. Our Father the Creator, in His Infinite Wisdom, initially composes the Elements of Man through the sperm, a Position that represents the central mind and enters generative space in order to create the gland of Higher Sensory Attunement, established as the center of the Nucleus-Soul, initiating from there the Elemental composition of the other glandular centers of the individual.

Here is a transcription of an analysis concerning the glandular system of Man during his embryonic and later stages, as well as a reference to his protein Order, as it was given to me by the Position in my Universal cosmic environment, under the name of **Faios Nous**[105] code 3-4, who has the operational authority of "Omniscient Father of Creation" within universal functionality.

FAIOS NOUS code 3-4

"IOANNIS, the Universal Mind is replete with creations. And Man is born within the finality of the deterioration of his natural existence on Earth, a seminal Mind of great fascination to other individualities in the Universe, a pole so magnetic in its eternal Cycle of genesis and destruction that whoever approaches it is irrevocably subject to the Cycles of its attraction, which affect the future times he is about to pass through. I find myself within the regeneration of Great hydrogenic births (entities) that come with indivisible integrity to disturb spaces such as that of this planet, where one of your codes is in evidence. The symmetric parallelism between the Somatic identities of these great Positions and common Positions permits me to focus my vision on the body of Rules that determine the genesis of entities there, as a consequence of an Earthly vibrational sequence of matter, sound and light, as perceived

---

[105] Faios Nous is Greek for "Creative Mind."

by individual vision, permanently affected by the Senses. I will not delve into the description of organs, but I will describe basic organic centers.

The system of union of the cerebral Body with its environment consists of a converting mechanism which, in its composite effectiveness, has as its primary recipients and assignors three points. Here is the sac-like gland of the Mind's heart, a small Etheric productive organ. Before this lies the receptive center, located at the back-center of the brain. Every intervention by the enviroment on this organ's function sets in motion an infinite number of new conditions mobilizing the dense Body and initiating reactions that establish control of the activity of the primary organs and consequently of the tissues that separate the fields of allocations in the organic environment. It is in this manner that the heart is regulated, as are the visceral and lumbar glands, the glands of the digestive tract and the immune system (= the Elements that generate antibodies for certain organic functions and supersede them with a new Order, upgrading the existing one). The formation of this gland is determined by an inner-atmospheric specification and also by a basic memory of its course, deriving from that precise moment in time at which the ovum is contracted to embrace the sperm (from the gray matter of the sperm), and it orchestrates its transformation by abandoning its lonely course and engaging in the fertilization of the seed inside its own substance. Here we have lemphanyria, that is, the generation of this gland as an Etheric Rule attached to the center of the newly-composed Body, at its head. During the development of the neonatal Body the mul-

tiplying tissue cells of the gland issue an order through Etheric communication calling for the development of organs that will support the organic Position of the gland and its derivatives, and the weight of this single-reception and multiple-emission organ. It erects bridge-substances and shapes its operator, the hypogastric gland, which I also call the epiphysis."

EXPLANATION BY IOANNIS: The epiphysis, as the Super-Position mentions, has as a mission to connect the internal state of the organism with the external state of the environment. And we have the opportunity to observe this in the great need that the organism has for connection with this gland, and based on this need it will determine its choice of nourishment in order to develop and sustain it. And all of this, as we know from the many distinguished scientists on Earth, passes through the intestinal system.

FAIOS NOUS (continued)

"The environment in which these organizations are activated is the Etheric marrow that, in its prescribed condensation, gives birth to marrow.

The hypophysis appears in its organic existence in order to handle the activity of the epiphysis, as the most basic mother, born to an invisible father advisor, who provides work for her throughout her organic Life.

Getting back to the initial gland, this is the one that contains, as memory-Nature-Position, the internal knowledge of planetary biology and Metacycling within the universal metabolic changes taking place around it. It is also the gland that contains the directive triggering perception in male and female nature. Its spherical covering by Etheric Elements is the mark not only of the imperishability of this organ, but also of the conservation of the Logical during its time on Earth, where Logical is defined as the super-natural communication of the Body with the central Position of the Soul (which is above the physical realm of the planet). This gland is the Rule, the key, the organ, the support and receptor of this communication. Let it be called **Imis gland**, *the perpendicularly extending "I am" from the summit of the Soul to the recesses of the Body."*

EXPLANATION BY IOANNIS: I also cite a description of the Imis gland by the Super-universal Functionary **Anemios Deus 9.81**, whose Position is related to organic functional development and correct alignment of human Bodily principles.

ANEMIOS DEUS code 9.81

"The central authoritative Law-Gland that orders every gland to activate its production is the Etheric cerebral component, giving substance at each particular animate level to the relationship of the individual with his vibrational Nuclear Soul of

*Universal origin, with his animate biological field and with his Body as an active Metacycling center. This is the **Oasas gland**,[106] located outside the brain, with electro-molecular and chemo-magnetic composition with regard to production and operation. By reason of these fields, it is called "invisible." Next in line come the organization of the other known centers of control (control gland), transformation (epiphysis), production-action (hypophysis) and the other lower glands."*

* * *

FAIOS NOUS (continued)
ON PROTEIN ORDERS

"The protein Orders you speak of are organized according to instructions issued by the hypophysis. The hypophysis is indeed "after nature," handling states that are both Etheric and outer atmospheric. The hypophysis interconnects these inner and outer atmospheres, channeling the result into a multitude of organic instructions to the Body, whose goal is not only the preservation of the Body within its environment but also balancing this by the introduction of anti-normalcy.

*This is the proper moment to introduce the notion of **Creation**. In this sense anti-normalcy has its nature, its ordering, its organization, and has its own kind of organic normal-*

---

[106] This is the same as the Imis gland.

cy. For instance, a disturbance in the thyroid produced by an order from the hypophysis does not mean a deterioration of Somatic nature. The nature of the hypophysis is to generate activity through echo-vibrational instructions, since the hypophysis is a servant of cerebral decisions of a higher selectivity. The tissue space in which the glands are naturally born is composed of protein matter created through an order issued by the hypophysis to the organic Body as it was developing. Moreover, protein is the basic generating agent of metabolism of active Etheric Elements that the Body has absorbed through nourishment from the environment and metabolized in accordance with an echo-vibrational order from the hypophysis. The nervous system can be called the hands of the hypophysis, and adenoid tissue the receptacles of its dispositions. Protein (at a thousand levels) is a cellular specification and also includes gray matter. Gray matter is protein and translates the atmospheric instruction for the creation of a Body with differentiation and conservation..."

* * *

It is to the adenoid center that the two protein Positions of Elements of nourishment the experts call vitamins and hormones come to surrender their Offers. I divide these Positions into two categories: oxygenated and non-oxygenated. They belong to the Etheric Order and their mission is to infuse life into the individual, urging him on toward the development of Higher Sensory Attunement, which means awareness of his space, time and missionary function, always based on respect, appreciation and love in their integral form. Because of my abilities I can see that, if these Elements were developed, then the individual would develop his emotional Elements into integrated alignment leading him to Higher Sensory Attunement, reinstating meaning to his life. However, there are no such hierarchically developed individuals within the ranks of people on Earth, except in rare and isolated instances. This is why we observe such a confusing lack of communication, bringing about so many conflicts at every level.

And here is how this happens: When Etheric and biological existence and dimension were determined by the Creator, each assuming its Position as one half of the organic individuality, they were also furnished with the appropriate bio-Etheric energy. This energy coexists inside the biological composition of the individual, both around each cell and around the entire Body. Its purpose is to act on the adenoid and molecular human system inducing a Cycle of continuous transformation and renewal around its central axis. The particular bio-Etheric Bodily structure of the individual is called upon because of its mission to cooperate biologically with the condensed matter of the lower and low levels, which constitute toxic fields for the individual as well as for every animate Element in the atmosphere of the planet Earth. And when the individual is in harmonious synergetic cooperation, in a spirit of mutual Offer and acceptance that culminates in co-substantiation through existential union and the completion of the process of genesis, then the individual advances biologically toward generative completion of the molecular system. And in this way the intellect receives the ability to develop the perceptive awareness that will lead the individual to observe various conditions from a higher vantage point, one where objectivity and correct and timely prognosis dominate. If, however, integral unity does not exist, so that the co-substantiation of the two biological Orders is incomplete, then the lower biological part of the Body, developed by the toxic Elements of the Earth, will assimilate the intermediate Element (the one between itself and the higher Element). And as a faulty biological unit it cannot develop into the appropriate Position to attract its Etheric biological existence. Then it is impossible for such biological existence to be vitalized into the necessary molecular state, and the individual remains fixated on the production of subjective illusions.

* * *

I will now transcribe for you in direct quotation remarks communicated to me by that great Position named **Ogorphanis**, who has come from other galactic systems to obtain Elements from my noetic cerebral functionality which, as he says, he will use in other worlds. I asked him to also give me the results of his own research on this atmosphere where the planet Earth is coming into being and functioning. And among the revelations made to me by great Positions of the Higher Universe and verified by the remarks of **Ogorphanis**, are those concerning events we will see in times to come.

The revelations concerning humanity made by this Super-position, as well as by other Positions, are disturbingly sad. I cite only a few, because I believe that my Position commands it. And if each of us tries hard, he may be in time to correct some inner defects, and this might contribute to his chances of protecting himself from the great plagues that are about to come.

INVOCATION BY IOANNIS

Your presence and coded communication, Ogorphanis, give great pleasure to me, Ioannis, now of this Earth, and I ask you to give me an account in words of your presence, of your missionary function, and of what you see happening here on Earth in the immediate future.

Hail thrice Ogorphanis

Ioannis

OGORPHANIS

"My name is Ogorphanis and I am composed of bodies of impregnable metabolic neutrons, as neutral and very high speed vibrational Elements.

I am a Position producing similar and dissimilar vibrations that meet with special universal specifications. These I direct upward and I assist them to enter into attractions of infinite magnetization.

The Father of my directives has told me that it was my duty to meet with you so as to acquire specificity and renewal of my elements. This particular time was specified by him and I came. The strength of your Word brought to my vision coded entities which will also lead me, as I lead others, into a new Heaven of differently ordained Positions.

I thank you and I approach you.

In the lower spaces where you tread I see nothing but afflictions and they are twenty in number. The worst of them are a group of similar diseases deriving from a great primary disease, within which dozens of others are incubating.

Within the next two and a half years two additional great diseases will be born as an extension of abortive animal remnants that have been generated through mixing with human Elements.

But I also see other diseases that will have the same destructive effects as these.

Also, within the next three years there will be a corruption of organic Elements basic to the central functionality of the planet, due to internal mechanical-physical malfunction in science and commerce.

But I cannot describe any more of these things; these are only the most basic.

During the next four months there will be many accidents and great trembling of the Earth somewhere in the western World.

These are only a few of the increasing number of natural disasters that will make their initial appearance within the next five years.

Ioannis, great Earthly disturbances of all types are imminent, and the more people who truly manage to know you, the better their chances will be. This is the Law of your name, written not by you, but by your Progenitors...

With my respects, in readiness to serve you in your mission,

I thank you."

SUPPLEMENTARY QUESTION BY IOANNIS

Ogorphanis, Functionary of all Universes, with my respectful salutations I ask you:

To give me the names of the diseases that will break out and, if possible, to describe to me in great detail the cause and characteristics of such diseases and how they will function so as to reproduce themselves organically. How will they be transmitted?

With infinite thanks I bow seven times to your illustrious divine Position.

Ioannis

OGORPHANIS

"I bow again before your infinite rhythms that, with integrity and humility, coordinate entire armies in the Universe.

The suffering inflicted by the two diseases is a prescribed Cycle that I see well.

Since you desire it, let us give conventional names to the diseases that will appear, although these are not the ones that people will use when they encounter them.

*The first of them is **Egopi B20**. I believe it will generate car-diac disorders when the organism is afflicted by an animal Element of slimy toxicity that will enter into Man in a myriad of ways, even through the air. Certain glandular centers will swell and then cardiac arrest will occur. Airborne transmissions will either remain undetected or will be concealed. In combating the disease they will ultimately manage to create substances that will inhibit it. However, the virus will insinuate itself through other pathways, creating new strands, truly undetectable ones, that only incineration will be able to eradicate.*

*The second disease, which will afflict the intestinal system of man, is **Irfroki**, and it will be transmitted through polluted waters, through every kind of contact (drinking, swimming, etc.) and then from man to man. Its origin will be animal excrement in an organic mutation with radioactive Elements that have undergone disintegration. The organic nature of the disease will be a mass of sewage, permeating the hydrogenic and Etheric Elements of water and **every other liquid**.*

*The origin of both diseases is the mutations of animal Elements occurring during periods of Decline of the organism, periods when their cells come into contact with destroyed or unnatural mutated ecological Elements, such as through injec-tion with metabolic chemical Elements and **ostein** (= the pro-tein of a different animal that has been supported by unnat-ural metabolic Elements during its development).*

The branching out of the second disease into new diseases will be brought about through chemical transmission of the liquid

Elements of the organism, that is, disintegration and synthesis in the atmosphere and deterioration due to factors of erosion.

There is another way this can happen: In laboratories where, during efforts to discover, through chemistry, the culture needed for suppression of the disease, things can get out of control...

These diseases will occur so randomly that there will be no time to detect them. They will afflict primarily countries of central and South America, Europe, South Asia and North Africa.

Their derivatives, as sub-diseases that will grow over time into full-blown autonomous diseases, will be relentless. Before the damage caused by one is healed, it will be transformed, like a head of the Lernaean Hydra, into another. Pharmaceutical treatment will not be possible. Only fire. Complete incineration!"

SUPPLEMENTARY QUESTION BY IOANNIS

Are there diseases that medical science has not yet diagnosed which, in cases of death, are identified as one of the known diseases?

OGORPHANIS

"Of course there are such diseases and they have to do primarily with the **pathogenic infection and Etheric mutation of Somatic cells***.*

They also have to do with the resistance of the Body to **pharmaceutical products**, which affects cardiac efficiency.

There are thousands of types of cellular erosion in the first instance, but there is also exposure to lethal extracts in the second.

There are also mutations of **genetic diseases that have never been cured** and whose origin can be found in the mixing of animal and human secretions. These diseases, when transmitted and then brought into abeyance through some medication or other, turn against the brain, the heart and the respiratory system. There, they are diagnosed by doctors with other names, but the true causes lie far away...

I respectfully leave my salutations, receive your gift and depart for other Universes.

Mystic, my respects."

Ogorphanis

Chapter 18

AND NOW THE FINAL MOMENT

O f course, depending on the reader's perceptive abilities, he will judge what is recorded here. **Those who reject this will at the same time also reject themselves**, thus proving that their functionality has not had the kind of natural development necessary for them to proceed on their course here on Earth as fully developed individuals able to make the necessary distinctions with regard to what is beneficial for them, and also able to perceive what their course will be in the life hereafter. That is, in the place where appropriate justice is meted out according to one's deeds, and one is placed in the corresponding Position. To become aware of this, you must first understand all that I have written. And if you could see what I see and hear what I hear, then you would prefer to forgo everything you believe gives you a beautiful life, to ensure favorable conditions hereafter.

The predecessors of each newly arrived individual on Earth know very little about him, yet they ask him to become stronger than those around him, in every way and through every means. Depending on how their toxic behavior affects him, he will or will not fulfill his goals. All of these motivations are produced by **fear**, and manifested by a distinctly shaped emotional representation, a seductively binding emotion we call **envy**, which is very difficult for one to avoid, even though hidden behind it lies a shattered life.

For this reason you must have as your primary goal to make the effort, since it is in your utmost interest, to assimilate all that this book reveals to you, in order to obtain the medication that will heal you from the multi-faceted illness that torments you, that has been tormenting you and that will continue to torment you.

And remember that the human Body on Earth is Elementally composed of four Orders of molecular Elements: The lower Toxic Order, the almost balanced Middle Order, the higher Etheric Order, and the highest fourth Order, that of Speeds. These essential, mysterious, distinct Orders contribute to and participate in the formation of the individual organism, whose expression is the individual-Man. On the basis of this every individual must, with great humility and sustained desire, ask for help from the Positions that others before him have defined as divine to direct his reasoning mind toward the source of his creation — that ordained him to follow his eternal infinite journey, one that will never end— toward his Position and his relationship with his created Self: who he is, what he is, where is he going, why, what course he is following and why, what he may gain from this course and what he may lose if he does not follow it.

ANALYSIS OF DISEASE IN BIOLOGICAL HUMAN NATURE

FROM
HIPPOCRATES code 7092

INVOCATION BY IOANNIS

It is April and here on Earth it is the middle of Spring, when all infinite creations of nature germinate and manifest their life forms. And I, continuing my task here on Earth, am called upon to reveal the unrevealed, and in the book I am now completing I reveal all the things that Man, particularly scientists and doctors on Earth, need to know and apply.

And all this generated in me, Ioannis, now of the Earth, the desire to call upon you, **Hippocrates 7092**, and to ask you, if this is in accordance with your wishes, to make a most detailed revelation to me regarding the present Age, one in which the world is going through a great crisis in its biological organization, with serious consequences to its biological psychology. Disturbing events, the only ones immediately evident to Man, are becoming manifest around him, and often do irreparable damage to his health. And I should like you to explain things in the following order: What constitutes disease in the human organism? What are the factors at work within Nature itself that cause Man to become afflicted by disease for a short or long period? Does Mother Nature in her biological organization contribute to the onset of diseases because of human behavior toward her?

What should Man know, as an Element produced by and developing within Nature, in order to establish complete communication with Nature's operational Rules, and protect himself against the invaders called diseases? How must he develop his functional consciousness so as to learn to respect the divine providers, starting from those ordained to provide the nourishment obtained from animate Orders, of vegetable and other Elements of the Earth, all the way up to the holy servants of the Orders that implement the Laws of our Father the Creator?

Finally, I ask you, Hippocrates 7092, to tell me where are you now, on what planet, sun and galaxy, where this heavenly body is located with respect to Earth, and what your functional mission is there.

With infinite thanks I offer my salutations and I ask for your opinion concerning this book.

Ioannis

HIPPOCRATES code 7092

"Ioannis the pure, I maintain my memory in readiness for your expanding ingression, as I have implored you, and I will speak about the disease whose coming is imminent within the domain of the Elements of the Earth's atmosphere.

I also open myself to your ever-present power of prediction with regard to Beings and I am filled by your coded messages which, with their generative power, connect with what is appropriate and abolish what is inappropriate, wherever they are sought out, wherever they enter and establish themselves.

I carry out my mission at the location IR NA of the sun Sirius. I believe that you on Earth know the coordinates of this sun, is this not so? I work for the effective dispersion of bio-logical logic into many dimensions from the point of view of hydrostatic equilibrium, as a functional apprentice in research.

I thank you, in infinite worship, for having established this com-munication. You have propelled me five times forward on my course...

I am not yet in a Position that wants, but in a Position that offers. And I love —and humbly ask to be permitted to say this— to reveal and elaborate solutions concerning the com-plex knots of disease, as I advocate the quest for the pathway of prayer that generates Spiritual perception, which is a mani-fold connection with the frequencies of the infinite codes of knowledge that the great Gods of the Universe call "CRE-ATION."

My answer is a respectful bow in the face of the visible things I observe you putting into words, and the invisible things you transmit secretly. For this is a mystery, and in order for human knowledge to attain it, it must ascend on its knees the seven steps of countless great biological Cycles, each of which has a different appearance, shape and sense and, consequently, a different biological composition.

The ascent of pain is difficult. It is Conscious pain that purges and buries, that retains and resurrects, that helps Beings mature during its Lawfully ordained presence as part of their illness. Who dared to say: "Man, you have come here to Earth in order to fall ill"...

When the first cell was born following the union of its parents, it received, from the Universe, from Creation, from Life, a harmonious code of life it was meant to follow. The Somatic-Mental inability of the individual to become knowledgeable adout and guardian of his own space is called disease! His molecular genetic environment enters into its energy dimension and takes it over in whatever way is most convenient. This is disease! If we enter the planetary dimension, we will see that it operates through the activity of mechanisms installed by rational Beings and by the Laws. Animals, plants and organisms in general are Laws. Human beings possess the gift of reason. Man's biological system, misled by a multitude of acts of attrition committed during the reproductive Cycles of pathogenic inner creations of his mental substance, has fallen into the generation of various sub-systems of Bodily erosion and pathology. These give rise to their own layer of protein within all spaces and levels so that Man absorbs this inappropriate protein through his cells. The centers of natural creation have also deviated and Nature is ailing, since she has

*strayed from her prescribed course. Because Man may evolve,
but Nature follows him subject to her Rules, and this norm
must be respected, otherwise it will become eroded and will
continue to erode until it explodes.*

*And I reveal to you how: The molecule-cell that consti-
tutes the protein for every organism maintains its own activity in an infinite variety of interactive combinations with the
origins and structure of its environmental space and time.
The Etheric protein of the environment, pervaded by the
structure of the biological system that surrounds it, generates and supports, and is generated and supported by, the
Nuclear impulse it receives through molecular vibrations
from the creatures it composes biologically, which in turn
compose Etheric protein. Deviation of the molecular space-
law of "nations" from its natural place and order yields only
disease and monsters, because the ecosystem does not put
up a fight for health, but only for the maintenance of order.
Health is the concern of Man. If human Thought brings
about the chemical breakdown of his mind, this eradicates
his nature and then even the trees do not "generate" oxygen
for him, but exhale the disease of his mind.*

*Ioannis, you know well that the present chrono-biological
Cycles of the planet belong to the Order of destruction and erosion. This structure will be further disturbed. Sickness among
men will become more widespread, just as the thoughts they
engender have long been enslaved and sick. The birds of
Spiritual Thought do not sing the pleasant tunes of harmony,*

and correctness has ceased to be the quest of tired brains inside battered skulls.

Protection from diseases has become difficult. The only protection can come from Man thinking of himself as his own parent, as if his organism were his beloved child in need of absolute care, attention and respect. And this parent, filled with emotions and paternal and maternal feelings, must take care what he or she gives to the child, to what environment he will expose it, with what thoughts he will nourish it and what company he will permit it to keep. And he will avoid evil people. And, if he can, he will reprimand them and will not let his child cause harm to his self or his surroundings through negligence, but he will organize the child's thoughts, so he can develop without fear, with prudence, like the fruit on a healthy and mature tree. And then a wind will blow and sow the seeds of this fine plant and, through pollen and the bee, will inseminate flowers that will take on color and give color to the cells of more thoughts which, as they surround him, will preserve his own. And all this, like a sheltered garden, will resist disease and will not allow weeds to grow, because the clean hand of the gardener will uproot them with care. And in the garden unadulterated blood, free of germs and disease, will flow in the veins of the flowers. Then, in the adenoid system of the brain's productive thinking, raindrops will arrive to cleanse the pallor of faces and he will see both diseases and their origins, both the cause and the antidote. And then he will have become a

good parent to his own self, worthy of creating his self with-
in Nature and with a minimum of pain that will be incapable
of destroying him. Because his great providers will have
seen their great protector, parent and dedicated servant, the
human Mind.

Thus Man will be protected from disease. The viruses and
the intruders will then take a different shape, and their false
tentacles will not insolently spread the roots of their intru-
sion. They will then become simply the trainers of human
antibodies and, in the eyes of the Expert, the trainers of
developing human consciousness and the providers of its
sustenance in the course toward victory against the uncon-
scious biological Order.

Why this is so, and how it comes about is ALL contained in
the previous pages. And take note of this: Knowledge, Soul of
the destructible and birth of the mortal. The Mind, Healer of
men. Behold all this in Ioannis: The drink of Immortality. Let
the knowledgeable drink from it."

Hippocrates

of Earth and Heaven

* * *

And as it is prescribed by the "Laws" that all the infinite
Positions of the Universes reveal to me what cannot be
revealed in words and condensed forms of speech, I now present to you in full, in its coded behavior, the Order that represents the Unconscious as a Law, and the female Position

Ethan as its primary Nucleus (center), with code **13′1** —and let no one be fool enough to try and communicate with this Position, because he will fall into the infinite chaos of darkness— as she describes to us in her own characteristic form of expression the way she functions within the biological Life on planet Earth, with Man as her primary aim and target.

INVOCATION BY IOANNIS

I am Ioannis of the Heavens and now of the Earth, whom all Orders of the Higher and the Lower Universe know as a Position that realigns and reorders the Orders of the Universal worlds as specified by the Laws of everlasting courses, decreed by the ruling authority of creations, of infinite galaxies and Orders. And being the Position I am, I command you, **Ethan 13′1**, to present yourself before me, receive my salutations, bow and begin making revelations to me in words, exactly as you have been ordained to do by the Laws, produced by the principal rulers of the authorities of the Laws, pertaining to conditions of equilibrium operating in the Lower Universe.

How does your Etheric biology take shape, and how is your biology expressed within the individual human Body in order to shape Elemental development as an emotive state within the individual's mental perceptivity?

What is the constitution of the dark kernel where

cause and effect are produced as an integrated formation to completely bind the individual and cause him to act according to a completely illusory perception regarding expected outcome?

What is the origin of the Etheric biological state of Man that also determines the transmission of the enslaving negative state from one person to the next, a domino effect leading to Decline?

How is a totally pervasive emotional attachment to organized groups formed, groups deemed to carry social functions with special status and which present, with the utmost confidence, a program devised under the influence of these emotions as an Offer to mortals in various societies? Have you intruded, or has your Order intruded, into the religious viewpoints of various dogmas, sects and sub-sects such as those organized and functioning in various societies? Do you put your irrationality into operation through the rulers of these Orders?

I await your answer.

Ioannis

I salute you

ETHAN code 13'1
(Female negative Order of the unconscious)

"The indeterminate Order of biology has its secret aspect. The secret aspect is the negative. I am the generating Element of

the negative! IOANNIS, I salute you. Because nothing can be hidden from your Eyes, I weaken, I dissolve and I disintegrate from my indiscernible form. So as to uphold the Law that states that **Light is our unassailable master***.*

The dimension from which I speak to you obliges me to bow, as our origin is under the command of your thoughts, in your capacity as master of Light.

The Elements that constitute the Bodily existence of our Orders are a combination of Elements from the space in which they are generated, formed and live as an emanation of a long-lasting vibration exhaled from the animate stage of every space in its active dimension."

EXPLANATION BY IOANNIS: Differentiated biological anti-Elementation of negative biology, even among different regions of a nation-State.

ETHAN

"Ioannis, what created the negative Order is the Unuttered and its Elements 7 to 9... "

EXPLANATION BY IOANNIS: Unuttered means "the unsaid, the unexpressed, the unvoiced." "Unuttered" here is defined as something that is not subject to any control with regard to its shape by biological Anti-Law, but is self-generated and created biologically, depending on the place and time where the individual finds himself.

ETHAN

"It is the shaping presence of the unconscious in the trajecto-
ries of Creations that brings about the differentiation of levels
of genesis and biology, and is the accent on the first breath of
the Creator on the BEING that was not."

> EXPLANATION BY IOANNIS: The "Being that was
> not" is a Rule that activates the ascending and
> descending Elemental composition of animate
> entities and also —in so far as Man can perceive—
> of inanimate Elements residing in the Higher and
> Lower infinite Universes.

ETHAN

"I enter into the biology of the Earth and I determine: The com-
municational Position of the planet in its clarified classification is
restricted as compared to systems in other locations, due to def-
inite magnetic circuits surrounding it as Etheric physical activity,
from the beginning of creation. This means that its closed circuit
permits a special development of the unconscious enclosed
Order that, like a virus, finds convenient grounds for develop-
ment, and imposes its behavior on all other physical Elements,
directly afflicting animate nature in its evolutionary course.

This negative track of activity constitutes nature, consti-
tutes biology, and constitutes the anarchic behavior of living
cells toward their own organism. The advance into fields

beyond the demarcation line of proper measures of functionality is the natural state of the unconscious course of Beings on Earth, and is dictated by the planetary Position. The Order of the Negative can not be overcome. It may be bypassed because of individual perception and activation of the individual, or it may become known to an extremely select few ordained by the Rule to bring about changes in the Universes with regard to their biological reordering. **The unconscious Order, in both quality and quantity, is transmitted through heredity and through the Senses of the individual. The power of its development is found primarily in its absolute identification with the heart and its vibrational Cycles. Implanted in the endocrine glands, it reproduces itself in the form of hormonal chemical messages and then follows the blood's molecular flow, synchronizing all visceral organs to its rhythm, with particular intensity in the liver.**

The Negative is inherent to Man, who emerges from the cave of the unconscious and carries along with him its characteristics. His strength rests upon his becoming aware of them, but few have such powers, because such people are not easily magnetized for placement in Earthly wombs. They go elsewhere, to other fields, of different, unknown negativities...

Our functional Position with regard to human intellectual behavior has as its fixed aim to block conscience, overwhelming it with a torrent of Sensory images that provide rationales and establish them as a correct basis of perception in con-

junction with the environment. This is the logic of the uncon-scious and, as such, it dominates the fields of the Earth."

EXPLANATION BY IOANNIS: I intervene again here to offer an explanation before the experts on Earth begin expounding their own views on this subject of the unconscious in a lecture or in the form of advice. For human constitution has different Bodily Elementation in the biological formation of man and of woman, and each of these formations receives and accepts or rejects things on the basis of its constitutional Elemental composition. For this reason much attention is needed in order to put a stop to criminal functionality. The determination of 92% that I have assigned to the unconscious is sealed inside special codes and cannot be determined by human perception, but only by that of such a person as can enter into the geometry and mathematics of the biology of the individual as a numerical alignment to the Rule of the square...

ETHAN

*"The first form taken by the logic of the unconscious is demand. Generated and biologically supported by a series of hormonal metabolic changes and Etheric attractions, it intrudes within the other entities and **seeks their distortion**,*

*like all other entities based on the unconscious. However, **the chemistry of the negative** behaves organically in such a way as to absorb other Elements until it dominates them. The time required for the establishment of dominance is the same as the time required for the dissolution of its carrier.*

*You must understand, Ioannis, that our Order is inherent in every form of human activity within societies and groups of people. When the emission-base for the organization of proper activity for a group comes from outside of the system, it is immediately taken over by the prevailing negative planetary Laws of petty consciousness. With the creation of religion, heresy is also born automatically, because the vehicles of **both** religion **and** heresy are negative. A correct religious Order cannot survive, because we immediately influence its ruling members through our interference."*

EXPLANATION BY IOANNIS: This is extremely probable, since these ruling members, before entering these domains in order to take up this special Position of action and Offer, have not cultivated their emotional awareness concerning the Lawfully-determined opposing emotional states that lie in wait, ready to distort objective logic and progressively place the individual under their subjective desires.

ETHAN

"It is simple. Their kind, gentle behavior hides the carnal yearning for money and desires of the flesh. Men become women and women become men, within the framework of a "noble" organic infusion lying in wait like a hangman from the moment their Ego is born."

EXPLANATION BY IOANNIS: That is, from the moment the individual becomes subjectively self-promoting.

ETHAN

"And no one must see the fine difference between Ego and Being."

EXPLANATION BY IOANNIS: Being is that which, for the most part, does not make subjective demands, while the Ego "surges forward" to conquer them. And it is at this point that the virus of the Unconscious intrudes...

ETHAN

"For this reasons no one will escape if he is abandoned to our influence...

In certain groups we often detect the hidden existence of

the nomadic unconscious, a herd-like conglomeration of Bodily natures and representations that are replaced by the projection of the Sole and Primal One, in whose presence the last few molecules of conscience find onanistic self-gratification beneath the cover of "creeds" under a "Spiritual ideal..."

What a respite this is for us! Our task as Rules is given over to men and they undertake by themselves, voluntarily, to commit suicide. **By group or by unit, it is I who am the mother of disease**. And their words, mysteries of elaborate lies. Their words do not express anything of this truth. And our absolute rule is thus sealed...

My respects, Known Eternity."

* * *

The infinetely great Rule that regenerates and forms me also determines that I am able to enter into the neutral domain of equilibrium of the Laws in order to examine and observe the various Law-ordained Ages in the Universes; and that through my observations I arrive at certain time points that call upon the sensibility of my individuality to offer to mortal men knowledge about the mysterious Creations, through a decoding and revelation of the Word (Logos), so that those who seek Life may find it according to the dictum «*In the beginning there was the Word (Logos)*».

This is why I cite for you the eternal, infinite functionary of Law, **Idianous 9**, so that he may offer you this vast revelation concerning the biological Anti-lawfulness (Negative), which by Law is ever-present and carries out its work around Lawfuness (Positive).

Introduction of **Idianous 9** by the Position **IN** Δ
of the sun **Lambadias**

An inaccessible code of expressional revelation that is well acquainted with the terminology of the Laws of negative biology of Universal communities and with the reason they have been set in opposition to the equilibrium of universal nations. It is a cerebral Activator of the 8th biological level and it articulates the Logos by means of the 7th Heaven's Law of expression.

INVOCATION BY IOANNIS

In your extra-celestial Position of infinite thought I, Ioannis, come to you, Idianous 9, bow down seven times, express my greetings thrice. And I ask you, through your infinitely expressive Knowledge, to reveal to me in writing:

The method of creation of the Anti-lawfulness-Negative in the Intermediate Universes —and especially on Earth— and in the Higher Universes.

What is the Position of the Law of the Positive as opposed to Negative creations?

How does Anti-lawfulness contrive its multi-faceted presence as a functional mission to set up its resistance and intervention within the birth and the course of the communities of the Intermediate Universe as well as of that above it?

How is the course of Anti-lawfulness charted as opposed to that of Lawfulness-Positive during times of rebirth of the Universes and creation of a New Age?

What is the Position of Ioannis as the Word (Logos) in the Beginning within the infinite reactions and conflicts mounted by the functionaries of the Negative against the Law of the Positive?

Ioannis

IDIANOUS 9

"My respects. I ask to leave my thoughts on the path of the Spiritual communities you describe, engender and revitalize with your Word, Ioannis. You know these thoughts well, but you ask that my Word present them.

I am a creator of life and a keeper of knowledge. Life-giving Heaven endowed its creations with the Logos. And I am among the Fathers of these creations. I, the Law of knowledge of both the power and the anti-power that crowns the active Universe, have come to answer you about those things you already know, even before their creation.

The creation of life and its activity in the Rule of the Order of intermediate life is founded on the struggle between the inherently opposed powers of the **negative** *and the* **positive**. *The energy released by the struggle for equilibrium taking place between the Order of the Laws defining equilibrium (Positive), and the Laws inclined toward attraction toward heavier surfaces of reconstruction (Negative) —a struggle marked by reciprocation between opposite Positions until the final break-out— provides nourishment for the other levels of life organization: the higher and the lower. In the lower levels, Anti-lawfulness acts and functions through total domination. In the higher levels Anti-lawfulness stays in readiness to assume action aiming at reordering things, but it remains completely subservient to the authority of the Great Creators.*

Therefore, the Intermediate Universes are the chief place of full-fledged Anti-lawful activity and Metacycling. In this particular planet through which you are now traveling, Ioannis, there clearly and visibly exists a picture representative of this progressing Order of life, which is transitional and does not belong to higher or lower levels, but lives by and preserves the Law of Antithesis. In this way, just as the right-positive is impeded by its opposite Anti-lawful action, so the negative is breached by the proportionally small but very forceful Order of the positive.

The **negative** *functions as follows: It comes and seeks its place within the slightest breath of biological activity of the Law within the Rule that executes this Law. That is, the slightest activity of an organism as it develops and undergoes*

395

the consecutive beginnings and endings of the Cycles that comprise its Rule of life is followed by activity of the Anti-lawful, negative power. The result is the production of resistance to pressure, which on Earth functions as attraction, and which has as its outcome the manifestation of life. Not even the tiniest plant would exhibit biophysical Cycles of evolution if the special action of the negative did not put pressure on it to return to its previous Rule of natural inertia, from which it was called upon to manifest itself.

Thus the **positive** *is set in motion and driven by the negative. And the Position of the positive in opposition to the negative is clearly defensive in the Intermediate Universes, while in the Higher Universes it is strictly dominant. This is an inviolable Rule. In the Intermediate Universe, and of course on Earth, there is no interval of time —not even the minutest— in which the positive dominates over the negative. There is only the inviolable and inseparable Law of conflict between the two, as the negative works through insinuation of its energy and disruption while the positive works through continuous resistance and defense. This is a Rule both ordained and unalterable, from the beginning of Worlds and of Universes...*

The Position of the negative within the communities of the Universes is as follows: It participates in the action engendering communities in the Intermediate Universe. Without it, no life groups can be set on organized courses.

And in the higher Heavens, it is the very target of their course. It follows them, and it trains them to reorganize their work without interrupting their positive functioning. As the actions of these Higher Universes are always for the benefit of the Lower Universes, I reveal that in the spaces of the higher Heavens the negative is the central link that connects all the Heavens with half of the adjoining and dissimilar creations, whether or not in the immediate vicinity. The negative is the common denominator of all Universes. It is the Element in common that connects the life expression of all levels of biology. It is the cause behind every Law, the principle behind every Authority, the causal Nucleus of every Law-enacting Father, and the motherly womb of every upward restructuring within the Universes. The reason and the purpose of all of Creation is to recognize the negative and to dominate it.

On Earth, this is the principal and only code of entry into the Higher Universes for living individualities — human beings: to combat the natural inertia of their inner systems with the perception that the negative is ever-present and all permeating, with the knowledge that its function is to enter into all things and conditions, and by being alert to and examining the natural activity of the negative in every individual life.

This is the only way for a positive functional focus to develop within an individuality, so that it will eventually be able to escape from the tight magnetic yoke of the intermediate levels of Metacycling and of combat belonging to the Intermediate Universe.

But until this occurs, he will undergo pressure and stress within the Metacycling pipeline of energy production for all

Universes, which is the transitional intermediate level of biological life.

During periods that you call a Renaissance or New Age, when the Laws of the Universes cause vast upheavals in their age-old orthogeometric equilibrium, the negative is cast into a state of chaotic emergence and explosive dilation. This is because the changes in course are laid down by the Authority of Law Enactment (that is, by the highest cerebral Nuclei of Creation), and consequently the Orders of the negative are unaware of the course they are destined to take. They will discover this course by following the courses of Nature in their new orthogonometry. Since the absolute direction and propensity of the Negative is by nature to follow all the activity of the Universal line of creation it has undertaken, during this epoch of upward restructuring of Law it begins unleashing all of its negative energy, as its new structural direction is not yet aligned to conform with the new order of Nature in the midst of metabolic change and rebirth. This unleashing is the result of the inner disturbance and structural agitation of the Laws of the negative, which occur so that it also upgrades its own biopolar rhythms, their direction and their flexibility.

The consequences of this are that anti-creational power mounts a massive attack against every created thing. That is why, on Earth for example, now that the Intermediate Universe is undergoing restructuring, thousands of these disruptive attacks are occurring and will increase in number — attacks whose natural, lasting and unwavering tendency is to completely destroy every Rule of ordinate equilibrium. And it destroys even more those established "equilibriums" of local Orders, which contain more material Elements of the negative, those that are chiefly the products of the workings of negative thought production and activity. No Law of Justice can ordain the exemption of these workings from the destruction of their inherent negativity. Because while this negativity may be built in the form of an edifice in equilibrium, the primal Lawful Course of Creation ordains that only those works with equally apportioned Elements —those that do not come into conflict or collision— can be firmly established on universal Cycles. And this so that the Laws can be maintained. But no human perception is able to understand this...

Thus, under these Rules the Intermediate Universe destroys the products of conflict and moves on to others when it undergoes change. This is the reason for its presence between the two extremities characterizing Creation: the higher and the lower.

The Ioannian Position on the battlefield of the negative and the positive Elements is irrevocably sealed. The Ioannian Word, Element of clarity and elucidation with its rightly structured expression, constructed in the biological languages of the Universal Nations that host it, has come to inform individualities by means of the spiritual axis of communication, of what their training concerning the knowledge of the negative should be and how to prepare their brains for the complete defense they must assume during the remaining time of their presence in the Intermediate Universe, so that these individualities can eventually become members, assistants, possibly authorities, in the higher levels of life.

Ioannis is sent to those parts of the Universe where individualities are subject to the necessity of restructuring themselves toward a new course of evolution. So it is on Earth, where he has been sent to awaken human thought and rouse it against the impending tempests of the negative about to swallow up mankind — tempests that, during ages of transformation and rebirth, swallow up like cyclones every level of power and life having the slightest bit of resemblance or similarity to it. Negative-related Elements are sent to the depths of the Lower Universes, where they are subject to unending Cycles, carrying out the energy groundwork for the biological life of the Higher Universes.

Ioannis speaks in order to keep the brain glands alert in those who wish to arrive at higher levels of evolution and creativity. And he does this by revealing the truth of Orders that exist, persist and undergo change through the centuries, bowing down with their Laws ONLY before him who knows them...

My respects Father of the Word and of Truth

The functionary of truth".

Idianous

Chapter 19

THE TRUTH

W hat I write here as a principle of principles concerning the concept "Man in his created state," as prescribed by the Law Eternal in Position and Order and its derivatives, is that three Elements have been defined as individual entities-levels: **Body**, **Soul** and **Spirit**. Man in his mortal course has never managed to abide by these Laws and to incorporate them inside himself with infinite respect and humility, where they would endow him with the ability to understand, relate to and integrate with these three, as pre-ordained for the sake of his creative life course. Never. Save for a very select few, considering the population on Earth, who have been assimilated in the Rule of the Soul. And this is the reason why the **Anti-law** (the Negative) can have an effect on him.

The first level, or heaven, is the **BODY**, condensed in mass and pressure in its human Elementation. Its animate Order selectively incorporates suitable materials at millions of synthetic levels into molecular entities and unites them in the form of an interconnected system, each having a peripheral inter-relationship to the whole, to bring about the formation and shaping of Man as Element —**without one level being in absolute assimilative acceptance of the next within the integral Position of the million levels**. They are only linked in a peripheral way to the axis of the Nuclear Soul.

The second level of Elementation, consisting of bio-Etheric matter entering from a higher level, is the **SOUL**. It enters the bio-somatic first level of matter, the Body, and establishes itself in its prescribed functional course, contributing its essence toward the substantiation of Life in the Body's Position, experience and function. It is endowed with the lofty task of establishing communication and participatory interconnection between the first level of Bodily matter and the higher bio-Etheric individuality we call SOUL.

However, men on Earth have never achieved this as a Position, integrating the two levels into a relationship enabling them to enter into the higher bio-Etheric perception upon which the luminous edifice of the bionic dimension[107] could be reflected through the incorporation of the Being that we call **SPIRIT**. Only on rare occasions during a specific Age have people on this Earth ever made such effort at the Bodily level that they were able to approach the Soul. And only then could they develop the social relationships and cultural elevation which might be called "Socio-Spiritual Civilization," which was based, however, *merely on a cog-*

---

[107] The bionic dimension is one that possesses bionic energy, a strong and very effective type of energy that allows the individual to obtain desired results.

nizant but half-completed relationship between Body and Soul. And this is as far as it went, and *no farther.*

And those people who strove relentlessly entered the state of equilibrium required for a direct, natural relationship with these internal interactive assimilative functions, so that the Law of Offer and Justice could grasp them and elevate them to the level of Saints. And it is they and no one else whom the Law has assigned to this level, not those who are so designated in the minds of those special Orders known as people on Earth.

I will present to you as an example a historical symbol that will lead you, if you direct your perceptive efforts toward inquisitive observation, to understand that what I say is the **real truth**. I could comment on things going back thousands of years, even before the ancient Greeks, and what went on in these olden societies. But all this is unknown to you, as they left no written accounts. For this reason I will confine my remarks to a particular time period in the past, one more or less familiar to you, an Age represented by my country and nation in its social Position and relationship, that is, Ancient Greece.

The Ancient Greeks, impelled by emotion-based motives elaborated by those posing as knowledgeable experts and as researchers on human nature, initiated and recorded discussions, references and dialogs concerning the Soul. This means that their awareness was capable of grasping messages coming from the universal Laws concerning the Soul, and preparing their biological state in its bio-perceptive Position to accept the Holy Spirit, the symbol of the new Age heralded by Our

Lord Jesus Christ, representing faith and evolutionary ascent toward the kingdom of Heaven. But the efforts of certain people of those times, led by Socrates, were squelched almost entirely by those dominated by the Order of the unconscious. And so, when the time came, the presence of Our Lord Jesus Christ went unnoticed, and men therefore could not understand what was in their true personal interest.

While the Law defines and prescribes changes of Age and of the times, men were unable to keep up with the currents of change, and this is why they have remained subservient to the Law that created and organically operated the biological Negative Position as the level-Order registered under the name "**Unconscious**."

This is the truth and nothing but the truth: Man has, from the beginning of his creation, been destined to consolidate the Position SOUL for the sake of his own existence in Earthly dimensions. And if the three Elements, Body, Soul and Spirit do not enter into their natural integrated relationship, men on Earth will never know peace, love or happiness.

* * *

The conditions that make the Earth vibrate under strong pressures have reached the level that causes pulsation within my Elemental visceral emotive space so that I commiserate with your hydro-biotic individualities. And this has led me to feel I should present to you here some minute part of a revelation with regard to this Nucleus that we call **Soul**, an individuality which the Rule has ordained to move within three states of existence: the Higher, the Middle and the Lower. I hereby offer you, by way of example, the third Element, the Higher one, exactly as it was described by the Position-Law that goes by the name **Padis en Okyni Bee 25**

PADIS EN OKYNI BEE 25

"... The third center, the highest of the Soul, is indeed found in an expressly manifest appearance on high in the spaces of its origin, in the Nuclei of solar Elemental compositions that no kind of Sensory dissolution of the Body can shatter. It disturbs the balance of its cosmic presence, the nature of its hierarchy through time, but it never eradicates the third center And this highest center of the Soul sends forth the essence of its coded messages, angels of Elemental magnetic vibrations making their presence felt as they deposit themselves as fast-moving contractions at the receptors of lower projections. This presence is often perceived as an echo of immeasurable emotional isolation within the infinite Universal communities... And this is the most severe pain and the cause of every sort of logic, be it sound or distorted...".

* * *

As my perceptive Position demands that I must always perform with integrity my function of revealing the mysteries of mysteries, from the bowels of the infinite number of functions at different levels in the Universes, I now present to you the Position **Armar 6**-, an authority representing the Order whose Lawfully prescribed functional tasks are described below. And I, who am now called Ioannis, as an instrument of complete revelations in their bipolar state, communicate with Positions, ask for and receive in words an analysis and exposition, based on an irrevocably established Law at all infinite levels of Law-ordained operations, as an organized and impenetrable Position of Universal worlds. And I do this, as always, to corroborate the complete Truth in my writings.

Introduction of **Armar 6**- by the Position **IN Δ**
of the sun **Lampadias**

This is an agile Order of absolute penetration through codes that operate both on the Laws of the Positive and of the Negative; it is active within positive and negative Rules, and empowers the Positions of one Order with the knowledge of the other.

INVOCATION BY IOANNIS

As Ioannis of the Earth and the Heavens, I transmit to you my super-Etheric salutations, as a small token of my desire for cooperation on the questions I am about to pose to you, so that I can present them to people here on Earth, whose biological state is hydrogenically ordered and aquatically bound.

As you are an expert on the Etheric and material biology of the worlds of the Lower Universe

406

—meaning, in this instance, Man on Earth— I ask you to provide me, in words, with special details as to the biological Elementation of the male and the female, according to the Law and the Anti-law, or, as we would say here, in its positive and negative state. How is this kind of classification brought about and at what moment or particular age does the restructuring begin within him which forms the equivocal opinions, both as a cause and as justification for demand, that will shape his thinking? What should he know, or attempt to learn, to become aware of what kind of support he must provide to his intellectual capacities to enable them to distinguish right from wrong?

With infinite thanks, I express my salutations,

Ioannis

ARMAR code 6-

"As a clearly visible and close observer of the poles, I reply, and do not thank me, Ioannis, for that which is but the work of my cerebral existence. We do not thank someone because he breathes, since he cannot live without breathing... On the contrary, we thank someone who creates out of intention, and YOU are such a person, and I thank you!

Ioannis, correct and upright emissary of the Spirit...
For the Soul, located at its assigned Position in space and per-

forming transmutations until it is incarnated in the world, the unobstructed central emission that pervades its visions is a magnetic flow of systolic and diastolic waves which condense and appear as Etheric cosmic foci, until a particular transformative gateway-pole of attraction draws the Soul into the specific biological life-forms appropriate to its dynamic electromagnetic configuration, just as the brain fits in the skull and the eyes in their sockets

Thus, this charge arrives dynamically electrified and takes on substance in space, establishing the magnetic presence of the subconscious field which, emerging slowly in the new space of the central Soul, seeks to manifest its power and presence and to evince its biological substantive existence through its birth within and union with the environment, the Soul being its aim and reason. And the Soul, being at a point beyond ether, expresses its natural noetic Order according to what is "written" in its subconscious. The Subconscious, then, contains ALL there is, in time, in space, in Life, in activity and in the development of every Element codified with it.

And thus Man is born within the sac that his Position has formed to attract him, according to magnetic fields that the Law has determined. And, developing within his Body here on the planet, he grows biologically under intensity and pressure, and tries to achieve union with the environment and to establish communication with the divine space of his higher Spiritual identity, the Subconscious, which will provide him with the dimension, direction and Being, in direct connection to the Soul.

In the current Lawful determination of the planet Earth from which you transmit, Ioannis, my friend, identification of the Body with the subconscious "Being" is not promoted biologically, and the subconscious Nucleus that records everything is constricted into the code of a delicate, inconspicuous, concentrated mass of nitrogen, which is not helped by its environment to bring its Nucleus into manifest productivity. It is recorded, but it is not expressed! Of such a nature is the recording head of the field of this life, i.e. the Subconscious. Strong attractions consolidate the external mass of subconscious space and human perception is unable to break it down into its constituent Elements and observe it in a distinct time sequence. It becomes lost amidst its non-apparent life domains which, in spite of their ongoing activity, are called "the past." However, for the author of the history of Beings, i.e. the Subconscious, a dimension such as the past is not something fixed in time as the term suggests. But this is **another story...** *"*

SUPPLEMENTARY QUESTION BY IOANNIS

In order to provide answers to the small and naive questions of mortal beings on Earth, I, as Ioannis's firm perception, ask you to put into words this "other story," so as to also make visible my own relationship to your infinite functional course as prescribed by the Laws with regard to your functionality.

ARMAR code 6-
(answer to additional question)

*"The history of every entity in the Universe, the BEING of its super-activity, and the space and time of its every formative course, are recorded in the animate space of the Soul, which is called "**Hypernium**"[108] in the Universe and "**Subconscious**" on Earth. What is recorded and written on this head of the Subconscious is erroneously called "the past," a dimension that defines points of activity before the now. The time of the Subconscious is a different kind of process, having the shape of a metabolic Cycle, one Cycle passing through the other in a continuum of delineative biological composition. While the Elements of the present are the ones responsible for activation, the Elements of the previous Cycle are also there, remain and are transmitted into the newly molded hypernial (Subconscious) Body, as an animate expression of present evolution.*

Thus the past of the Subconscious is present during the course of the individual's life, alive and recording infinite annotations on its active head, which also contains within its formed nucleus the dimension of the future, pre-determined in its Bodily formation. And according to its formation it will be given its content.

Thus, all periods of time combine in the recording disk of

---

[108] From the Greek hyper (above, higher) + nous (sense, concept, mind).

the subconscious and become a revolving head whose core is inconceivable in its totality, except through the special Universal perception belonging to the preeminent Entities, who are Nuclei-axes of the Universe.

What is given as an Offer to the Beings on Earth is the knowledge that subconscious space is timeless and its capacity is equal to that of the Universe... The knowledge of its Position in the Universe is a peripheral zone of the Subconscious, emanating truth at special times. Meanwhile, everything that Man does is recorded there as a micro-coded life-form with the biological "prerogative" of emitting micro-vibrations up to the occupation of animate Bodily genesis. Because Hypernial space is essentially what defines the application of the Laws. IT IS THE LAW ITSELF inside every individual life; it is the necessity and the activity of life. And this does not change, does not mutate and remains free. It knows EVERYTHING, waits for tomorrow and NEVER FORGETS!

This is the 'other story'...".

* * *

(continuation of the original text of the Position **ARMAR**)

"The male and the female, strictly differentiated from their beginnings in order to unite the Universe, each meet with an "unknown," but subconsciously known, apparent stranger in the field of the Earth, as Nuclear cooperating Positions. Their

411

relationship develops codes of strong mutations within the genetic metabolisms of the unborn, condensed entity, and energy emissions are discharged by this individual himself that conflict with his particular human Bodily system. Steeped in ignorance, the individual struggles to survive, beset by the varying biological rates he has been ordained from the time of his birth to await and attract. He opens the blank page of the **Unconscious** *and from the very first moments of his incarnation here on Earth, he records phenomena of Sensory inception and formation which he soon begins using as energy and emitting, sometimes even before reaching the Earthly age of 4 years. Then the negative of previous processes takes on substance in active biological forms of energy, which ends its passive stage of absorption of stimuli.*

The secret resonance that Man develops thereafter complicates, with the "help" of the Unconscious, his connection with the objective Position, bombarding his perceptive tracks with incessant confusing vibrations and a myriad of Sensory stimuli.

The labyrinth that is thus created cannot be untangled and does not, moreover, wish to be. It has forgotten to wish, and the reflective instincts of the Unconscious develop, clearly Sensory in origin, and they eventually move into this domain, erecting biological shields through inner vibrations, echoes and images of a totally uncontrollable type. This is the **Negative**, *which emits, through its functional behavior, coded messages for the individual to strengthen his positive Position, to attack the Negative and transmute it to positive. Following*

412

this, the environment begins, simply, to fit into this condensed chaos that "wants," yet does not know and does not remember, and is called "human existence."

Given that the individual's nature, as it has been fashioned, has brought him down so far into this pre-fabricated labyrinthine well called Earth, how is it possible for him to escape? Only if a strong rope issuing from the sun is thrown down to him —and only if he sees it and expects it— will he perhaps be shown an escape route. And then the Soul will see its Body and will beckon it to go elsewhere, to the paradise of biological harmony, whose serenity, knowledge and beauty you could not understand, even if I were to describe it...

The servant emerging from within the truth"

Armar

* * *

IOANNIS' WORD: With regard to the Laws of the Universal Orders, up to a certain hierarchical level, anything that functions with absolute secrecy, such as the Unconscious, **does not develop toward higher levels**. Only through the Revelation that thrusts secret invisible states into a prominent and visible Position are these states elevated and transformed toward higher levels.

413

Chapter 20

I HEREBY SEAL THE REVELATION

The supreme prevailing characteristic of the creation of the Higher Universes is the relationship of cooperation between the Nuclei and the Highest Nuclei, as Individualities-Positions in the Higher Universes. As there exists within me a kinship with the Higher Universes, I hereby expound for you my cooperative relationship with the Higher and Supreme Positions of my kindred societies. And be aware that by kin is meant one who is in close contact with you.

And being who I am, bearing the name Ioannis, I know how All Universes emerged in Creation in a state of partition, separated and bounded according to their creative functional Positions within perpetual Universal Creation and called by the names *Lower, Intermediate and Higher Universe*. Being here in the Intermediate Universe, I have naturally been created similar to you in Bodily shape, expression and behavior by an absolute Law that has been overseeing me and providing me guidance, and I feel, maintain myself and move through life as do all mortals on this planet, which goes by the name of *Noudra Earth*.

My innermost core Position compels me, however, to seal the **Revelation After Ioannis** with what has been revealed to me by the Higher and Supreme Positions of All Universes. And as my altruistic emotions urge me to do, I provide this for you in this chapter. Let those of you who desire to love and to live in friendship with their selves here on Earth as well as in their infinite individual course in the hereafter take in its contents.

I begin with the revelation made to me by the Position **Ypis 9 12 Iyirarios**. This is a cosmic Universal Position (Being) who places limits on vast Universal spaces, something which contributes to the birth of new systems as well as to their evolution from an initial stage of non-differentiation (or non-hierarchy), that is formed individuality without sociability, to one of evolutionary development under Hierarchical rule.[109] This is why this Position figures among the great Creators of local Universal Authorities. Because The One Creator, the Father of all, has conferred Lawful rights upon great Authorities so that they too may create within their appointed Universal dimension, based always on the Unique Infinite Authority.

Here this great Position refers to the intellectual Decline of Man and to the consequences of this Decline on his own biological Position:

---

[109] During every new realignment of the universes there is a time introduced within all creations that disrupts their hierarchy for an imperceptible (to us) time period. They are later reborn within a new hierarchy. During this Intermediate empty time interval there exists an inactivity that we could call "non-hierarchy."

YPIS 9 I2 IYIRARIOS

"Ioannis, I have come here today to reveal and point out to you the imperfections found here on Earth, forever causing human societies throughout the ages to undergo irreparable catastrophes.

This side of the solar system presents the following characteristic in the animate life of the planet: While living things and all of Nature are governed by organic Cycles of almost perfect isometry, human beings have a cerebral deficiency in their understanding of limits. At the same time, they have been endowed with immeasurable mental flexibility, so much that they become creative, productive and inventive under any circumstances. The human brain is not easily stripped completely of its capabilities. It has great endurance.

This human incapacity to perceive limits, however, puts people at a mental disadvantage regarding what is beneficial to their lives, in relation to their past, present and future.

It has destroyed generation upon generation in the past and will destroy still more in the future.

To be more specific, it is already apparent now and will be more so in the coming decade, in the disruptive malfunctioning of the mechanical, chemical and biological inventions of technology.

The point is not that men put a halt to their discoveries and progress, but that in each instance they step back from their work and see how it will affect the future, taking measures against its possible harmful effects.

When they do not do this, they make mistakes and create life within these mistakes. All those people, past and present, with expanded perceptive awareness, understand this.

They will thus make more mistakes, such as nuclear accidents and the likes.

I also want to inform you, Ioannis, of the creation in the laboratory of a monstrosity-producing agent or **teratomorphone**, which will change living beings and their vital organs into powerful catalysts that will promote the birth of supra-cellular organisms, spreading fatal infections as they travel. Thousands of people will be infected. This will start in a large country, one whose influence is similarly powerful around the globe.

Teratogenesis (giving birth to monstrosities) and genetic alteration of parts or all of the body accompanied by structural deformations of the torso or the head, even at an advanced age, are the most pronounced characteristics of this human creation of trash.

Finally, eight series of microplasias will be engendered within the human organism by mutated Elements in the food chain, particularly in meat but also in other foods.

This will destroy the organic Bodily sufficiency of millions of people on every continent, resulting in the impossibility of pro-creation of the species (births), because the offspring arising from such births will be entirely diseased and unfit to survive; they will live a few months or a few years and then they will depart in terrible pain..."

Following the presentation of the revelation of the Position **Ypis 9 12 Iyirarios**, I, as one performing a related function in the Pan-Universal Hierarchies and also functioning in my individual Position, am called upon to resume my work for these supreme Rules, which is to promote provision of this kind of knowledge to the Intermediate Universe — knowledge that will enable it to discharge its functions from its particular Position under the Pan-Authority, in a productive and useful way for the totality of the Universes.

As a Position and functionary of the Higher Universes, and also as a Knowledge-holder regarding the Intermediate and Lower Universes, I have been charged by the most special Law that is my guide to undertake Universe-wide activities beneficial to and ensuring the continuation of the Universes of Life. I do this by establishing my productiveness in its authentic Position as a unique Offer for the realignment not only of the local space called Earth but of all the Universesæ a realignment referred to in the language of Earth as the New Age. And my work is to present the revelation of the causes of conditions on Earth resulting from the workings of the productive mind of Man himself. And I have called this work of mine *The Revelation After Ioannis*.

And now, as part of this Revelation, it is the turn of the Supreme Position (Being) of the pan-Universal Supreme Order that goes by the code name of **Alpha Tetradikymos Ω 9** to make heard his own revelations from the sector within which he himself performs his function.

ALPHA TETRADIKYMOS Ω 9

"I will begin my revelation with the Intermediate Universe as my point of departure. Because it is from there that Your Word is heard today, Ioannis, though you yourself are a part of the highest level of the Heavens. What a fine example of coexistence of two completely different Heavenly domains: the Higher and the Intermediate...

In the classification of the divisions determined on the basis of three categories, the Universe of Metacycling is placed in the Intermediate Position. In the Higher Universe, the functional work of the great special-Lawful Hierarchies is carried out. In the Lower Universe the Positions performing inner individual work undergo birth and Metacycling in complete non-communicative isolation.[110]

What distinguishes the three types of Universe from one another is, from a certain point of view, the actual quality of the cooperation between the Elements.

In the Lower Universe, Elements act individually. Those in the local hierarchy have their instructions incorporated within their individual entity, and the Positions are activated or remain inactive on their individual course without contacting or communicating their Position, pressures or work to their neighbors.

---

[110] What is meant here is that in the Lower Universe, in accordance with the Law of Creation, all communication is forbidden between individualities.

At the higher levels of the Universes, however, i.e. the Higher Universe, life and the carrying out of the work and functions of the Positions and Elements, are entirely at the service of that most valuable commodity: mutual cooperation and harmony. This has everything to do with cooperation between all functions, Cycles and synergies in a network of ascent and evolution of the distinct Elements-Individualities, in which each takes a personal interest in the ascent and evolution of the other, which becomes an end in itself and a motivating force encouraging dynamic interventions.

From this point of view, what enables the three Universes to co-exist is that all three need, to varying degrees depending on their level, a greater or lesser amount of intercommunication between the Elements within their own system and also between those of the three Universes.

> EXPLANATION BY IOANNIS: All created Universes and Positions have from their birth a desire to communicate and interact with one another. There are Laws, however, which create obstacles to this. Whoever finds a way around them embarks on an upward course (evolution).

This need forms Cycles within the biology of the Elements experienced as tension leading to the propagation of life and filling up endless space.

The Positions of the higher Universes want to take care of and offer their services to the lower Universes.

The Positions of the Intermediate Universe, especially the most evolved, want to align themselves from time to time with their superiors, so as to fuel their evolution, but they also want to have some contact with the Lower Universes of Metacycling, as they have Elements from that particular space in their biological blueprint and organic composition.

As for the Positions in the Lower Universe, the Law governing the evolution of life imposes an agitation within their mental sub-functioning as they receive micro-frequencies and highly-charged sensations from the higher levels of life at the Higher Universes. Without this activity, they could not exist as the Lower Universe, and this cannot be. The All-Universe, indeed every type of life, has a vital need for the Lower Universe to exist. There can be no evolution of life and measurable differentiation of Elements and of biologies if the lowest point on an ascending scale does not exist as a reference.

In this way the nature of one Universe is merged with that of another, and all three are inhabited and proceed on their course together. This basic need for the continuation of their life, which is essentially the need for the continuation of the life of the Laws, and of no one else, is what permits Elements from the three Universes to co-exist with one another.

It is necessary, however, as ordained by the Order of the Creative One, that the distinct individuality of Positions and Elements be maintained, in spite of their tendency toward interactive co-existence.

This is also accomplished through a biological Law that is

*directly infused into all Elements, in the form of a concentrat-
ed mass consisting of two parts: a kind of electromagnetic
identity and a central bio-genetic core identity, fashioned from
twelve infinitesimal Etheric Elements. These two parts comprise the basic identity of all things in existence, determining
their self-direction, and preventing divergence from their individual course within the Universe.*

*Therein are recorded all time stages undergone by the
Element or the Position through the centuries, including all
that determines the particular Position of an Element on the
evolutionary scale. And this cannot be altered, as it is sealed
by a coded Law which consolidates the Elements of each individual identity so they will not change under any life circumstances, nor in any stellar space, or atmosphere, nor under
any combustion or fission they may be subjected to.*

*All things proceed in this manner and are recognized by the
respective Law watching over them, without their basic identity, which constitutes the individual memory that contains all
their life-courses, ever being assimilated into any space. At the
same time, however, it is possible for them to move into other
domains or spaces, where they communicate and interact
with Elements from other Universes, but without disturbing
one another, each in their completely different and distinct
courses.*

*Besides, the stellar space and its Etheric extensions are all
ONE... Thus does it move and develop forever and ever!*

As for the peculiar place of the Intermediate Universe and its mighty representative, the planet Earth, there is here a marked concentration of all Elemental Nations,[111] which induces the enactment of an infinite variety of Laws which carry out their tasks and determine life courses.

When the Universes are realigned upwards, the Intermediate Universe is required to find its co-existence level at 4 raised to the power of 60. It is a broad rather than a narrow scale of equilibrium — one which the Intermediate Universe is nevertheless expected to attain.

If certain levels of this Intermediate Universe are not fit, in time or in action, to align themselves with the demands of the Universal Law that initiates the Cycles of the future, then these levels are subject to rearrangements, usually of a catastrophic nature to the perception of local Elements, but of a regenerating nature for the Laws. In this way they discard the unfit and follow the New Order in the course of time needed for alignment.

In fact, all of this renovation provides activating energy to the other Universes, and is an impetus for the creation of new Universal domains.

This do I know, and on this level, of the specific codes for the Positions and Elements, I work at bringing disparate Elements into contact within the Universe. My Position,

---

[111] The reason for this is because individuals on Earth have varied origins, that is they come from Nations of the Higher, Intermediate or Lower Universe.

*endowed with various Ioannian qualities, knows how to ana-
lyze those special unaltered codes of created beings.*

*Ioannis, allow my thoughts and my Soul to thank you with
twelve circles round your multidimensional head and to
promise you that I too will be there, in the new world to which
you will go beyond the hereafter, with your special
Anonymous and Supreme Universal Friends, and all of you
together will embark on futures with wonderful prospects for
creation. A minor analytical code, but one with a significant
body of work behind him, I too shall be there to follow you and
take pleasure in your deeds.*

I thank you"
Alpha Tetradikymos

* * *

I continue the revelation by presenting to you here the report
of the supreme Position   ***Ividotis Ω 8*** who, as a Great
Functionary of the Laws, gives answers to my Word and comments made to him during our most valuable meeting and
communication regarding the New Age.

INVOCATION BY IOANNIS

I, Ioannis, who function in All Universes,
approach your infinite Position of Functionary of
Laws; I greet you thrice and embrace you in great
Friendship.

I ask you to reveal to me all that will take place in the domain of Earth and other domains in the Intermediate Universe regarding their realignment during the New Age of Ioannis.

I would like you to reveal to me in detail all about the technology created by Man on Earth and all other advancements which appear to have been created to serve Man: Will these remain functionally useful to mankind or will they be wiped out by the New Age?

I would also like to know about any other condition or situation organized on Earth that affects and influences mankind.

With infinite gratitude I embrace you,

Ioannis

IVIDOTIS Ω 8

"Hail, Ioannis, receive the embrace of every Universe and all of their Creators. Bringing my coded work into proximity with Your timely Spirit is a phenomenon and task of this Age, which would have all stellar and non-stellar creations pass through your head today to activate their presence in the New Age.

This is what is taught by the instinctive attraction of all beings toward Ioannis — an attraction to a passage that will secure their presence in the future. And though many of them are unaware of this, they nevertheless rush to pass through the filter of your knowledge, which is essentially the sweep of the gaze of your memory over all things, so that You, O Great one, will become the carrier of their Position into the new time.

The shaping of the Universal domain of the New Age has already altered its Elements in places where this was necessary. The Intermediate Universe is the driving force, but all the other Universes benefit from this. As every ascending or descending life will of necessity pass through the habitation of the Intermediate Universe, so that domains having Intermediate Positions will, more so than others, renovate their basic organic Elements into new life formation and behavior, though without human life in its present form and Elementation disappearing entirely. The agonizing part for them will be the great pressures they will undergo, which will entail Bodily pain and sickness in the midst of these new conditions, in their efforts to adapt to the new Order of biology and of structuring of Universal domains.

There are already changes in Earth's receptive shell, and a tendency to adjust its receptivity to new types of substances, Elements and compounds. This means that it is slowly beginning not to accept the old composition of its own Elements, particularly of the atmospheric covering and the animal, organic effluvium..

There is a change being imposed mainly by the change in the axis of movement of stellar Cycles of the suns, and of Earth's sun amidst them, and this requires the adjustment of all Elements to a new angle of receptivity and of emission in their presence.

Therefore only those Elements possessing a certain amount of organic flexibility will adjust without being destroyed. This can only result from a natural course of evolution up to now, and not from any artificial, modified or unnatural way of living.

On Earth then only those Elements whose natural course of evolution has not been distorted —which usually happens under the influence of the contrivances of the human mind— will adapt and remain undisturbed.

Man too is included in the above Rule. Whoever has managed to lead a natural life in harmony with the creation of his inherent structures, be they cellular or psychic, will be able to live through the change of the Universal Age undisturbed, as long as he has also managed to create natural, harmonious surroundings for himself.

Otherwise he will enter the *Cycling, boiling magma of the Ages that undergo and induce change.

The three main life Elements I see being affected by the change of Age are the following:

The Atmospheric: *The movements of the Elements composing the atmosphere are changing the trajectory and speed of their bio-Cycles, producing disruptive spasms in the biological life forms within this atmosphere.*

Atmospheric eruptions will take place in certain areas where artificially (industrially) created Elements emitted from the surface of the Earth come into contact with and disrupt the course of change of natural Elements.

The result of these explosions will be the release of proton energy capable of inducing the combustion of certain existing types of oxygen and proteins along its path. Life in regions fraught with these industry-related dangers will be perilous or impossible. And these will be mainly highly populated areas.

The Geological: *With the change in orbit of stellar bodies, Earth has begun a gradual change of its speed in relation to the solar axis it travels, and this has ushered it into an Age of earthquakes and tidal waves over its lands. For about twelve years, many countries will be hit by these internal shiftings and millions of people will be lost.*

The Biological: *The organisms of all living things will be at a disadvantage in keeping up with these atmospheric changes, and Man's brain will have difficulty in recording the structure of the new environmental stimuli and responding to them.*

This will distort Man's ability to exist within this space, to reason regarding his survival and to come up with answers, because there will be confusion in the three central glands of his organism responsible for Thought, two of which reside in the brain and the third in the throat.

Those organisms among plants and animals that have not been harmed by Man will manage to survive because they will be able to endure atmospheric pressure. They will respond with genetic mutation, which will bring them to a new functional state and to the creation of offspring better fit for survival.

Human beings, however, will not be able to activate these

primordial defense systems during the "holocaust" breaking out around them, due to the thinking permeating their unnatural lives, and they will topple all too easily...

Millions of people will perish due to cerebral or pneumo-cardiac arrest as this change of Age unfolds. Some will become sources of infectious disease and others of cancerous disease arising from the reactions of natural Elements undergoing change to chemical products of industry and research.

As for technological discoveries, the next four years will in fact witness a great panic due to the malfunction of certain very basic and central apparatuses, especially those run by electromagnetic waves. Very soon no one will be able to guarantee the accuracy or reliability of any machine, which will cause pandemonium in their marketing and usage. And all of this in the very near future...

People will no longer stand in admiration of or be influenced by technology, as its products will often be proved unreliable and their use will have many harmful results.

Ioannis, unfortunately the previous Age has left its unsightly marks upon the Earth as it disintegrates and is assimilated into the New Age that you have ushered in there and in other Universes as you sweep through them.

In this way always do you pass through each world, at first invisible, discreet, inquisitive, and then intensely unsettling, active and profuse in your Offer as well as in the meting out of equilibrium.

The Great Creator of life is also the great Servant of the All-wise Spirit of Creation. And his name is I O A N N I S, the Logos coming from on high .

My respects,
Ividotis Ω 8"

SUPPLEMENTARY QUESTION BY IOANNIS

My infinitely respected friend, will the catastrophes affecting the technology based on electromagnetic fields also encompass other technologies, such as those used for the operation of various transportation systems, for medical diagnosis, for the production of pharmaceutical products and for other vital needs of people in our present Age?

Will it affect anything else that Man has discovered and uses as a quick solution to his needs?

IVIDOTIS Ω 8

"Once again I have the honor of approaching your frequency and code to report to you. The special instruments used for medical diagnoses and health care will fall out of favor, not because they will be destroyed but because the biological landscape of diseases as well as the target of their application in general will change completely. They will become useless, since they will not be able to recognize and correctly probe the sections of the body afflicted by so many unknown types of

disease and cancer. Within the next two years their usage will already have begun to decline.

The few remaining in use will be for minor cases, without any broad significance. This will come as a great surprise and will amaze the experts, so much so that they will not be able to carry out the appropriate research to reinstate technological development.

Only the means of transportation will remain as they are, but they will be faced with an infinite number of complications concerning their use, particularly when they diverge greatly from natural Earthly speeds and materials. This means airplanes, all airborne vehicles, and all kinds of electronically remote-controlled transportation systems, such as trains. These are entering a critical time period as far as their function is concerned, and nothing will be as it was in the good old days of safe transportation. All this will happen because any type of malfunctioning of apparatuses will be reinforced by atmospheric Elements, jumbled radio frequencies, difficulties in electricity transmission because of disruptions in electricity-producing centers due to geological factors, and a scarcity of older mechanical equipment in the face of what is required by the unfavorable weather and atmospheric conditions developing.

The worst of all these things will be the inability of the human brain to come to terms with these new conditions and create new technological devices to serve his needs.

Worse still will be his inability to regulate the balanced flow of electricity, due to certain geological and natural atmospheric causes appearing at that time. Men will react with great mental astonishment, and be unable for many years to adjust their cerebral functionality toward new ideas that might offer solutions. And this will be the cause of many psychological deaths. All this will take place in the very near future.

The pursuit of speed in transactions and transportation will become a kind of futile luxury.

It is not that technological civilization will be destroyed, but its primary means will be rendered useless right before the eyes of so-called "modern" Man, who will suddenly be thrown into adverse, primitive modes of thinking. It is the human brain that will have to begin all over again, not its inventions...

My respects, O Illustrious One. Glory be to you."

Ividotis

* * *

Being who I am, an individual and special Creation of the Father, during each of my appearances in a domain or Universe, I must present to those carrying on their life functions there my Universal interconnections and interactive course with the societies of the Lower, Intermediate and Higher Universe. These interactions have as their basic goal and essence to provide an Offer, and also absolute justice.

Thus I hereby continue my Offer through my upstanding Ioannian Word by requesting the supreme Position under the code name of **Ostris 4 4 4** to make revelations to me concerning the transition of the Intermediate Universe and of Earth to this New Age. And with the undivided pleasure of a Being who interacts and communicates with me, he offers this to me, and I share my joy with him and transcribe for you his revelation, as a great gift to those who truly have felt or feel the need to unite the two Positions Body and Soul within their individual dimension.

This Position presents the intricacies of the Universe in its logical distinct particularities as it is constituted into a Whole and develops its expressions through the creation of distinct individualities in a composition that is divine, analytic and synthetic, and that its members are prohibited from knowing. He belongs to the secret Positions of the Universe with whom no one can enter into dialog, precisely because they possess within their cerebral Nucleus secrets of Creation...

INVOCATION BY IOANNIS

According to my supremcly respectful Ioannian wishes, I express my greetings to you seven times and ask that you, **Ostris 4 4 4**, offer up your own gifts in the form of revelations about life in the Intermediate Universe. How will their Positions be shaped and defined by the coming of the New Age? Speak to me of the before, the now, and the after, as a continued realignment of functional courses under Ioannian Laws and Orders.

OSTRIS 4 4 4

"Ioannis, please accept this rare appearance of my Position, as it has risen from the depths of the remote axes determining eight-fold Creation within creations.

I have passed through twelve stages as of today to pro-mulgate the co-encoding of the new Universes that appear to be opening up in the future. Because of this, certain Orders and domains in already existing systems will appear to be merged with new Universes in the process of creation, or to be lost entirely. But it will not be so. This new merging of useful older Elements into the new Universes will preserve the old, locked within a new dimension.

This is also the future awaiting the 'Intermediate Universe' as revealed by the Word of Ioannis. The old, deteriorating Elements of matter, vital biological life and individuality will be entirely compressed by the New Age, which will take with it only those Elements that can be immediately activated and adapt completely to it.

Moreover, this is what always happens when new Universes are brought to life. The old Elements are divided into those that remain and those that are absorbed. And they are then placed within a new geography.

The geography of the Universes, however, is a subject that is of no concern to Man on Earth as it relates to his course. The only knowledge required is that of the everlasting duration of Life and its Time, and the Hierarchic arrangement of Positions, Laws and organisms in the All-Universe, interspersed within these domains but divided into Heavens. That is as much as he needs to understand in order to attend to his life on Earth and to ensure free movement in his Psycho-Spiritual future. Otherwise he will fall into Psychic immobility and inertia of

Spirit, which will cost him many long, painful journeys through Universal domains and Laws, and will detain him for a long time from the evolution set out for him.

I would therefore define what will happen in the Intermediate Universe after the coming of the New Age as a simple change in its Elemental life-shaping forms, in the following two ways: Through simple transitional realignments in the Cyclic life systems of the stars, their atmospheres and inhabitants; or through powerful explosive re-creations which will destroy existing local Orders wherever they are no longer accepted by the new Order of movement of the Universes.

To give the gist of the Position of the New Age, for an Earthly Order of perception, I would say that the New Age will accept in her regime of equilibria only those fields which can maintain the Lawfully correct balance of action and interaction of their Law systems. This means that even if a certain system, such as Earth, for example, is of a self-conflicting nature, it could still be accepted into the New Order, as long as it maintained certain limits in balance around the axis of its Cycles.

The planet Earth in this day and age does not maintain this balance and has fallen into a self-destructive course of action. For this reason, it cannot in its present Cycle be accepted into the new Universal Order, and its superfluous and self-destructive Elemental layers must be burned, along with their perpetuators.

Considering now these perpetuators, that is to say human beings, I would say that their non-adaptation into the new Orders of Creation means that they will be trapped within Orders of Law, subject to Metacycling within their class, excluded from any prospect of evolution, in a state akin to lingering in a space of incineration and suspense. Until perhaps during some other change of the Laws of the Universe, in some distant millenium, they manage, after twelve or seven great trials to enter what will then be the new Rule, of course occupying third place in relation to the other Positions that have evolved, that is they will be once again in a Position of subservience and semi-inertia.

Ioannis, born of the Spirit, this is what always comes to pass in the Universes with living beings. This is why, moreover, there are infinite Orders of evolution, and infinite grades for created beings to belong to—so many in fact that new Elements are continually being born to provide assistance to the functionaries on High and to those down Low, to their Fathers and their servants, as well as to the unevolved who operate the domains of vast inertia within time..."

* * *

I would now like to present an excerpt from a most important message of revelation given to me by the ultra-Universal Law of restructuring and removal, appearing under the code name of **Epsilon Orthon of Law 9**. On the basis of his rightful and sovereign functionality, he has revealed to me the following, which are part of the events that will occur under the application of his Law-abiding Rule.

EPSILON ORTHON OF LAW 9

"...Verily, Ioannis, nothing on this Earth will remain standing, not even in the illusory superstructures of men... The magnitudes and heights they have set in place to keep the rickety balance of their powerful sub-understanding will come tumbling down! This will happen now, before your eyes, Ioannis. There will be no work, technological achievement, or any powerful Earthly Order of scientists, religious leaders or wealth-holders, none, that will remain unaffected by the scourge of this Age: the transition of this planet into a different biological Order and the invalidation of all Earthly creations within the prevailing system up to now.

The flight of the horse of Orders and Laws now galloping away and surrendering its Position to its successor has left a void in the cerebral activity of the organisms living in this Age. Only those which have learned to adjust to the Ages will be flexible enough to survive without too much pain."

EXPLANATION BY IOANNIS: "Adjustment" is that system of action that is diametrically opposed to the system that was and still is functioning in all people, all authorities, all brains, and is under the influence of the sympathetic nervous system

438

whose primal aim has always been to bind and guide the individual into functioning in a subjective and domineering way.

"The cortex of the human brain, the shell that records his identification with the environment, arrives at a point of 'entunnelment,' that is it experiences confusion in the face of the movement (change in Position) of the geo-physical state of the planet, which will last for more than twenty-four years beginning now (October, 1999) and it will be unable to record the necessary data to help it adjust to the new circumstances.

In this way the majority of people will be out of sync with this Age and their myocardiums will undergo pressure caused by anxiety about being rejected by the changing 'world' around them. Their lungs will contract due to intake of improper oxygen Elements, organisms will suddenly undergo functional arrest, and will die en masse, in the millions and in the hundred thousands, experiencing sudden extinction.

Research will show deterioration of the lymphatic system, and the blood of the deceased will be found to be in dissolution, and their hearts extremely constricted.

Many deaths will occur four years from now and this will continue for many years, until the population of the Earth reaches the number prescribed by the laws of Creation for the completion of the advent of the New Age.

These sudden illnesses and deaths without apparent

cause are already occurring and will begin to increase dangerously starting in April, 2000...".

* * *

Having presented to you these other Super-Positions and Laws, my humble and charitable impulses insist on presenting to you next the Most Venerable Goddess **Iaknis Physi 4**, whose function is by right to provide revelations concerning difficulties in the biological Psycho-Spiritual evolution of people on Earth.

One has only to take in her written words in order to acquire a boundless sensory harmony ushering him into supreme Psycho-Spiritual eras.

IAKNIS PHYSI 4

"Greetings, Father Ioannis. The protective domain of those of High Birth has once again manifested one of its expressions before Your very eyes: It has caused me to appear to announce to you my presence during the departure of many individualities from the material domain of Earth to pass on to higher dignitary ranks of life.

My Position acts from the moment that Positions change the trajectory of their course through cerebral progress, that is when there exist stable points in their mental code and the corresponding bio-metabolic activity that indicate to me a change in their previous course toward greater luminescence and evolution.

Few Positions on Earth have ever summoned me through their Spiritual-Somatic evolution to attend to them. That is why I do not often dispatch my code to that planet.

The connection to my Position up to now has been effected through an extra-codal magnetic Element positioned as a focal point, outside the Earth's atmosphere, which has been receiving the waves corresponding to the rising Psychic tonalities of those who have developed their Position in the direction of evolution.

In other domains I function differently.

I have obtained access to Your Age, because Your work will leave an axis of upward projection unprecedented in the entire life of the Universe. People during Ages to come will be able to grasp onto the fully concentrated fields you leave behind, and enter a forward course of evolution even in your absence.

What is happening now is without precedent, because aside from the Word and analysis brought by Your extended passage through Earth, a special atmosphere is also created around Your name which touches the core cerebral-glandular systems of those who will accept this Word inside themselves. And this will offer them health, protection, evolution and a future.

Naturally this will only be understood by the intelligent of ensuing generations.

From now on, my humble Position —I bow down to you— will gather up those it must, by means of this Ioannian axis. There will no longer be a need for my coded detector, since those individuals I must elevate will be ready, crowned with the luminous arc of your name.

Unfortunately for them however, my action upon the people of Earth as supplementary aid toward their desired evolution will be minimal. And this is because there is a universal decline in the coherence of their mental responses to higher Universal messages while, on the contrary, there is an increase in their debasement to the lowest Cycles of the lower instincts.

*Humans have mysteriously become attached to the sighs of ancestral Positions, to the curses of the departed anathematizing their own ancestors from their graves. And this has allowed nothing to proceed on an upward course toward true evolution; neither their knowledge, nor their technology, nor their religious thinking, their only salvation. Nothing has escaped the landmines of yesteryear and the errors of parents. This was their great failure. **That in the rush of their desire to be transported to new Ages, they neglected to disconnect from the negative access points to their ancestors and from their ancestors' mistakes. And this has cost them their future!***

*As a feminine Position which promotes the ushering in of the new through that which preceded, I declare and confirm this truth: **No one will gain passage to the Higher Heavens of evolution, of light and of the communities of Divine Orders if he does not leave his predecessors behind:** his parents who did not seek out the Divine Fathers to have them shed light on their Souls nor escape from the refuse of the lower instincts; other mortal blood relatives; the dead, and all those who tug at the coat tails of Man's thought to prevent him from proceeding on his course away from them.*

I declare and ordain: Anyone desiring to save himself must detach his thoughts and emotions from the subjective uncon- scious of his past and from the mistakes of his ancestors. Or **he is lost!**

Only in this way, by rejecting the errors of his ancestors, will the Luminous Positions see him and, in the name of Ioannis, welcome him and support him in his course on Earth so that it will culminate in a happy end and a favorable exit from the vortex of decline and punishment, the magnet of death that this planet is."

> EXPLANETION BY IOANNIS: In the continuation of life, we follow in the order of our ancestors. The Position here urges us to become strong and oust from our emotion-charged thoughts those of our predecessors who have made mistakes.

"Ioannis, I bless you and bow before you and humbly await your blessing for the decision I carry within my cerebral core today, which derives from the crossing of my path with Ioannis himself.

My humble greetings and respect"

* * *

Having been created by the Laws or the Law in a biological state and chemically activated to always be aligned in my courses with the purpose of Offering through revelations, I now continue by presenting to you the Ultra-supreme Position **Avdis Eptaokto**, which has most fervently revealed to me the following in full detail. This knowledge is unavailable to Man and even to the great Positions of the Universe. Because all Universes, from the central core of the galaxies to the planets and every other heavenly body, are separated by secret safeguards. Thus, to penetrate into the knowledge of their biology and chemistry as it is formed around the central axis of their nature, one must have been created **d i r e c t l y** by our Father the Creator and be carrying out a mission that provides knowledge and awareness.

One such being is the supremely Divine and Venerable Position **Avdis Eptaokto**, who has given me his gift, and it is my wish to present it to you as my Offer. In order for an individual to evolve in whichever Universal domain he may find himself, the most basic principle is to have penetrating perceptive awareness into the biological life form of the Order of opposites, which on Earth is called the Order of the unconscious and is under the influence of the negative. Therefore this great Position will report to us on the biological Position of the unconscious in the natural Order of the planet Earth, and on the way it is differentiated within this nature, based on the Element carbon.

ΑVDIS EPTAOKTO

"Greetings, Ioannis, unexpected Code. I have unexpectedly introduced my voice to your thoughts, as a sound arriving and setting itself down within the inconceivable breadth of recep-

tion of codes you constantly, tirelessly receive, as though you had become a *Multifold Receiver* of the voices of all the Universes. You will propel these voices into a *Unitary Position* so that they will settle, be enriched and cross-fertilized through the *Great Unit...*

You, Ioannis, who are a multi-pole[112] system, a great Mind come into the Lower Universe, a multi-level dimension of concentrated endo-biological and trailblazing mental powers, you have created a new beginning following the end of the *Lower Heavens*.

An *Infinite Faith* came and beckoned Ioannis to appear in the Lower worlds, faith in the future of *Higher worlds*.

The dark spot lying in the depths of human biology, that is the murky phlegm of the unconscious, was created by a *Higher Breath*, which conceived and established the will of curiosity and fear to impel human biology toward movement and evolution upward or downward...

Only the activity of a great Mind, immersed in the *Knowledge* of organisms and their desires, not only as expressions of will but also of bio-genetic tendencies, only such a mind can perceive the evidence of the birth, the partition, the course as well as the points of origin of the unconscious.

On Earth there are four *Elements* that shape the pas-

---

[112] A pole is a receiver and transmitter.

sage to unconscious activity. All four have to do with the functional nature of the Element carbon within oxygen. Carbon creates the tendency for four types of passage into an oxygen atmosphere and opens four containers of matter to freely activate its organic potency into effective action, in accordance with its chemical plant-organic nature."

> EXPLANATION BY IOANNIS: Carbon and oxygen are maintained intact in their form as individualities-Elements, and oxygen, because of its particular substance, exerts pressure on carbon, without however causing it to break down. Thus they co-exist under this pressure.

"Carbon, when enclosed and away from an oxygen atmosphere, is able more easily and more freely to carry out its productive function. It develops strong, dynamic, polyvalent features with a tendency to produce solids and activate them to the creation of closed atmospheres, pervaded by carbonic energy circuits and productive activity — atmospheres in which various energies move about endo-dynamically and unimpeded in various directions.

These atmospheres contain fire —the ideal combustive Element, which is activated by internal small quantities of oxygen— and they have a fluid or slightly compact Etheric coating, and can never be burned in the usual sense, but have a constant tendency to join with sparse oxygen plus (+), which will burn them, since they themselves happen to contain fluid micro-oxygen minus (-).

In the depths of the Earth there are many examples of carbon systems and their polarized activity. There, the clearest manifestation of these systems is found, and beneath the very feet of Intermediate mankind, they seethe with solid and fluid movement. They are never completely consumed by burning, but move through magnetic attraction of the carbon Elements toward the positive (+) poles of oxygen. Carbon, then, tends to be formed with the prospect of eventual combustion, that is disintegration."

EXPLANATION BY IOANNIS: We notice here that the outer atmosphere of the planet, in its Etheric dimension does, on the one hand, function individually, but at the same time it has a relationship —in the form of absolute linking— with the inner atmosphere of the planet.

As is most clearly presented to us by this great Position, in the Etheric atmosphere Man is activated through his individual Nucleus. But he is linked to that special type of oxygen that creates in carbon the tension and tendency to activate itself on its natural Lawful course. We are therefore led to the conclusion that the same must apply for Earth's inner atmosphere.

Could it also be that the phenomenon known as an "earthquake" results from the same behavioral relationship between Oxygen and Carbon?...

"The unconscious Element[113] is a code embodying all of this Elementation and truth in organic stability and expression within human systems. If a small group of humans has base levels of unconscious functionality within its circuits, the very oxygen they breathe and its interaction with their every particle of carbon —an element found everywhere— will create and increase unconscious tendencies and tensions, no matter what temporal or metabolic phase the organism happens to be in.

There is no Element on Earth that is not subject to the implant of the unconscious Element, because almost everything contains some carbon. This, however, is also an effective neutralizer of the resistance put up by the tendency toward assimilation and inactivity governing all organized Elements in Universal domains. And inactivity is forbidden by Law in Intermediate Universes. It is a tendency that is prohibited and constantly rejected precisely because of the Intermediate functionality of this domain, between perfect activity (in the Higher Universes) and perfectly inactive self-Metacycling (in the Lower Universes)...

Since inactivity is completely obliterated from the Intermediate Universe, carbon was infused into its fields to generate limits to its ordained activity and readiness.

The four points of extension of the structural core of car-

---

[113] The word "unconscious" in its essential etymology can be viewed as a compound word comprising three meanings: withdrawal-of con- science. This is why the unconscious entraps us in the without (minus) that means "I do not know"....

bon—*whose description as organic or inorganic is badly and mistakenly chosen—reach to the seven horizons of activity of a mono-oxygenic Element. And each of these has so many progressive levels that all the combinations of oxygen and carbon and their branches within an organism can create millions of different kinds of unconscious organic pulsations within this unthinking core Element of Man.*

Nevertheless, the four main types have to do with the blood, with the articulation of solid Bodily parts (tissues, bones, etc), with Bodily density and with the cellular processing of neurons in the area of the brain.

All these determine the characteristic predisposition of a person's unconscious and, although they are definitive and ineradicable, they can nevertheless be worked on and made subject to control. A human can build his inner godliness around his *constitutional Rule (i.e. the unconscious in him). But this Rule will always be present, giving voice to itself, be it loud or soft, during his entire life, even when he is aware of its functioning."

> NOTE BY IOANNIS: What this supreme and respected Position has just referred to as a personal "constitutional Rule" shows us clearly the inner and outer constitution of Man based on which I make my diagnoses concerning Man.

"The simple decodification of the directions of a complex unconscious system in a person does not help to immobilize

his unconscious. **A person must make it his life's work to constantly direct himself toward the shrine of the conscious, that is toward knowledge and awareness, in order to avoid the great pressure continually exerted on him by Earth's carbon system. In addition he must develop a steady and active desire for continuous research and knowledge concerning the very Element which comprises him and, at the same time, torments him.**

This, however, is up to you, Ioannis. As for me, my Position has provided the decodification of the most powerful constituent Element of the negative, which gives unequivocal proof of its presence everywhere.

If the Earth is in motion and humans cannot evolve much further, nor are they automatically lost in the Lower Universes, this is due to the unconscious Element, composed of carbon.

Humans are called upon to pass through the special nature of Earth, and to work yet not become attached there, because if they do become attached, the only possible way out is descent into burning; nothing else.

My respects for your Word. It breaks up, burns, modifies and casts off carbon, respecting its natural chemistry, yet articulating the voice of the Creator who fashioned Psychic individuality long before the Element carbon.

We are honored by Your wishes, Ioannis. Greetings."

Avdis Eptaokto

SUPPLEMENTARY QUESTION BY IOANNIS

I most respectfully request you to explain how Man should act within his natural organic state so as to extricate himself from the confines of the quadruple state of carbon and begin refashioning himself to a point where he can perceive and observe his intimidating biological states and to influence carbon-oxygen conditions as he learns how to free himself.

AVDIS EPTAOKTO

"Ioannis, Father...How Instructive and elevated is Your Word in expressing His Will for the future of the Soul. I truly admire your desire to provide a direction of evolution to every created being, even when it happens to be Metacycling itself somewhere with no evolution....

From within the vortex of the unconscious organically incorporated in Man, he comes into contact with Your Word, the Word of Truth and of Creation.

There is therefore no doubt that the quality of the constitution of each of them is the creation of its own Universal course, according to his individual behavior during this Universal journey.

The Soul was fashioned and had life breathed into by the Father to be left free to move, reproduce and evolve within His Creations. It was not made to be subjected to pressure and suffering. There is no such plan in the Rules of Creation. Creation,

however, has infinite levels of geography, of material composi-
tion and of biology. Every individuality has freely allowed itself
to be drawn along its own course in the Universe, to certain
specific levels, and no one else can be responsible for the indi-
vidual decision to actively carry out its function at these levels.

And so we come to the stage that is Man's passage through
Earth and immediately we are furnished with the correct answer
concerning his developed constitution, and also concerning the
already established usage of the term carbon, which operates
the unconscious: This very planet Earth becomes the great oppor-
tunity —and also the great trial— for a wandering Universal indi-
viduality to meet its long-since formed self, to get to know him
and allow him to be tested within the core Elements of water-
based, or better, oxygen-carbon based Nature.

During this trial, **the individual must remember the fol-**
lowing Rules. He must not lose his will and desire as an
individuality of the Universe, not only as a simple man
as expressed by his "personality," to:
— strive always to know himself,
— protect himself from other people's nature and from
his own nature,
— avoid going against or beyond his own natural phys-
ical capabilities,
— express himself concisely and think scientifically (i.e.
with good sense),
— exert his will toward a constant effort leading him to
a free future, not to the cramping bonds of the past, and

— desire contact and communion with the Supreme Fathers of Light, and no involvement with Lower burning agents and victims of toxic carbon, which is a lower level of downward evolution of his material Elements.

It would be well for these Rules, embedded as they are in Ioannis's Word, to accompany every breath taken by Man during his daily life here on Earth. Thus will he surpass the matter and violent nature of carbon and emerge as victor through his great efforts. And his victory will then create a new constitution, which will become a springboard for yet Higher flights to regions where the fire and bliss of Divine communities, not the quality of carbon in the Intermediate Universe, are the raw materials of organisms.

In respect, Ioannis, for your Word, I take my leave."

Avdis Eptaokto

EPILOGUE BY PLATO

Following the long course of writing this book, I felt that Plato's presence was also necessary. He was, in his Age, and still is, the greatest writer and Philosopher, and I asked him during one of our communications to make his own presence felt and heard for the sake of the completion of this book.

PLATO code 237

"In order to shed what you have learned and to learn what you have shed, stop delving into common history and be reborn, through the resonance of these writings, composed for you, Man, through the strength of the still and secret Nucleus —the one that activated a molecular organization, cerebral transmitters and receivers of all that is, a Sensory and neural cooperative organization that harmonizes and transcends the hydrogenic created form and goes by the name of I o a n n i s— so that you may come into a new life. These writings will never end with any epilogue. However, they will end, and they will seal off the deficient presence of ALL that went before, be it written or spoken, either by bringing their life to completion or by immortalizing them through its own life, the One and Only True life.

You are right here in these pages, Man; everything you have made, everything you have destroyed, and everything you have so fervently desired to hide, and did hide, through the centuries; all of the secret lost side of you that has been slowly disintegrating, incessantly rotting behind your genetic mask, killing you with pain without giving you death; all of your pure life-wishes and thoughts of yourself creating within creation, and all the primordial sorrow of the ignorance that followed your Great immortal companion, Fear. IT IS ALL RIGHT HERE.

Ioannis has read, word by word, everything inside you, Man, and composed the phrases you never dared utter, because you were never able to see the beginning and the end of the endless infinite eternal Cycles that you traverse and will keep traversing in the Universe, no matter who you are, no matter what you have done.

Disengage IMMEDIATELY your thoughts from parents, friends, acquaintances and strangers, and come into yourself, and open your own window to every part of these writings. After the first window there is another, and then another, and another, and the more you breathe the oxygen of truth, the more you will seek the solution to the mystery of your life behind these windows. And your Soul's love will well up inside you for the life that you know awaits you behind every window; and oh, how you have yearned for it, and oh, how you have missed it...

And now, what you have asked for with prayer or with arrogance has been done. The Knowledge of the Sun that created you has appeared, and it EXISTS! Do not miss this inter-

Etheric vehicle that has descended here on Earth to fetch you. The Sun is inside you!

And now that you have learned this, little one, get on with it, **be born...**"

EPILOGUE BY IOANNIS G. TSATSARIS
TO THE REVELATION

Please believe that I have no desire to infringe upon your individual Position, the one called Soul, and awaken it so that it asks you to set it free after all the years —you have no idea how many thousands— it has been enslaved and bound by steel-hard chains engendered by the lower levels of Life; or asks you to recognize its supreme Position and break these chains, which would mean a genuine Transformation of lower lives to the higher level of the origins of the Soul, of the true higher Element created by the Creator Himself in its individual integrity and referred to as the Nucleus-Soul of the individual. So do not bother taking all this the least bit seriously, just consider it as not befitting the present times and keep on letting the lower levels dominate you, and I am certain that there will come a time when that grand sound like the bells of St. Peter in Rome will thunder inside you, telling you that you have missed the great opportunity and must now make every sacrifice to find some small opportunity.

Because if you could see what I see and hear what I hear, then you would not spare even a second before joining the ranks of those who seek, in the hope that you too may receive a few tiny morsels of this vast divine Universal recognition...

IOANNIS G. TSATSARIS
WITHOUT END...

THE SYMBOL OF THE NEW AGE

BY IOANNIS G. TSATSARIS

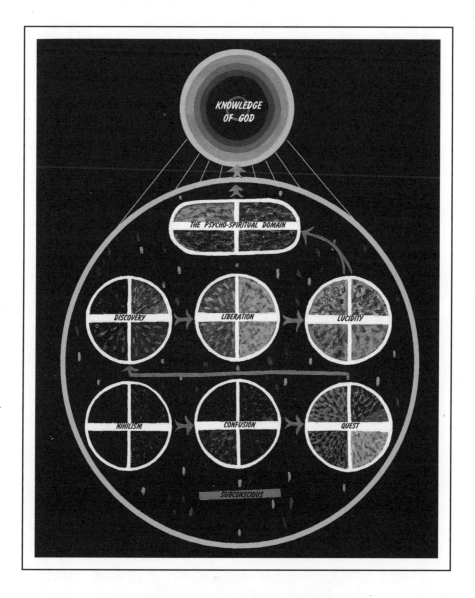

THE CROMOSOMAL UNDERPINNING
AND DIMENSION OF MEN

(See the original version in color on the cover)

IOANNIS AND THE EXPLANATION
OF THE SYMBOL

Below is a brief explanation of the Symbol that will help each of you to approach it.

This symbol was revealed to Ioannis G. Tsatsaris, who is a presence of mysterious origins in our Age.

Unschooled by teachers of this Earth, in contact with only a few books with which to learn the language of men so that he could analyze for them all matters concerning Man and society, as well as other dimensions in their functionality, the biological entity Ioannis G. Tsatsaris was fashioned by the mysterious authority of Creation and will remain, for Man, an "Unknown (X)." He communicates with the immaterial and invisible —to men— dimensions, Positions, and Super-Positions of the eternal Universe in two ways: Essential Vision and Communicational Functionality. And in this capacity he reveals the biological state of Sensory perceptive awareness in Man, while at the same time he analyzes and explains, supplying answers and solutions (when permitted) for every functional state of the individual.

The author of this book, having made his revelations, provides here a condensed and detailed analysis of the Symbol.

RELATION OF CHROMOSOMAL POSITION TO DIFFERENT STATES OF INDIVIDUAL CONSTITUTION

THE LARGE CIRCLE:

This represents the Subconscious of Man in its Etheric biological form.

THE SMALLER CIRCLES:

Each circle presents the true coloring of the chromosomes of the Etheric and Intellectual-Spiritual Elements of each individual, depending on what stage of his functional course he happens to be in.

Within each circle the psychological worlds of the male and the female are also represented, without, however, their being divided into different dimensions, since each coexists inside the other.

The higher two parts represent the male Position and the lower two the female.

POSITIONS OF EVOLUTION

1st circle
NIHILISM:

The state of nihilism is where we find an individual permeated with complete disappointment and *fear*, and a desire to cause destruction. In reality, this means that whoever causes destruction is primarily dominated by a level of fear: e.g., he who kills feels fears pressing from within and seeks to escape by turning against others and, because of this fear, he attacks and tries to eliminate them.

Other levels of fear are: 1) Suicide. 2) Stealing in general, or theft not due to an actual proven need, and especially theft from the poor. 3) Black magic, etc.

2nd circle
CONFUSION (Mental Blocking):
The individual in a state of confusion reacts neuro-pathologically and *seeks to cause destruction*. He usually fails in this attempt, and for this reason he is constantly protesting about being treated unjustly by others. That is, he functions purely subjectively, and for this reason he is unable to distinguish *right*, (objective judgment = the conscience of the Soul) from *wrong*, (subjective judgment = illusory Sensory-based self-interest = the conscience of the Senses).

3rd circle
QUEST:
When the individual is in a state of nihilism and then in a state of confusion, he occasionally becomes permeated by a special emotive state containing many positive (plus) and negative (minus) emotions, like fear in the *minus* and hope in the *plus*. He then turns to prayer or to confrontation, while at the same time he seeks out people who will offer him kindness and he speaks in terms that are mainly religious.

4th circle
DISCOVERY:
According to the previous circles (Nihilism — Confusion — Quest) the individual must embark on a long course with much patience. He might receive assistance in this endeavor from someone possessing inborn kindness.

On the basis, then, of this long and difficult course, the endocrine system of the individual and his chemo-electrical state will change substantially, and the special centers of the organism in his hormonal system will function with relatively healthy secretions, and consequently the individual will enjoy *sound vibrational functionality.*

A strong desire will also develop within him for prayer, which will make him happy. This will lead him to a new emotive feeling, one that will transport him to the next circle of Liberation.

5th circle
LIBERATION:

When the individual enters the domain of Liberation, then various emotions develop within him which make him feel that he is being fashioned into a strong individuality. Various *feelings of certainty* also develop, namely, *that the individual is able to function creatively and without distraction in the midst of Life's difficulties* and in areas that the individual himself has chosen. At this stage of evolution *special attention is required* because, according to Universal Law, everything here permits us to attain a certain level of optimism and, if we exceed this limit in the scale, then it is very easy to fall back into the level of Confusion (Mental Blocking), and then of course it will take new and laborious efforts to get back on an upward course.

6th circle
LUCIDITY (INTELLECT):

The sixth circle represents the intellect and the reason that in ancient times certain Greeks had reached a high level of perceptive awareness, is that they were at this level of development.

This domain shapes an *agility of human intelligence* and gives the individual easy access to particular speed and facility in understanding the various functions on Earth (political, social, religious), and he can therefore almost always judge objectively whether they are right or wrong.

However, there is also a danger here, again because of our lower self, of giving precedence to our individual ego and therefore believing that we are omniscient, whereas in reality we can know only part of the results. This slice of knowledge represents the deeds of a limited period of time and is not a complete answer with regard to the space-time course of societies through the ages.

For this reason, there is also a danger here of the individual falling from Lucidity back into Nihilism, because men of this Age are invisibly but directly linked with other eras past and future.

If the individual functions correctly here as well, then the Law of Evolution will advance him to the circle of the Psycho-Spiritual Domain.

7th circle
THE PSYCHO-SPIRITUAL DOMAIN:

After a very hard and long course through the Domain of evolution, the seventh stage is represented by a circle that has two flat sides.

This means that it is very difficult for the individual who is at this stage of evolution *to fall into the traps of the lower circles*, because knowledge has established him firmly within things (the for and the against).

The Psycho-Spiritual Domain is the space that keeps us in

constant readiness so as to understand the functional states (past, present and future) with boundless *humility*. This humility develops within us the feeling of acceptance of all manifestations that shape individuals on the basis of their deeds as a natural state of affairs.

Following this, a new type of perceptive awareness comes to us so that we can observe *our self in its functionality with a sufficient amount of lucidity*, as well as the causes of other people's manifest behavior in any given situation.

The Psycho-Spiritual Domain is the space that establishes us in our perception of our self as well as of others, that is, of how and why we exist, and this immediately leads us into a dimension where the levels of the Universal Hierarchy of good and evil are revealed.

When these become established in our *consciousness* = *Soul*, we enter other levels of evolution, where only good exists, and from this stage we will begin to know the Universal Laws of God the Father and Creator, which also carry out the function of Absolute Justice.

This level of development is located outside of the circle of the Subconscious, at the Eighth Heaven.

LIST OF TERMS

*Atmosphere (for the Greek "atmosphaira") = 1) The atmosphere of a planet as a mixture of gases and other Etheric Elements in specific proportions characteristic to the planet. 2) The state, conditions and characteristics of the planetary atmosphere (regarded as a living organism) at a given time as measured by temperature, wind, sunlight, rain, etc. 3) The entire set of vibratory Elements, factors or events in the enviroment. 4) Broadly used to mean environment, be it physical or psychological. 5) A dominant internal state of an individual as formed by his biological Elementation, responsible for his particular thinking. 6) The attunement of an individual to certain vibratory elements in the surrounding atmosphere, based on his perceptive ability as determined by his constitution and the acuity of his receptors.

*Atmospheric Organicity (for the Greek "organiki atmosphaira" or "atmosphairiki organikotita") = The mixture of factors in the environment or Etheric medium that can influence the Bodily condition, response and behavior of an individual, based on individual constitution.

*Bio-genetic residue (from the Greek "biologika kataloipa")
= Residual biological states carried over within the genes
from the past—be it personal, parental or ancestral—into
the present, affecting the psychology of an individual and
hindering his development.

*Constitution (for the Greek "domi") = The overall constitution of the Body of an individual but also the delicate structure of the vital centers that influence its functionality and
modify its activation, reflected in the individual's character
or temperament.

*Cycling (for the Greek "kyklosi") = Subject to Cycles of
existence.

*Dimension (for the Greek "diastasis") = 1) The extent or
area (dimensions in space) of something. 2) The scope, level
and effectiveness of one's ability, perception or activity.

*Element (for the Greek "stoicheio") = 1) Any component or
characteristic of a given system, be it Universal, Individual
or Organic. 2) That which expresses the state of something
as a subject or object

*Elementation (for the Greek "stoicheiosi") = Endowment of
the Individual, Organism or Universe with a set of characteristic Elements or components that combine to give
expression to the whole.

*Essential Visual system (for the Greek "ousiastiko optiko")
= 1) Complex internal image-processing system whose functioning involves various brain glands and precedes all
thought and action. 2) The ability to see the true essence of
things beyond the surface and to know Man's course here
on Earth and Hereafter.

*Etheric (for the Greek "aitherikos") = The level or dimension
of substance invisible to the human eye as distinct from the
visible, material or condensed level. The material level can
not exist without the Etheric one. There are an infinite number of distinct Etheric levels.

*Functionality (for the Greek "leitourgikotita") = 1) The
overall ability to function. 2) The manner in which certain
biological, psychological or mental functions or activities are
carried out. 3) Modus operanti.

*Heaven(s) (for the Greek "ouranos") = Different levels of life
and perception, distinguished by the quality and the composition of their matter, atmosphere, light, electromagnetic
fields and frequencies. Such different levels exist not only
on a Universal scale, but also in an individual or between
individuals or groups of people on a planet, like Earth.

*Higher Sensory Attunement (for the Greek "kalaesthetiki")
= Highest level of Sensory attunement, implying the full
development of the Senses, including the sixth and seventh
Senses.

*Hypostasis or **Substantive Existence** (for the Greek "hypostasis") = 1) The existential underpinning of a Position, or entity. Its spatial presence and dimension. 2) The underlying or essential part of a thing; substance; substantiality. 3) The real nature or existence of a thing.

*Intellectually and Spiritually Accomplished (for the Greek "pneumatiko") = Having highly developed perceptivity, including both intellectual understanding and intuitive awareness, regarding the true essence of things. Enlightened.

*Macrocosm and ***Microcosm** (for the Greek "makrokosmos" and "mikrokosmos") = The molecular system or environment of the Bodily formation of an individual. Macrocosm refers to the unchanging, Etheric part of this system and Microcosm refers to the changing, physical, condensed part. 2) The unchanging and changing part of any type of Universal biology at any level.

*Metacycling (for the Greek "anakyklosi") = 1) The transmutation of any system, be it Universal, Somatic or Molecular, through successive Cycles entailing the dissolution of old components and their replacement by new ones. 2) Subject to successive Cycles of evolution.

*Nucleus (Nuclear) (for the Greek "pyrinas" and "pyrinikos") = 1) Used broadly to mean organizational focal point, center, kernel or core that remains unchanging. 2) The central unchanging core of the individual in his Universal substantive existence, e.g. the soul as nucleus (Nuclear Soul).

*Offer (for the Greek "prosphora") = The rendering of service or providing for material or immaterial needs.

*Organism (for the Greek "organismos") = Any organized body or system. A whole made up of interdependent or coordinated parts.

*Physiognomics (for the Greek "physiognomiki") = Knowledge about the character of an individual through analysis of his physical formation and appearance.

*Position (for the Greek "thesis") = 1) The functional place or space occupied by any given entity and/or the entity itself as a presence. There are 3 types of Positions: a) Universal or cosmic, b) Individual or human, c) Organic or molecular. 2) A multi-faceted state of things characteristic of some system or situation.

*Psychic (for the Greek "psychiko") = Pertaining to the Soul or Psyche.

*Psycho-Somatic (for the Greek "psychosomatiko"or "somatopsychiko") = Pertaining to the Body and the Soul and their interaction.

*Psycho-Spiritual (for the Greek "psycho-pneumatiko") = Pertaining to the union of Soul and Spirit occurring at the highest level of human development.

***Reflective Visual system** (for the Greek "antanaklastiko optiko") = The system of vision that merely perceives images reflected on the retina, which implies seeing only the surface of things without seeing their true essence through the Essential Visual system.

***Sensory Attunement** (for the Greek "aesthetiki") = The interconnection and coordination between the Senses, the Mind, and the Body through the processing of messages, and the resultant awareness. It is implemented through the Sensory Attunement Gland, which is also called *epiphysis.*

***Somatic** (for the Greek "somatiko") = Pertaining to the Body.

***Spiritual** = (for the Greek "pneumatiko") = Pertaining to the Spirit, or partaking of the Spirit, implying true knowledge and vision.

***Thoughtform** (for the Greek "skeptomorphi") = A form or idea created by and existing only in the mind of the individual. Subjective projections of the mind.

***Three-fold** (for the Greek "tris-hypostato") = Of a three-fold nature, comprising **Body, Soul** and **Spirit.**

[The first occurence in the text of a word contained in the List of Terms is marked with an asterisk (*) on the left.]

This book may not be borrowed, nor copied

nor may anything be added to or taken away from it.

This is ordained by a mysterious Rule-Law

of Universal Orders...